Surrounded by Idiots

REVISED & EXPANDED

Also by Thomas Erikson

Surrounded by Idiots

Surrounded by Psychopaths

Surrounded by Bad Bosses

Surrounded by Setbacks

Surrounded by Narcissists

Surrounded by Energy Vampires

Surrounded by Liars

· · · ·

Surrounded by Idiots

REVISED & EXPANDED

**The Four Types of Human Behavior
and How to Effectively Communicate
with Each in Business (and in Life)**

Thomas Erikson

ST. MARTIN'S
ESSENTIALS
NEW YORK

First published in the United States by St. Martin's Essentials,
an imprint of St. Martin's Publishing Group

EU Representative: Macmillan Publishers Ireland Ltd, 1st Floor,
The Liffey Trust Centre, 117–126 Sheriff Street Upper, Dublin 1, D01 YC43

Translated by Ian Giles

www.stmartins.com

The Library of Congress Cataloging-in-Publication Data is available upon request.

ISBN 978-1-250-42045-9 (trade paperback)
ISBN 978-1-250-39894-9 (hardcover)
ISBN 978-1-250-42046-6 (international, sold outside the U.S., subject to rights availability)
ISBN 978-1-250-39895-6 (ebook)

Our books may be purchased in bulk for specialty retail/wholesale, literacy, corporate/premium,
educational, and subscription box use. Please contact MacmillanSpecialMarkets@macmillan.com.

Originally published in Sweden as *Omgiven av Idioter* by Book Mark

First U.S. Edition: 2025

10 9 8 7 6 5 4 3 2 1

Contents

The Danger of Being Surrounded by Idiots

HOW IT ALL BEGAN

Reader be warned:

Since my readers' views on anything and everything mean such a great deal to me—for without you, dear reader, I would have achieved nothing—I wish to explain before the book begins just what it is you are holding in your hand.

This is an expanded anniversary edition of *Surrounded by Idiots*. In practice, this means that many parts of it are reworked and updated from the original edition of *Surrounded by Idiots*. Time flies, the world changes, and as an author I have a duty to keep up. This book is actually rather different from the original in that it includes the answers to the majority of questions people have asked me after reading the first. This is an expanded, heavily revised book specifically aimed at the reader who wishes to improve their relationships with the people around them. I've added a number of new sections that didn't make the cut in the original version on the grounds of length. I have also revisited and revised many other parts of the book, although some remain largely intact. The language has been updated and clarified, but this should really only be regarded as the application of new makeup.

In short, this is simply a more complete and—I believe—better book.

But it's also important to note what it is not: This is not a brand-new book.

Right, that's out of the way. If you've read the original edition of *Surrounded by Idiots*, then maybe you don't need to buy this book, too.

Both editions are basically about the same thing: how a deeper understanding of the four colors—what's known as the DISC model—can genuinely make your life easier in the most incredible ways.

If this isn't what you're looking for, then now is the moment to check whether you kept the receipt.

The original Swedish-language edition of *Surrounded by Idiots* has been translated into the most languages of any Swedish book since the late, great Astrid Lindgren was still writing. It may be a decidedly different tale from that of Pippi Longstocking, but it's reached every corner of the globe with translations into close to seventy languages.

It's a completely surreal experience, and as a writer, I am humbled by it, but the content of the book evidently speaks to people everywhere on the planet. It's clear there are many people out there who feel they are surrounded by idiots.

Personally, it strikes me as deeply unfortunate that despite all the tools at our disposal today, we continue to struggle so badly to get through to each other and to communicate meaningfully.

It is my firm belief that the world would be a more beautiful place if only people better understood each other's differences. Perhaps that's my inner romantic speaking, but I really do mean it—many of the conflicts unfolding on the surface of this planet are down to misunderstandings and indifference.

From a global point of view, it's hard for any one individual to do much about this, but I'm driven by the old maxim: No one can do everything, but everyone can do something.

If I can help to simplify communication between people in their everyday lives and make life a little easier, then that's something I will gladly do. I believe it's more important than ever that when something goes wrong, we stop and ask questions instead of immediately leveling accusations at each other left, right, and center. Including that of being an idiot, to name but one example.

That being said, I want to briefly set out why I decided to write a book about idiots in the first place.

After a few years spent in banking, where I did admittedly encounter an awful lot of idiots, I finally got it together and became a management consultant. I had met a fair number of admirable people in the world of consultancy—often within the sphere of what is generally known as inspirational or motivational speaking. Education was another sector I often came into contact with, and I was always equally impressed with them. These consultants always seemed to have the answer to everything. They were smart, quick-witted, confident, and determined. They even wore nicer suits than the ones I had been able to afford on my old banker's salary.

The job itself offered a lot of freedom but it was extremely demanding. In effect, I was at liberty to spend my time however I pleased so long as I was bringing money in for the company and not only securing work for myself but also getting bookings for other consultants as often as I could.

But it was also scary because there was no system to follow, unlike in a bank where everything was regulated. A tremendous amount of my potential success really did hinge on me and my own performance. For the first time in my life, I began to doubt my own abilities.

I remember one day, about six months in, sitting in an armchair in our small library seeking inspiration from a book and instead nodding off as a result of pure exhaustion and stress.

The CEO happened upon me and woke me up, saying we needed to have a little talk.

But things got better. Little by little, I mastered the craft: selling; having the confidence to call pretty much anyone; meeting senior executives from well-known companies. I was barely thirty years old and starting to get a sense of how it all worked at this company.

In just my second year I was named peak performer of the year, and I figured my fortune was made. This was going to work out. I'd finally found the right place. Maybe this was something I was actually good at.

And sure, things were going absolutely fine. I worked like the devil and took on every task I could. As I added assignment after assignment to my résumé, my self-confidence also grew. And with that increasing self-confidence there came new opportunities to make a fool of myself.

On one occasion I crossed paths with a guy who ran his own business. Sture was in his sixties and had founded and built his own company from the ground up over the course of thirty years. I had called him completely unaware of his legendary hot temper, and scheduled a meeting in which I envisioned selling him a project I thought his company needed.

The needs analysis was actually extremely simple. Sture had an obvious need to get something off his chest, and it wouldn't be long before I realized what the actual problem was. We started out discussing what was and wasn't working in the company.

One of the very first quips Sture made was that he was surrounded by idiots. I remember laughing because I thought it sounded funny. But he really meant it. And he stuck to his guns, insisting he was literally surrounded by idiots.

After he'd said as much several times over, I remember raising a hand and stopping him. *Obviously, you don't really mean that your coworkers are idiots, so what exactly do you mean?*

Sture persevered. Idiots was exactly what he meant. The place was full of nitwits.

Amused by the entire conversation, I requested examples.

The color rose on his face as he told me that the people working in Department A were complete idiots—the whole bunch of them. There was only one person in Department B who understood anything at all, while the rest of them were a bunch of clueless losers. Department C was worst of all—it was staffed by people so strange and aberrant it was beyond Sture how they even made it to work in the morning.

The more I listened to him, the more I realized that there was something very peculiar about this whole story. I asked him whether he really thought he was surrounded by idiots. He glared at me and then explained that very few of his staff were really up to scratch.

Later on, I discovered that Sture was more than happy to let on how he felt to his coworkers, too. He had no hesitation in calling someone an idiot in front of the whole company. This resulted, among other things, in his employees steering clear of him. No one dared to meet with him one-on-one and no one ever wanted to impart bad news to him because he usually shot the messenger. Metaphorically, in case you're wondering.

At one of his sites, someone had rigged up a warning light in the lobby. It was discreetly positioned above reception and when he was inside, it would be illuminated red. When he was off the premises, however, it would be illuminated green.

Everyone knew about it. Staff and customers alike would automatically glance at the light to check what they might encounter when they crossed the threshold. When that light shone red, some would simply turn on their heel and come back later. (With the passing of the years, I've come to wonder whether Sture might not, in fact, have been aware of that light. I suspect he liked the mythic status it gave him.)

Anyway, as we all know, when you're young, you're full of brilliant ideas. So I asked the only question I could think of: *Who let in all these idiots?*

Of course I realized that he himself had hired most of them. What was worse was that Sture knew that I knew. What I had implied was: *Who's really the biggest idiot here?*

His face turned beetroot red in a split second, and he leaped to his feet, pointed at the door, and roared: *Meeting over!*

Sture kicked me out.

What I didn't reveal in the first version of this book is what happened right after that meeting. In the car heading back to my office, I felt shaken up. When I got back, my own CEO appeared like a flash and wanted every last detail about the meeting and how it had gone. You see, there were very great expectations for this deal.

I remember staring at him while I searched for words, before eventually having to tell him the facts of the matter. So I said: *Look, I'm going to tell you the truth, which is . . . that guy was . . . a complete idiot. He didn't understand a thing.*

But the incident got me thinking. Here we had a man on the brink of retirement. He was evidently a skilled entrepreneur and highly respected for his knowledge in his specialized area of business. But in truth, he was incapable of dealing with people. The only resource in an organization that cannot be duplicated—the employees—was one he did not understand. And anyone who couldn't be understood, well . . . it went without saying they must be idiots.

Since I was from outside the company, I could easily see how wrong his thinking was. Sture didn't grasp that he always compared people to himself. His definition of idiocy was simply anyone who didn't think or act like him.

He used expressions that I also used to use about certain types of people: "arrogant windbags," "rude bastards," and "tedious blockheads." Even though I would never call people idiots for no reason, I too faced clear problems with certain types of people.

And then it hit me. It was an utterly appalling thought to have to go through life constantly thinking that I was surrounded by people who were impossible to work with. It would be such a huge limitation on my own opportunities in life. What would my own encounters with others be like if that was my mindset?

On paper, Sture had it all: a profitable company, wealth, prestige, status, power. But he was deeply unhappy.

I tried to look at myself in the mirror. The decision was an easy one to make—I didn't want to end up like Sture.

So I plucked up the courage and called him again, and managed to schedule a follow-up meeting.

As we sat down for our second meeting, Sture said the following to me, word for word: *I haven't left the shotgun in the car this time.*

This relationship could undoubtedly have gotten off to a better start.

After a particularly poisonous encounter with him and some of his miserable coworkers, I had a knot in my stomach. Everyone was pissed off. Some of them were brokenhearted. And all this had emanated from Sture's inability to deal with people.

Right there and then, I resolved to acquire the most important knowledge of all—how people work. Given that I was going to be crossing paths with people for the rest of my life and since I was always going to be dependent on other people, it was easy to see that I would benefit from such a skill.

I was true to my word. I began to study more specifically how we can understand people who initially seem difficult to understand. Why some people are quiet, why others never seem to stop talking, why some always feel compelled to impart the truth while others never do. Why some of my colleagues always showed up on time while others rarely did. Why I liked some people more than others—because I did.

The insights I began to stow away were fascinating, and I haven't been the same since I embarked upon this journey. The knowledge I gained has changed me as a person, as a friend, as a colleague, as a son, and as a husband to my wife and a father to my children.

This book is about what is perhaps the world's most common way of describing the differences in human communication, and I have been using variations on this tool for more than thirty years with spectacular results.

The first edition of this book received its fair share of criticism. Me, too, for that matter. Not to mention the four-color model—the DISC model. Most of that criticism has come from people who don't like that it simplifies human behavior.

Which it does. On the other hand, so does every other model of this type. The human psyche is fascinatingly complex, and I am aware of the shortcomings of this particular method. I'll touch on these later.

But—and this is something I will stand by—the four-color model is good enough. It's been out there for decades. Of course, it wasn't invented by me and I can't take any credit whatsoever for its creation or the way it works, but I do like it as long as it is used for what it is intended for.

For me, it's more important to use a method that is effective and works than to search for a method that is 100 percent exact.

Then there's the obvious: Methods for creating an exact description of a living person's psyche do not exist, and I would be surprised if any such method were to come into being in the future.

How do you get really, really good at dealing with different types of people? Learning the theoretical part doesn't make you a world-class communicator. It's only when you start *using* the knowledge that you can develop actual, functioning expertise in the area.

It's like learning to drive a car: Studying theory is not enough. You have to get out on the road with everyone else and experience what it's like to be surrounded by . . . other motorists. Some of them know how to behave and that's great. Others aren't quite as on it, which means you have to know how to react. But it only works once you're behind the wheel. Only then do you realize what it is you have to do.

As a wise man or woman once said: *In theory there is no difference between theory and reality—but in reality there is.*

Since I started studying how people function and really took pains to understand all the possible—and sometimes impossible— permutations, I've never been the same. Nowadays, I'm nowhere near as dogmatic as I was and I don't judge someone simply because they aren't like me. With a little luck, I can engender the same respect in return.

My patience with people who are my direct opposite has been much greater for many years now. I wouldn't go so far as to claim that I'm never embroiled in conflict, just as I wouldn't attempt to convince you that I never lie, but both phenomena are rarities these days.

I hope you don't interpret this as boasting. It's taken me decades of study and practice to reach this point and I am acutely aware of how much I have left to learn.

I do have one thing for which I should thank Sture and his mad warning light: He was the one who sparked my interest in all this. Without him, this book would probably never have been written. Without him and his catchphrase, stuck like a broken record, I would probably not even have given this book its title: *Surrounded by Idiots*. And who knows, dear reader? Without that, you and I might never have met.

Statistically speaking, nonfiction books are rarely read in full. On average, people only read the first three chapters. That's a pity if you ask me, given it means you miss out on a heck of a lot of the knowledge contained in each book.

What can you do to increase your knowledge? A start could be reading this whole book rather than just the first three chapters. With a little luck, in a few minutes' time you'll be starting the same journey I embarked upon some thirty years ago.

And, dear reader, that wouldn't be such a bad thing, would it?

Thomas Erikson
Behaviorist, mentor, lecturer, and author

1

Communication and Why
It's So Important

1.1 IN ALL COMMUNICATION, IT'S THE RECIPIENT WHO IS IN THE DRIVER'S SEAT

People see what they see and they hear what they hear.

You knew what you wanted to say, so you said it as you saw it in your head. Setting aside for one moment how you expressed yourself, what you chose to emphasize, the tone of voice you adopted, and what your face looked like as you said it—what came out came out.

But what remains of what you said to someone after it has been filtered through that person's frame of reference, views, attitudes, experiences, prejudices, and preconceived notions is ultimately the message that has been understood. They may, for various reasons, perceive what you are seeking to convey in an entirely different way from what you intended. Of course, just how much is understood varies depending on whom you're talking to, but it's very rare that the full message arrives exactly as you pictured it in your head.

Perhaps it's even a little depressing to have so little control over what the recipient understands. No matter how much you want to hammer it into their thick skull, there's really not much you can do about it, and therein lies the rub. Naturally, you can consider this one of life's many challenges. God knows we can learn from facing down our challenges, but there's no way to change what makes the recipient tick.

Most people are probably aware of and sensitive to how they would *like* to be treated. But as you and I both know, the world is rarely that simple. By *adapting yourself* to how other people want to be treated, you will become more effective in your communication.

1.1.1 What Does It Matter How We Treat Each Other?

You can help people understand you by creating a secure arena for communication—on their terms. That means the recipient can expend their energy on understanding what you're saying instead of consciously or unconsciously reacting to the way you communicate.

People really are very different. There are so many dimensions to consider that simply thinking about it can leave you a little perplexed. We all need to develop some flexibility so we can vary our communication style and adapt it when talking to people who don't function in the same way we do.

Because that's another truth: No matter how we choose to communicate, you, the individual, will always be in a minority. Whatever your type of behavior is, the majority will work in a different way. And there's always going to be more of them.

My mother was wrong. Don't treat others as you'd like to be treated. It's a nice thought—but a misguided one. Sorry, Mum.

You can't base everything on yourself. This flexibility and ability to interpret other people's needs and adapt yourself according to these observations is what characterizes a good communicator.

Being familiar with and understanding another person's behavioral style and way of communicating means that your guesses become more sophisticated in terms of how that person might react in different situations. This understanding also dramatically increases your ability to get through to said individual.

1.2 NO SYSTEM IS WATERTIGHT

By the time you've gotten your hands on this book, a lot will have happened since I wrote it.

Surrounded by Idiots makes no claims whatsoever to being comprehensive when it comes to how we humans communicate with each other. There is no book that can do that, since it would be impossible to fit all the different signals we are constantly broadcasting into one book. If we included body language, the differences between male and female dialogue, your position in your sibling group, cultural differences, and every other way there is to define difference, we wouldn't be able to get it all down on the page. It would be the world's longest book.

We could add psychological aspects, graphology, age, and astrology into the mix without achieving a picture that was 100 percent complete. Neuroscience—that's brain research to you and me—is making constant advances.

Tricky. But as far as I'm concerned, that's also the charm of it all. Not everything can be quantified. People aren't Excel spreadsheets. We're too complicated to be fully described. Even the simplest, most uncultured, lowest-ranking individual in our respective scales is more complicated than can be expressed in a book. But we can avoid the worst mistakes by understanding the basics of human communication.

There are simply no theories, tools, or aids that can fully describe a person. "We see what we do, but we do not see why we do what we do. Thus, we assess and appraise each other through what we see that we do." So said psychoanalyst Carl Jung. Different behaviors are what create dynamics in our lives. Everyone has to behave somehow or another. Certain behaviors will be ones you recognize in yourself, while there will be other types of behavior that we either don't recognize or don't understand. As you know, each and every one of us also behaves differently in different situations, which can be a cause for joy or irritation for those around us. It can certainly be refreshing, but it can be confusing at the same time.

There aren't really any behaviors that are right or wrong in this regard, and most behaviors can probably be considered as perfectly okay. What I mean by this is that there is no such thing as correct or incorrect behavior. You are who you are, and there's really very little point pondering over why that is. You're good, no matter what you're like. Regardless of how you choose to behave or how you are understood, you are okay. Within reason, of course. Manipulative behaviors and generally psychopathic or narcissistic actions are very much not okay. But then again, you knew that already.

1.2.1 This Is Just How I Am, Okay?

In a perfect world, it would be easy to say, *I'm a particular kind of person and it's okay because I read it in a book. That's just how I am and this is how I act.* Sure, wouldn't it be great not to have to restrain your own behavior? To always be able to act and behave precisely as you feel at the time? You can do that. You can behave exactly as you wish. All you have to do is find the right situation in which to do so.

There are two situations in which you can be you, only you, and nothing but you:

1. The first situation is when you're alone in a room. Then it doesn't matter very much how you speak or what you do. It doesn't hurt anyone if you scream and swear or if you want to sit silently and ponder the great mysteries of life or wonder why Bill Gates is the biggest farmland owner in the US. In your solitude, you can behave exactly the way you feel. Great, right?
2. The second situation where you can completely be yourself is when all the other people in the room are exactly like you. Feel free to follow your mother's advice and treat others as you want to be treated. Excellent advice and very well intentioned. And it works, too—as long as everyone is like *you*. All you need to do is make a list of all the people you know who believe, think, and act exactly like you in all situations. Then all you've got to do is give these people a call and start hanging out. Exactly like you, remember.

In any other situation, it might be a good idea to understand how you are perceived and to learn how other people function. I don't think I will make headlines by saying that most people you meet aren't exactly like you.

The words and expressions we choose to use vary. The title of this book alone demonstrates our different interpretations of mere words. I've received several emails from people who think it was a poor choice of title. They say we shouldn't call each other idiots. And on the whole, I'm inclined to agree, while also noting that humor and irony are probably not for everyone.

But when you use the wrong word, well, maybe you are an idiot. What do I know?

Well, I know this: We're all the idiot in *someone's* story.

1.2.2 Surrounded by Idiots—or Not?

Hang on just a second. What does this actually mean?

Somewhere along the way, I picked up the following analogy: Behavior is like a transmission. It doesn't work with just one gear. The more gears you have at your disposal, the smoother the drive. Just like with a gearbox, sometimes one of the gears is the right one, but other times that very same gear is very much the wrong one. It's fine to start the car in first—starting in eighth would be a little tricky. In other situations, it's hopeless trying to use first—for example, if you're doing sixty miles per hour.

In some situations, every single person ends up stamped, labeled, and categorized faster than you can say "stereotype." On the other hand, before you draw your labeling gun and start firing words like "stupid," "lazy," or "generally weird," let's explore the option of not putting labels on each other at all.

The benefits of not labeling people are just as amazing as finding extra french fries with your meal. Firstly, it makes life more exciting. Instead of simply seeing someone as "annoying," you might discover that they are an unexpected source of entertainment.

Then there's the whole thing about avoiding embarrassing situations. Labeling someone as "dumb" can quickly turn embarrassing when it transpires that the individual in question is a professor of astrophysics or a chess grand master. It's like pinning a note that reads "kick me" on their back and then realizing said individual is, in fact, a champion kickboxer.

But it's not all sunshine and rainbows when it comes to avoiding labels. Sometimes it feels as if our brains are programmed to automatically apply labels to people, as if we need to pigeonhole each other if we're to deal with each other, period.

Who is she, really? Age, fashion choices, profession. Married, single, cohabiting, straight, or something else. A college graduate? That much you could probably have figured out from the start. In what major? Oh, she's one of *those*. Does she live in a condo? Oops. A house, then? That explains it. Well-traveled or a couch potato? Kids? Why? Oh right, no kids? How come? Washes her car every Sunday? How dull. Never washes her car? Eww. Dirty.

And so on. Applying labels to each other—we do it all the time. I suspect it's baked into our DNA. We quite simply have to find ways to relate to one another; otherwise, it ends up being too difficult to keep track of everyone.

But next time you're tempted to pull the trigger on your labeler, stop to think about the advantages of refraining. You might find that life is a little more fun and that you make more unexpected friends along the way. And who knows, you might even avoid being labeled as a "label junkie" in the process.

But what does this have to do with our beloved idiots? Well, you see . . . in this book I also apply labels to people. And there are those who are opposed to the idea of sorting people into different personality types. Perhaps you're among those who believe people shouldn't be categorized in that way—that it's wrong to pigeonhole people. Even if—as I said—everyone does it.

Sometimes they may do so differently from the way I do in this book, but we nevertheless all note our differences. And the fact of the matter is that we are different, and pointing this out can in my view be a positive thing, provided that you do so in the right way and, most important, for the right reason. Anyone who labels people out of downright prejudice is on the wrong track. But I believe those who do so in an attempt to understand are onto something.

Not that this comes without its risks. Used incorrectly, any type of tool can be harmful. I think it's more to do with who is using the tool than the tool itself.

As such, consider this book an introduction to how human behavior works and a dialogue on how we can adapt to each other in the best possible way. The rest of it is up to you.

1.2.3 Note the Following

Behavior . . . is relatively predictable. But:

- Every individual reacts according to their own routines to similar situations.
- It is impossible to predict every possible reaction before it happens.

Behavior . . . is part of a pattern.

- We often react in ways that are consistent. As such, we should respect one another's patterns. And understand that our own . . .

Behavior . . . is changeable.

- We should learn to listen, act, speak openly, and reflect—as the prevailing situation demands. Everyone can adapt.

Behavior . . . can be observed.

- We should be able to observe and understand most forms of behavior without being amateur psychologists.

Behavior . . . is understandable.

- We should be able to understand why other people feel and do what they are doing right now. Everyone can think about why.

Behavior . . . is unique.

- Despite what we have in common, each person's behavior is unique to them. Everyone can succeed on their own terms.

Behavior . . . is excusable.

- Reject personal envy and griping—it helps to talk about it. Learn the arts of tolerance and patience, both with yourself and others.

Behaviors . . . are like a toolbox.

- Every type is needed. Depending on the situation, a tool can sometimes be right and sometimes wrong. A ten-pound sledgehammer is good for knocking down walls, but it's not the best if you're hanging a painting in your living room.

2

How Our Behaviors Came into Existence

2.1 WHY DID WE END UP THE WAY WE ARE?

Where does behavior come from? Why are people so different? How come we're not all the same? You tell me. In short, it's all about the combination of nature and nurture. The foundations of the behaviors we exhibit in adulthood are laid before we're even born. Hereditary temperaments and traits of character influence our behavior, and these trigger a process at the gene level.

Scientists are still squabbling about exactly how this works, but I think we can safely agree that it matters. Not only do we inherit traits from our own parents, but we also inherit them from their parents, not to mention in varying degrees from other relatives. At some point or another, we've all heard that we speak like or look like an uncle or an aunt. As a child, I resembled my uncle Bertil—something to do with my red hair. To explain how this is genetically possible would take a tremendous amount of time. For the moment, let's simply accept that this inheritance lays the foundation for our behavioral development.

What happens once we're born? In most cases, children are born impulsive, intrepid, without any inhibitions whatsoever. A child does as it pleases. The child says, *No, I don't want to!* or, *Yes I can!* They are immersed in the thought that there's nothing they can't do. This kind of spontaneous and sometimes uncontrolled behavior is, of course, not always desirable to the child's parents. Then hey, presto, what was once an original pattern of behavior begins to transform, in the best- / worst-case scenario, into a copy of someone else's.

2.1.1 What the Science Tells Us

To begin with, we would need to find enough researchers who are sufficiently in agreement in order to know what the science is actually telling us. But fear not—there are clues. Our behaviors, no matter how diverse and complex they may be, originate from just a few different, identifiable sources. Of course, these sources are psychological, but they are also biological and social.

The nature-versus-nurture debate is one of the oldest chestnuts in psychology, especially in the study of human behavior. It revolves around the relative contributions of genetic inheritance (nature) and environmental factors (nurture) in human development and behavior.

In recent decades, consensus in the field has shifted toward a more nuanced understanding that emphasizes the interaction between genes and environment rather than seeing them as separate or opposing forces.

There are a lot of ways to look at this issue, including through the lenses of interactionist perspectives, epigenetics, gene-environment correlations, brain plasticity during critical periods, quantitative genetics, cultural and social factors, and neuroscience.

Biologically, our behavior is influenced by our brain's synapses and chemistry—and what we eat seems to be of greater significance than previously thought. All sorts of things affect how we process information, how we react to stimuli, and even how we communicate.

It's clear that we inherit a great deal from our parents. But which traits end up in your DNA? Are they the same as your sister's? Why or why not? I don't know. You don't know. No one knows. Yet another excellent question to which we don't have an answer.

Basically, why an individual ends up the way they are still remains something of a mystery. And perhaps it's not all that important, given that you and I are already the way we are. We're hardly likely to change to any great extent at this juncture in life.

Psychologically, our upbringing, experiences, and environment all play a significant role—and don't forget the social dimension.

There is increasing recognition of the impact of cultural, social, and individual experiences in shaping behaviors.

Our interactions, our culture, and our collective norms all influence the way we express ourselves. Context naturally plays a role. An individual might change a little (or even a lot) when they switch jobs, start a new relationship, move to a new neighborhood, join a club, or do just about anything else.

The prevailing view of the field at present is that human behavior is the product of complex interactions between genetic and environmental factors. This is not a question of nature versus nurture, but rather how one interacts with the other. The consensus is that almost all traits and behaviors are affected by a combination of genetic and environmental factors.

Understanding where our behavior comes from helps us understand and sometimes even predict why people act the way they do. As you read this book, remember these roots—the biological, psychological, and social factors. This isn't just about putting labels on each other; this is about understanding behavioral origins and learning how to navigate and react to them effectively. It's also about doing this without judging people, which is one of my core values.

2.2 MY CORE VALUES

And now for a smooth DJ transition: How to interpret the behavior you observe is an undeniably fascinating subject. Let's disregard the whole nature-and-nurture thing for now. Deep within me, in what eventually became my personality, are my core values—elements so deeply embedded in my character that it's barely feasible to alter them.

These are the things I learned from my parents as a child or that I learned in school when I was very young. In my case it was different variations of "study and do well in school so you get a good job when you grow up" or "fighting is wrong." The latter, for example, means that I've never laid a hand on another person. I haven't fought since third grade, and I seem to recall that I lost then. (She was really strong.)

All of us carry many such core values. We know instinctively what is right and what is not. No one can take my core values away from me. They're just there.

2.2.1 My Attitudes and Approaches

The next layer is my attitudes, which are not exactly the same as core values. Attitudes are things I have formed opinions about based on my own experiences or on conclusions I have drawn from encounters in the latter part of my schooling, high school, college, or my first job. Even experiences later on in life can form attitudes. Everything I experience with other people will either reinforce or confirm my previously formed attitudes. Unfortunately, we rarely change our minds.

2.2.2 My Core Behavior

Taken together, both my core values and attitudes affect choices I make in my behavior, forming my core behavior—the person I most want to be. My core behavior is what I use with full latitude without any influence from external factors, when it's just about me.

I'm sure you've already spotted the challenge this poses: When on earth are we ever completely free from any external influences? When I discuss this issue with groups in different contexts, we usually settle on one situation where this is true: while we're asleep. We are otherwise subject to various influences more or less all the time.

If I'm comfortably reclining in my favorite chair with a good book on a Sunday afternoon and recharging my batteries ahead of another intense week of work and all that entails in the form of responsibility, there will always be someone else on my mind. As I tear through the pages of this novel I've been wanting to read for ages, I'll be listening out for my wife. Stereotype or not, if she catches sight of me idly sitting there, then you can be sure she'll find me something more useful to do.

But people are different. Some don't care. They're always themselves since they've never stopped to think how others might perceive them. A liberating yet worrying thought, if you ask me. How you're perceived by others is sometimes the key to success rather than failure.

The stronger your self-understanding is, the greater your probability of adapting to the people around you. The self-preservation instinct, if you like.

2.2.3 Adapted Behavior

What the rest of us usually see is adapted behavior. It's an interpretation of a specific situation and a choice about how to act—this is the behavior that is put into practice. Think of it as a mask you wear to fit into a given situation: the mask you think is the right one based on the form of adapted behavior that will allow you to blend into that situation. That gives rise to an interesting reflection: Different people in the same situation put on different masks. Why? Well, we quite simply interpret the very same surroundings in different ways.

What's more, we may naturally have several masks. It's not at all unusual to have one at work and another at home. And maybe another one when visiting the in-laws (a wise choice, if you ask me). I'm simply noting that our interpretations differ and we then act accordingly.

2.2.4 Surrounding Factors

Consciously or subconsciously, surrounding factors cause me to choose a particular course of action. I don't claim in the course of this simplified explanation to have fully accounted for the many factors that create a person's behavioral patterns, but it serves as an introduction.

Take a look at this formula:

Behavior $= f(P \times Sf)$

- Behavior is a function of Personality and Surrounding factors.
- Behavior is that which we can observe.

- Personality is what we try to figure out.
- Surrounding factors are things that have an influence on us.

Conclusion: We continually affect one another in various ways. The trick is to try to figure out what's there, under the surface.

2.3 WHAT'S THE CONCLUSION TO ALL THIS?

As I touched on in the last chapter, some are opposed to the idea of sorting people into different categories according to their behavioral types. You may feel you shouldn't categorize people like that and that labeling people is wrong. But we do notice our differences. This is just my way of doing it.

The fact remains that we're all different, and if you ask me, pointing this out can be a positive thing if done in the right way. Improperly used, any tool can be harmful. It's more about the person using it than the tool itself.

What Are the Four Colors—Really?

3.1 AN INTRODUCTION

At the end of this book you will find a description of how the system at the heart of this book came into being, but since you probably want to dive into its most interesting elements—how everything works in practice—please feel free to read on.

In the main, there are four primary categories of behavior types, and we will look at how you can go about recognizing them. It won't be long before you picture certain faces when reading about specific colors. Sometimes it might even be your own face you see.

It's a pretty fun exercise, but remember that we have to start with the basics. Just like when baking a cake, it's good to know what adding milk will do to your batter, not to mention flour and every possible spice. What happens if you add extra eggs to the mix? That's only something you can fully understand once you know what an "egg" is.

Every single person you meet has a range of different qualities, and sometimes you may wish you had some of them. You may even occasionally be envious of people. Everyone you meet—without exception—knows things you don't. They have mastered things you haven't.

Maybe you'd like to be more decisive, like a Red, or perhaps you wish you had an easier time getting along with strangers, like a

Yellow. Maybe you'd like to be less stressed out and more easygoing, like a Green, or perhaps you wish you had the skill to organize your notes in the way that comes naturally to a Blue.

This book is going to teach you how to be like that and in which situations one or the other will work best.

Of course, it also works the other way around. You might read things that make you realize you boss everyone else around too much, like Reds tend to do. Or maybe it's that you talk too much, like Yellows. Perhaps you take it just a little too easy and can't engage with anything—the flip side for Greens. Or maybe you're always suspicious of everything and see risk everywhere, like Blues. This book will teach you to identify your own pitfalls and what to do to circumvent them.

No matter what you read or otherwise see: Feel free to take notes, underline passages in your copy of this book, and make sure you get what you need out of it.

3.2 TASK-ORIENTED VERSUS RELATIONSHIP-ORIENTED

So just how different can people be? Let's see if we can dissect this. The DISC model starts by observing the divide between task orien-

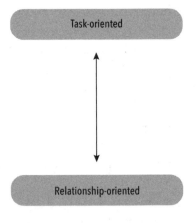

tation and relationship orientation. There's no right or wrong about veering toward one or the other, but it does entail differing points of focus.

3.3 WHEN YOU'RE MORE INTERESTED IN TASKS THAN RELATIONSHIPS

Being task-oriented entails focusing on the task at hand. While this will be very apparent in a workplace, you may also spot the signs outside working hours.

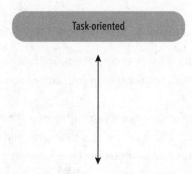

Instead of devoting lots of thought to who ought to be involved in a project to build a new fence—a job that's going to take half your holiday—you look at the hard facts of what needs doing. There's digging to be done, not to mention piling, casting, and so on. You calculate how much lumber you'll need and attempt to guess how long the whole caboodle might take.

Then you get to work. It's not necessarily that you're uninterested in others, it's just that the job comes first. Maybe you get your best friends involved, but that's not the most important factor, either.

What really matters is getting the job done. Who knows who simply isn't important, as long as you get help with that damned fence. Sure, you might talk about sports or holidays as beads of perspiration form on your brows, but that'll only be outside working time. During your lunch break, say.

3.3.1 The Advantages of Task-Oriented Behavior

Task-oriented individuals tend to be fairly neutral about what it takes to get the job done. They don't easily get caught up in emotional issues, they don't lose focus in the way that relationship-oriented people can, and they have an easier time moving forward.

They're less likely to stand docilely by and listen to emotional outbursts or to tolerate any other forms of drama. They're more level-headed about the task itself—be that building a fence or running a household budget—and they're less likely to be as emotionally affected when people around them face problems.

3.3.2 The Disadvantages of Task-Oriented Behavior

Since so many tasks require cooperation, individuals who are overly task-oriented may fail to take into account the views and perceptions of others.

Someone feeling stressed or downright tired simply doesn't matter that much to them. The goals of the task-oriented individual come first: The fence must be completed. Of course, it's understood that stuff comes up, but they'd prefer not to hear the whole story about sick kids.

There's a risk that these people will press ahead instead of listening to others. Moreover, since the majority of the population is more relationship-oriented than task-oriented, this can give rise to conflict, as task-oriented individuals may be perceived as insensitive, harsh, and bad listeners.

3.4 WHEN YOU'RE MORE INTERESTED IN RELATIONSHIPS THAN TASKS

Relationship-oriented members of society think differently. They're more focused on the people and relationships involved in the fence-building project—let's stick with our metaphor—than the grind itself. Of course, this doesn't mean they're not interested in getting

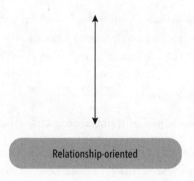

the job done. They too want a fence. But relationships matter to them.

They find it much harder to call their old buddy to ask him where the hell he is—work was supposed to start at 9:00 A.M. sharp. In fact, odds are it won't happen. They treasure their relationships and that means broken promises are accepted with more understanding.

When that friend replies that he was on a bender the night before and can't drive today, a relationship-oriented person will have an easier time stomaching this, even though a promise has undeniably been broken.

In order to work well as part of a team—whether it's at work or elsewhere—you need to be cognizant of your fellow human beings, know who they are, and understand them a little. Only then will the task be done with aplomb and everyone will feel able to pitch in.

3.4.1 The Advantages of Relationship-Oriented Behavior

Listening to the views and ideas of others comes far more naturally to these individuals. They have no trouble remembering to look around and consider what others might be thinking.

They ask questions. *What do you think? Could you do that?* And also the obvious stuff—*How are the husband and kids? Family doing well?*

They quite simply exhibit a natural interest in their surroundings— and not just because the fence needs building, come rain or shine. They're also more inclined to try to gain support from their families for different ideas and projects before they get started.

A relationship-oriented individual who has embarked upon a fence-building project will quite likely have sought advice from their family, while their task-oriented counterpart probably wouldn't have bothered.

3.4.2 The Disadvantages of Relationship-Oriented Behavior

These people are, however, more inclined to listen to people they like than to those who actually know how to do things. If someone in the neighborhood isn't pulling their weight in the annual spring-cleaning drive on the street, this immediately poses a problem for a relationship-oriented project manager.

If a neighbor is dragging their heels and barely lifting a finger, nothing is going to get done. That necessitates negative feedback, which is something a relationship-oriented person is reluctant to give. Who wants to be criticized? After all, they might end up in a conflict situation.

They'd rather maintain a good vibe and will happily sidestep any potential conflicts. This can be to the detriment of the very project itself. The street (or should that be the fence?) might never be finished.

That's one dimension, and it's actually quite simple to manage. Things get a little trickier when we add the next axis into the picture.

3.5 INTROVERSION VERSUS EXTROVERSION

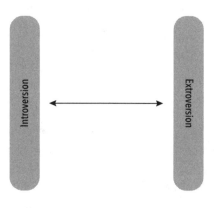

The biggest challenge is encapsulated in the next dimension: introverted behavior versus extroverted behavior. This is where it gets really interesting. You see, there can be real clashes between these dimensions. When things go awry, much of it can be traced back to this difference.

3.5.1 Being More Extroverted than Introverted

Being an extrovert entails being receptive to impressions from outside. A rather simplistic way to put it is to say that extroverts draw their energy from what goes on around them. Activity alone boosts their energy.

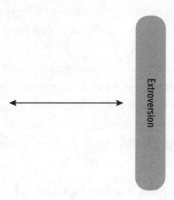

Extroverts move swiftly from thought to action and devote less time to reflection. Not infrequently, they are results-oriented, and they like it when things are happening. Inactivity is a negative thing.

Their energy is outward-focused on other people and the world at large. Diversity is good and they imbibe a lot of strength from the outside world. This often causes them to surround themselves with people. Their energy comes from activity and from constantly coming up with ideas.

Forcing an extrovert to sit down on the sofa to "recover" creates more stress than the situation requires. For many of them, solitude is a boring drain on their energy. They like to talk to others and prefer the spoken to the written word. Experiences are important; otherwise, they're unlikely to keep up.

It was probably someone with this personality type who cooked up the idea of open-plan offices. They wanted to pave the way for dynamism, quick decision-making, and communication across boundaries. The beating pulse of that setting energizes them. (Alas, they went on to fill these offices with introverts—so it goes.)

3.5.2 The Advantage of Extroverted Behavior

Extroverts are fast. Very fast. They get a lot done. Sometimes it's good, sometimes it's bad. But they don't sit still and wait. They need to stay active.

Extroverts rarely waste time on overanalyzing data and details or on taking in too much from their surroundings. Not infrequently, their egos are big and they quickly make up their minds about any given question.

This makes them natural decision-makers, and they're happy to take risks. They're often fearless and dare to dominate larger groups of people. As a result, we see large numbers of extroverts in leadership roles. They're seen and heard. Their receptiveness to external impressions also provides the impulses for many new ideas.

3.5.3 The Flip Side of Extroverted Behavior

Pace isn't everything. Sometimes speedy decision-making can cause trouble. Things proceed at breakneck speed and go horribly wrong because these people are driven to keep going; they stand up for their ideas even when it's become obvious that they don't have a clue what they're talking about.

You see, their egos are so big that they sometimes take up too much space and forget to listen to what others think. Their own ideas tend to be the only ones acceptable to them.

They're used to arguing, which in turn makes their views sound better. They know how to express themselves plainly and the result is that this occasionally wins people over to the wrong side. They're no more right than anyone else—they just sound like they are.

3.5.4 Being More Introverted than Extroverted

Then we have introverts, who are more active on the inside. The technical term for this is "passive behavior," but you'd be wrong to interpret that as meaning they don't do anything. You just can't see it in the same way you can with extroverts. There's a lot more going on under the surface than you might realize.

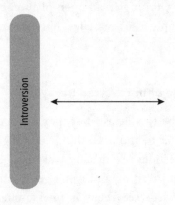

Introverts tend to bide their time. They're thinkers. They think ahead and can spend a long time assembling facts and impressions before they make a big decision. The path to a decision is just as important as, if not more so than, the decision itself.

Introverts are energized by being able to withdraw and find themselves in their own heads. They crave privacy: Forcing them onto the dance floor or dragging them around endless cocktail parties will always result in serious inner tension.

They direct their energy inward toward their own world and whatever is going on there. That means they need a serious amount of peace and quiet in order to concentrate. They're often thoughtful and those ideas they do propose tend not to be drawn from inspiration but are instead based upon reflection. They will have thought it over until they came up with something. And reflection is something they want and appreciate.

For an introvert, the written word supersedes the spoken, whether they are sending or receiving, so there's no guarantee they will participate in discussion. They will, on the other hand, send you a follow-up email with their thoughts. In fact, they may well have been taking notes.

These are the people who have a serious beef with the open-plan offices. The constant interruptions and sometimes boisterous environment mean they have to restart every single thought they have. They can't think properly in those conditions.

For an introvert, working in an open-plan office is like working while tipsy. They simply lose their edge. I know many introverts who straight out hate it.

3.5.5 The Advantage of Introverted Behavior

Introverts may not be the fastest, but they don't tend to do things by halves. They prefer to approach things thoroughly, which means their answers to questions are usually well thought through. They have no problem with waiting and won't get in others' way. On the contrary, others tend to see them as unassuming. Introverts will rarely express their demands without having their ducks in a row.

An obvious advantage to those around them is that introverts don't fight for space with everyone else. They're more than okay with letting others talk. Consider them more as observers than actors. Of course, there's more than one type of introvert—we'll get to that soon.

3.5.6 The Flip Side of Introverted Behavior

It's obvious that introverts sometimes wait and wait and wait and observe for a little too long. Not being in a hurry can sometimes be a strength, but if you never make it out of the starting blocks, then it can be a real weakness. Not infrequently, introverts will remain silent during meetings without sharing their views.

Don't forget they have just as many opinions as anyone else. It's just that they're not always noticeable. This can result in extroverts, in particular, assuming that introverts are on board.

This can be a serious mistake. Silence should by no means be regarded as consent in this case. It might simply mean that the individual in question isn't comfortable expressing their views. Or perhaps they haven't yet reached a conclusion. Probably the latter.

In a confrontation between two spouses, the extrovert might say, *Why didn't you say you didn't want to go on holiday to Denmark?* And the introvert might very well reply, *You didn't ask*. This is more common than you would think, even among intelligent grown-ups.

These are the fundamental basics of DISC theory. As you can see, we have a couple of crucial differences that affect the overall picture to a large extent.

3.6 SO WHERE DO THESE COLORS COME IN?

We can identify four core behaviors using the dimensions of task-oriented / relationship-oriented and introvert/extrovert. And once you combine these dimensions, this is the picture that takes shape. It also explains why there are variations within each dimension. For example, not all task-oriented people are the same. Nor are all introverts.

3.7 WHAT GOVERNS EACH TYPE OF BEHAVIOR?

So we have two versions of task-oriented individuals: introverts and extroverts. We have two types of extroverts: task-oriented and

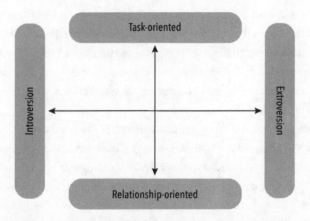

relationship-oriented ones. We have two types of relationship-oriented people: extroverts and introverts. Not to mention the two types of introverts: relationship-oriented and task-oriented. This is where it starts to get interesting. Don't forget we're still looking at the basics here.

This is what each respective field stands for:

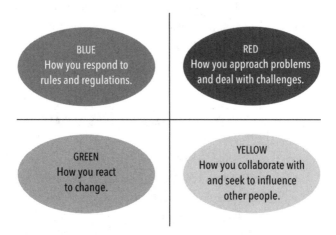

Reds—task-oriented extroverts—are motivated by solving problems and difficult challenges. The tougher the demands, the better. If something goes a little too smoothly, they become utterly suspicious. What's the catch? Why was this so easy? It's supposed to be hard—real hard. Life is meant to be difficult. You're meant to feel something. It might even hurt. Pain hardens these people. They like pace and action—on the double!

If Reds are all about action, then Yellows—relationship-oriented extroverts—are all about interaction. These are the people who constantly have to persuade everyone else of their own views. They can't leave the room until everyone is on the same page. And they see sunshine even when the rain is pouring down. Yellows also appreciate speed and sizzle.

Greens—relationship-oriented introverts—are all about stability and the willingness to change. However, a darker shade of green will entail a strikingly limited interest in any change at all. For some it's considered foul language. Not even wholly necessary changes will be looked upon kindly. These are the people who say things like *It was better before—well, maybe not better before, but it's worse now; Better the devil you know; The grass isn't always greener on the other side.* New ideas tend to be dismissed with a brisk *Everything's just fine, thank you very much.*

Blues—task-oriented introverts—have an appreciation for rules and regulations. They follow the rules and always know what's right and proper. They read the instructions in full before they even unbox their new IKEA bookcase. Preferably in three languages. These days they are confused because IKEA usually only has images in their manuals.

These four approaches, together with the differences between introversion and extroversion and the focus on tasks and relationships, give rise to certain, quite specific behaviors.

3.7.1 Different Characteristics per Color

RED	YELLOW	GREEN	BLUE
Dominant	**Influential**	**Stable**	**Compliant**
Compelling	Talkative	Patient	Conscientious
Ambitious	Enthusiastic	Relaxed	Systematic
Strong-willed	Persuasive	Self-controlled	Dissociated
Purposeful	Creative	Reliable	Faultless
Forward-looking	Optimistic	Calm and composed	Conventional
Problem-solver	Sociable	Loyal	Seems uncertain
Trailblazer	Spontaneous	Modest	Objective
Innovator	Expressive	Understanding	Structured
Impatient	Charming	Long-winded	Analytical
Controlling	Full of zest for life	Steady	Perfectionist
Convincing	Self-absorbed	Careful	Needs time
Performance-oriented	Sensitive	Discreet	Reflective
Powerful	Flexible/adaptable	Supportive	Methodical
Results-oriented	Inspiring	Good listener	Seeks facts
Initiator	Needs attention	Helpful	Quality-oriented
High tempo	Encouraging	A doer	Scrutinizes
Time-conscious	Communicative	Persistent	Follows rules
Intensive	Open	Reluctant	Questioning
Obstinate	Relationship-oriented	Thoughtful	Thorough

3.7.2 Characteristic Traits

	RED	**YELLOW**	**GREEN**	**BLUE**
	Dominant	*Influential*	*Stabilizing*	*Conscientious*
Behavioral pattern	Compelling	Optimistic	Thoughtful	Reflective
	Honest	Spontaneous	Understanding	Faultless
Manner	Businesslike	Visible	Discreet	Formal
Way of working	Diligent	Engaging	Personal	Structured
	Ambitious	Personal	Relaxed	Organized
	Formal	Flexible	Friendly	Specialized
	Efficient	Stimulating	Informal	Methodical
	Precise	Verbose	Unobtrusive	Taciturn
Work rate	Fast	Relatively fast	Relatively slow	Slow
	Determined	Spontaneous	Stable	Systematic
Prioritization	The task	Relationships	Maintaining good relationships	The task
	The outcome	Impact	The people	Their way of working
Scared of	Losing control	Loss of prestige	Confrontation	Making a fool of themselves
Actions under pressure	Dictates terms	Goes on attack	Gives in	Withdraws
	Self-assertion	Makes ironic remarks	Agrees	Avoids
Seeking	Results	Inspiration	Stability	Methodology
Wants to know	How it works	How it can elevate their status	How it affects their personal relationships	How to logically explain an action
	When it will be ready	What it costs	Who else has tried it	How it works
Wants to maintain	Success	Status	Relationships	Credibility
Want you to be	Honest	Stimulating	Pleasant	Precise
Want themselves to be	Decisive	Admired	Liked	Faultless

This grinds their gears	Inefficiency	Passiveness	Insensitivity	Surprises
	Indecisiveness	Routines	Impatience	Capriciousness
Appraise people based on	Results	Public recognition	Adaptability	Precision
	Logic	Compliments	Deep relationships	Accuracy
	Measurable progress			Energy
Their decisions are	Definitive	Spontaneous	Considered	Reflective
Want	Success	High status	Peace and quiet	Credibility
	Control	Flexibility	Close relationships	Time to prepare
Good as	Project managers	Innovators	Doers	Reviewers
Manner	Businesslike	Engaging	Friendly	Law-abiding
Work rate	Determined	Spontaneous	Stable	Systematic
	Fast	Relatively fast	Relatively slow	Slow
Support their	Goals	Ideas	Emotions	Thoughts
Distinctive features	Can be tactless	Seeks agreement	Listening and nodding	Gets hung up on trivialities
	In a hurry and performs many tasks simultaneously	Eager, open, and friendly	Creates a safe, stable atmosphere	Everything in its rightful place
		Good at selling and stimulating	Often unidirectional	Preferably written rather than verbal
Communication	Often conveys own views as facts	No immersion in details	Prefers to listen to others	Does not reveal their views
	Often says exactly what they are thinking	Avoids difficult people or tasks	Speaks calmly and systematically	Uses significant volume of facts in their argumentation
	Often unidirectional to others	Emphasizing interpersonal relations	Answers if addressed	Diplomatically polite
			Acting cautiously	

Leadership	Outcome-oriented	People-oriented	Supportive	Observant
	Good on points of order where there is no need for consensus	Good at providing constructive criticism	Good as teachers and instructors	Good at keeping track of things around them
	Acts impulsively	Not overbearing	Follows the rules of the game	Compares different options
		Considerate		
Lives in	The future	The present	The past	Their thoughts
Wants to	Start over	Join in	Get to the finish	Immerse themselves
Trusts	Their gut	Recognition from others	Themselves	Specialists' skills
Struggles with	Sitting still	Loneliness	Unforeseen activities	Urgency
Also wants	To be understood	To gain attention and be entrusted	Their work to be considered as significant and valuable	Praise for the outcome of their work

3.7.3 An Everyday Example of What Effects the Colors Can Have

Imagine an elevator. You know the deal—everyone behaves the same. But have you ever wondered why that is? Here's one possible explanation.

RED
Enters the elevator. Repeatedly presses the button.

YELLOW
Regards the ride in the elevator as a golden opportunity to have a chat with people they haven't seen in a while. Holds the elevator door open for a while to wrap up a conversation with someone who isn't getting in.

GREEN
Presses the "hold door open" button to ensure everyone can get in.

BLUE
Silently calculates the total weight of everyone in the elevator and compares this with the stated maximum weight capacity on the posted sign. May opt to take a different elevator.

4

Red Behavior

4.1 HOW TO RECOGNIZE A REAL ALPHA AND HOW TO AVOID GETTING IN THEIR WAY

4.1.1 What Should We Do? Let's Do It My Way. Now!

This is the behavior type that Hippocrates's theory of human temperament described as "choleric." If we consult the thesaurus in Microsoft Word—you know, right-click and scroll down to synonyms—we find the following: irascible, hotheaded, hot-tempered, quick-tempered, short-tempered. Oh dear.

You quickly notice a Red person because they never make even the slightest effort to conceal who they are.

A Red person is a dynamic and driven individual. They have goals in life that others may find difficult to imagine. Since these goals are highly ambitious, achieving them seems close to impossible. Reds strive forward, always pushing themselves harder, and they almost never give up. Their belief in their own ability is unsurpassed. They carry inside them the firm belief that they can achieve absolutely anything—if only they work hard enough.

People who have lots of Red in their behavior are task-oriented extroverts and they enjoy challenges. They make quick decisions and are often comfortable taking the lead and taking risks. A prevalent perception is that Reds are natural leaders. And that does make sense: These are people who willingly take command and put themselves in the vanguard position. They are so driven that they hurl themselves forward regardless of any obstacle in their path. Their disposition is ideal in competitive situations.

It's not unusual for a CEO or a president to have lots of Red in their behavior. That's not to say that Reds make the best leaders, but they definitely have sharper elbows than everyone else. They are simply able to put up with the fact that it's lonely at the top, but also quite windy (because the higher up you reach in the hierarchy, the stormier or more brutal it gets).

This form of competition is present in everything Reds do. To say they constantly want to challenge and compete is probably not entirely true, but if a chance of winning something arises—why not? The exact nature of the competition is unimportant; it's the competitive element that keeps Reds firing on all cylinders. After all, the taste of victory is just so much better than . . . well, the bitter taste of failure.

Pelle, one of my former neighbors, was so competitive that he would spontaneously develop entire new interests. I like puttering about the garden and spend a fair bit of time doing so. Lawns are my specialty, but I'm also partial to planning flowers beds by thinking about colors, shapes, heights, and flowering seasons. The whole thing gives me a real energy boost. Long story short: I like it.

As our tale begins, Pelle didn't like gardening, but once he'd heard other neighbors pass comment on my sumptuous garden enough times, he got the bit between his teeth. He started one project after another, always with a single but very clear objective: to outdo me and my green thumb.

To his wife's delight—not to mention astonishment—Pelle dug new flower beds the length and breadth of his garden, planted an inordinate number of unbelievably fabulous plants, and devoted himself to getting his lawn up to golf-course standard. It was truly refreshing to see him out there working morning, noon, and night throughout the summer.

The only thing I needed to do to keep him going was to drop the mere suggestion that I was going to buy more plants. That would make him hasten to the nearest garden center quicker than you could say "bad loser."

It was the tulips that finally seemed to push him to his limit. I planted fifty bulbs beneath a tree in my garden. He asked me how many I had put down and I couldn't help myself: I told him five hundred. And off he went. But his wife intercepted him and managed to put a stop to it.

You can also recognize Reds by other behavior patterns. Who talks the loudest? Reds. Who goes all out when explaining something? Reds. Who's always the first to answer a question? Reds again.

Who, during an otherwise quiet and pleasant dinner, makes dogmatic comments on just about any topic? And who will judge an entire continent based on something they saw on YouTube?

When you're in the presence of Reds, you can be sure things will always happen. They can't sit still. Idle time is wasted time. Life is short so let's go! Do you recognize the type? Always on the go. So step aside; let's get cracking!

4.2 TELL ME WHAT YOU REALLY THINK

Reds have no problem being blunt. When asked a specific question, they often say exactly what they think, without any frills. They see no need to wrap things up in a bunch of empty phrases. When a thought pops into their heads, everyone knows it immediately.

They have opinions on most things, and they trot their thoughts out quickly and efficiently.

A common observation is that Reds are brutally honest, because they dare to express their personal truths to people. They don't really understand what the fuss is all about. All they've done is tell it like it is.

If you need someone with extra energy, you may want to invite a Red to your book club. They fight tirelessly on when others have long since given up. They're just so much faster at reading. And while we're at it, don't you think the folks at the local history society are being rather lackluster in their efforts? If they're determined to succeed, that is. A task that seems humdrum or meaningless may well end up being ignored entirely by a Red.

I call this phenomenon "slog or split." If the task is important enough, a Red will slog through fire and water to complete it. But if they feel it serves no purpose, then it goes straight into the bin.

So what do you say? We might as well push on—full steam ahead!

4.3 CAN I WIN SOMETHING? IF SO, I'M IN

Reds like competing. They appreciate the slight antagonism that is part of being competitive and the glorious moment of winning in pursuits that have no importance except in the minds of Reds themselves. It can be getting to the red light 250 feet away first before stopping, or it can be finding the very best parking spot out of the two thousand available. Or it can be winning the pentathlon of party games at a fun gathering where the real intent is to allow people to get to know each other and none of the other participants are actually competing. . . . Well, why not? For a Red, all this comes to them naturally because they see themselves as a winner.

Let me give you an example. I once worked for a company where the CEO was a Red. She was energetic and efficient—and incredibly dynamic. No meetings were as short as those with this CEO. But her weak spot was the competitive element. As a young woman, she had played a type of floor hockey called floorball, and every spring at this particular company they held a floorball tournament. It was very popular, even before she joined the company.

Naturally, she had to take part. None of her predecessors had done that, and some of the employees had their doubts about what would happen with the company's top dog in the competition. But that wasn't the problem. The problem was that as soon as she had a stick in her hand, she became a changed woman: Blazing with competitive drive, she flattened anyone who stood in her way.

This carried on for a few years until someone dared to tell her that she was going in a little too hard—no one else was playing for keeps, after all. It was mostly about having a bit of fun on a Friday.

The CEO didn't understand. She grabbed the latest flyer for the game and pointed out that it was called a floorball "tournament." Tournaments are competitions, and if you compete, you are in it to win. Simple as that!

Now, I know what you might be thinking—that's a solely work-related example. Right?

It goes without saying that she competed in business while at work, but she also competed with fellow motorists while behind the wheel, and with her husband when playing a game of Monopoly. No area was too insignificant to become a competition. She even raced to see how quickly she could finish reading a book. What the rest of us do for relaxation she had transformed into a competition. One hundred pages an hour was a reasonable pace. Why, I hear you ask? Well, why not?

It even emerged that her husband had banned her from playing the Memory game with their children, who were five and six years old. Since they had better memories than she did, they won most of the time, and in her frustration she would really intimidate them.

Before you conclude that this woman sounds unsympathetic, we need to look at her intentions. This kind of intensive and competitive behavior often upsets other people because they think it's all about dominating and suppressing others. Nothing could be further from the truth. Her intentions were almost never malicious. She just wanted to win—sometimes at any price.

This is one of the greatest challenges for Reds. It's not uncommon that other people feel irritated or intimidated by them because they're such powerful personalities. Later on in this book, I'll share some simple ways to deal with these individuals, but I can already reveal that it's pretty straightforward.

4.4 RED PEOPLE ARE IN A HURRY. PERIOD. MOVE ON.

"Quick" is synonymous with "good" for Reds. If you're at a meeting of your local retirement association or maybe at the movies to see the hottest release of the year and you suddenly realize that someone else there is completely occupied with doing something else, you may have encountered a Red who has simply lost interest. If you look closer, you will realize that said individual's thoughts are elsewhere—on the next step in the process being discussed, for example. Because Reds are quick thinkers, they move on long before everyone else.

Few things annoy Reds more than sluggishness. If a meeting or a discussion drags on, they may interrupt and ask if it's really necessary to prolong the issue: *We've already discussed this for twenty minutes. Get it together! It's only a few million in investments. How hard can it be?*

If you think about it, they're often right. When other people find it difficult to make a decision, Reds are prepared to make quick decisions in order to keep things moving. If you have a Red on your team, nothing will ever be discussed ad infinitum. After all, it's always better to do something rather than *nothing*, right?

The advantage is obvious. We're talking about people who never waste time on anything that doesn't move them forward. As soon as a task becomes unclear or is taking too long, a Red will ensure the momentum is regained and spur things along, whether it's a project, one of their regular tasks at work, or constructing an entire building. Chop-chop! Life is short. Let's get going!

Let me tell you about a work-related example of this that had a happy ending.

About twenty-five years ago, I began working for a small con-sulting company with about a dozen employees. It was a polished organization with a great spirit of entrepreneurship and excellent momentum in its business dealings. One of the reasons they were so efficient was that the founder of the company was a Red. Nothing could move too quickly for Björn. No meeting took longer than was absolutely necessary.

In my second or third week in the new job, I was sitting in traffic when my mobile phone rang. I looked at the display and saw that it was Björn. I answered the way I'd been instructed to when I started at the company—with a greeting, my name, and the company name.

Impatiently he interrupted me and spat out his question.

"Were you looking for me?"

"No," I replied, taking a deep breath as I prepared to say some-thing else. I didn't get the chance.

"Okay," he said, and hung up.

Eight seconds. Ouch.

Unpleasant? Well, at the time we didn't really know each other. I must admit the whole episode had me quite worried—at least on that occasion. I was only a few weeks in at the company and already I'd had the big boss himself on the phone sounding grumpy.

Once we got to know each other—and I learned that Björn was a Red—I asked him why he was so abrupt on the phone. Obviously, he didn't even remember the call, but he said he was probably just trying to find out if I was looking for him. Once he knew I wasn't, there was no further need to talk. Wasting time on pleasantries or drawn-out farewells wasn't for him.

But at the same time, here was a person with the capacity to work far more than normal. Björn managed to do more in an average working day than most people in a week. He still has an exceptional ability to make the most of his time—whether he's working or at leisure. If he has a gap of five minutes in his schedule, he manages to squeeze in an email, and a phone call, and go through some papers. From the outside, this may seem like the unnecessary pursuit of efficiency. But a Red detests inactivity. Things must happen. Add to this a sense of constant urgency, and a great deal will get done.

Interesting enough, we came to be the best of friends and now hang out more in our off time than we do in professional contexts.

4.5 THE SKY'S THE LIMIT—OR IS IT?

For a Red, a realistic goal isn't very interesting at all. Why isn't it interesting? Because it is entirely possible to achieve and thus no great challenge at all. You see, if we don't push ourselves to the breaking point, then we haven't tried hard enough. Reds love difficult tasks, so their level of ambition is usually boundless. The ability to manage difficult situations and challenges is the defining attribute of Red behavior.

When a person with Red traits sets their goals, several things happen. First, they want to know how well a specific task could be performed given the most favorable conditions. If all nineteen parameters were met and they all put in a little extra effort, the results would be phenomenal. This means that anything below that level is boring, since there is unquestionably the theoretical potential for it to be achieved. Moreover, if someone else has successfully achieved the impossible, then all is clear in the Red mind.

Nothing is impossible—the impossible just takes a little longer. More than likely it was a Red who came up with that expression.

Naturally, it's also about the purpose of what is to be achieved. It's not enough to lay your hands on the most expensive house in the neighborhood. If a Red doesn't like the house, then they'll ignore it. Since they prefer to make all the decisions themselves, they're unlikely to be fooled into doing something they don't feel like doing.

But that isn't really the problem with Reds. Reds put higher demands on themselves than any of the other colors do. And they're always prepared to work hard. I wouldn't go so far as to say that no other color works as hard as Reds do, but I would venture to say that a Red would give anyone a run for his money.

Ambition, which is intrinsic to Reds, shouldn't be confused with a lust for power. Reds have no problem taking positions of power, since they are fearless. As I previously noted, expressions like *It's lonely at the top, but also quite windy* don't scare them. They just don't care. But for a Red, power isn't an end in itself. It's more about driving forces than behaviors. Power does, however, come in handy for those who like to make their own decisions and avoid having to wait for others.

A Red can, in fact, be quite unassuming. It's true that they have strong egos, but status and prestige don't have the same importance to them as they do to other colors. The reason is simple: A Red usually doesn't care what others think. They're not here for someone else's sake—they're here for their own sake.

4.6 LET ME SPELL IT OUT FOR YOU

Reds give it their all. When they have an opinion about something or just want the rest of us to agree with them, they pull out all the stops.

I was once at a dinner with a table full of people who didn't really know each other but knew the hostess in slightly different ways. I think it was probably one of those occasions where they throw strangers together just to see what happens.

Anyway. People were in high spirits and everyone was having a good time. It was in the middle of a recession, and we were all concerned about the national economy's lack of direction. While we were waiting for them to serve the coffee, we were chatting away about this and that.

At one end of the table sat Elisabeth, who had strong opinions about everything. In an unequivocal voice, she suddenly stated that Company X was still expected to earn in the region of $60 million a week, recession be damned. Some dozen people around the table, most of them highly educated and quite capable of independent thought, all nodded in unison. Just think—$60 million! Per week!

While Elisabeth quickly moved on to another topic, I began thinking about the figures a little bit. Not knowing where this figure came from, I remained silent. While it might be true, it might also be— ahem—a little far-fetched. I honestly didn't know. I started trying to work out how much $60 million per week added up to in a year. There wasn't enough space on my napkin for my workings.

A few days later, my questions were answered. I was in a taxi on my way to my next meeting when the driver turned on the radio. On the news, they said Company X had an estimated turnover in the region of $750,000 per week. I guessed that Elisabeth had sourced her information from the news. I also realized that three-quarters of a million dollars per week was far more realistic than the figure of $60 million she had referred to. Not to mention the obvious difference between turnover and profit.

But wait a minute. A little reality check was needed here. Why didn't anyone react? No one around that dining table even raised an eyebrow or called her information into question. It wasn't just down to the red wine intake—so why?

Because she sounded so convincing! Her facial expression was definite, her countenance was determined, and her voice did not quiver in the least when she presented the figure.

And that is how Reds work. When they believe something, they let people know this is the only truth that exists. Now there may be some sticklers for detail out there who would say this is deceptive behavior, given that we now know the company was turning over $750,000 a week rather than some $60 million.

But I'm convinced that Elisabeth really believed what she said. Sure, she'd gotten the wrong end of the stick somewhere down the line. And sure, she wasn't interested in the details. My point is that by sounding so utterly convinced when she declared that Company X was pulling in one to two years' revenue per week, we all fell for it.

Or, in the words of a good friend of mine: *There are two ways to do this—my way and the wrong way.*

I'm sure you can fill in the rest.

4.7 ONLY DEAD FISH FOLLOW THE STREAM

So Reds are both groundbreaking and strong-willed. Why not also add "results-oriented" and "decisive" while we're at it? For Reds, it's not enough to do things like everyone else. And just because it's tough doesn't mean we should avoid doing it.

Reds aren't afraid to make decisions. Why would they? What

could possibly go wrong here? When everyone else hesitates, think-ing and weighing up the risks, a Red plows on with the controver-sial decision. A Red's determination is usually unyielding. Once their mind is made up, it's full steam ahead.

Their fearlessness enables them to tackle things that make others hesitate. This is often evident when things get rough, and they are un-daunted by tough choices or tricky decisions. It's no coincidence that many entrepreneurs are Reds. Setting up new businesses—especially if they are based on completely new business concepts—is, in our current global economy, not for the faint of heart.

It's not a bad thing to have a force of nature in the driver's seat. It takes a strong mind to move things forward, someone who under-stands that risks are part of everyday life and that everything boils down to hard work from morning to night—for many years.

Reds understand this from the beginning and are in no way intim-idated by it. Do you need someone to get to the bottom of something with your condo association? Maybe you've fallen out with your electricity supplier who is claiming there's nothing wrong with the meter at all. Or maybe the contractor who repaired your cabin roof did shoddy work and now won't take responsibility for it.

When you try to get things straightened out, all you encoun-ter is a wall of call center operatives and an "info@" email address, and you're about to give up when you suddenly remember the guy who lives on the second floor one building over. Isn't he pretty Red? Wasn't he the one who dared to go against the super at the last meet-ing and get the trash policy changed? Yes, that's the guy.

Get the guy from the second floor into the process, and then you'll see things begin to happen. You might have to motivate him a little, explaining that he has a lot to gain from it himself. But he'll make things happen. And some of what happens will be good—really good. The contractor who messed up will start returning your calls. And your guy from the second floor won't lose any sleep just because someone got angry with him in the process. He couldn't care less. It's a "them" problem.

I've used this method myself, but I usually dispatch my wife in-stead of a neighbor.

She's delightful in every possible way, but I am sincerely relieved to have her on my side. She takes no prisoners when it comes to stupid people.

Generally speaking, a Red's strengths are very powerful. They are extremely clear in their communication, and you don't have to look far to identify Red behavior. Of course, over the years many Reds learn to restrain themselves somewhat—my wife, for instance, no longer allows herself to lose her patience when out in public—but it doesn't usually last very long. When at liberty, Reds will soon be back to full throttle—and all that entails.

4.8 THINGS WERE MOST DEFINITELY NOT BETTER IN THE OLD DAYS—FORGET ABOUT THEM AND FORGET ABOUT THEM QUICKLY

Good to know: A Red doesn't try to stick to their original point of view once they realize that a better solution exists. They are rapid thinkers and have no problem shifting their ground at short notice. One of the advantages of this is that they don't reject other people's ideas if they don't have any of their own. It's worth looking into *anything* that can propel development forward.

Sometimes decisions will be made a little too quickly, but the will to constantly change creates a strong dynamism and flexibility. If anything has been static for a long time—say, for a few weeks—they will dial things up a notch. Or two.

Some people will find this stressful, but when you ask a Red why they changed something that was, in fact, working, the answer could well be *Because I could.*

Naturally, there are downsides. By way of a minor concession to those of you who are Red and who don't have time to wait for the separate section on these: You Reds get bored more quickly than everyone else of what you have achieved and can't wait to get on to the next thing. Just as a Green or Blue begins to get used to the furnishings in a new home and thinks they have finally grasped how everything works . . . well, their Red partner will already have outlined the next step.

Or you might simply come home one Friday night to find the TV room has been relocated to a completely different floor of the house. How did that actually go down? (Asking for a friend.)

4.9 SOME EXAMPLES FROM REALITY OF RED BEHAVIOR

So what do you say? Do you know any Reds? Are there any in your midst? If you'd like to get better acquainted with some well-known Reds, you can always consider Simon Cowell, Hillary Clinton, Mother Teresa, or Darth Vader.

Oh yes, it's true. If you consider Mother Teresa's deeds, the strength she needed, and the fact that she had to deal with world leaders to achieve what she did back in the day, then you'll realize she was extremely determined and forceful. A typical Red.

Yellow Behavior

5.1 HOW TO RECOGNIZE SOMEONE WHOSE HEAD IS IN THE CLOUDS

5.1.1 That Sounds Like Fun! Let Me Do It!

In the Hippocratic world, we have now reached the sanguine person. What other words can be used to describe them? We might say they're optimistic and cheerful, a person with a bright outlook on life. The thesaurus even suggests the epithet of "man/woman of opportunity" . . . How about that? It's an excellent description of Yellow behavior.

These are people who live to live, always finding opportunities for enjoyment. Life is a banquet, and Yellows will see to it that they savor every single bite. They're driven by merriment and laughter. And why not? The sun is always shining somewhere.

And speaking of the sun, do you know anyone who purely sees sunshine where others see actual dark clouds? Have you met anyone who can laugh even though they haven't had any good news for months? If you have, you've met a Yellow. Have you been at a party and wondered why everyone flocks around one person in particular? It doesn't have to be a celebrity. At the center of that circle there may well be a Yellow holding court for all who wish to be entertained.

Yellows make sure the atmosphere is at its zenith, so that every event becomes a marvelous party. When the fun stops, they move elsewhere to find a better atmosphere.

Recognizing a Yellow is ridiculously easy. They're ones who are talking all the time. They're the ones giving answers rather than asking questions—often answering questions that no one has even asked. They're the ones answering a question by telling a long story that may or may not have anything to do with the issue. But it really doesn't matter, because they'll leave you in a cheerful mood. Besides, their unshakably positive attitude also makes it impossible for you to feel upset for long.

I would even go so far as to argue that Yellows are more popular than other colors.

How can I say that?

Well, see for yourself. They entertain and put people in a good mood, and fun things always happen around them. They know how to capture everyone's attention and how to keep it. They make us feel important. They're just nice to be around. They're easygoing and engaging. The whole package.

They are also very typically touchy-feely people. Like Reds, Yellows are very willing to make quick decisions, but they can rarely provide a rational explanation for why. A more likely response would be *It just felt right*. Sure, gut feelings shouldn't be underestimated. Studies have shown that gut feelings are right more often than you'd expect. But that's not the kind of gut feeling we're talking about here. Yellows often make decisions based on feeling simply because no thought was ever involved.

At this juncture, allow me to make a confession. I have a sister who is a Yellow. She's so easygoing that I've never heard anyone utter a single negative word about her. Ever. I may be biased, but I have never met anyone who doesn't immediately like her.

It's slightly annoying but mostly incredible. She has a unique ability to connect with every person she meets.

Marita always has something entertaining to say. However, some of these things are so peculiar that I have to ask her what she was thinking when she said them. With a burst of laughter, she usually replies, *Thinking? I wasn't!*

Her husband, Leif, has similar traits when it comes to positivity. Visiting their home is in many ways liberating. Their almost incomprehensible ability to see the bright side in everything they encounter is so invigorating it releases my own easygoing side. I'm never as happy and relaxed as I am when visiting them, of all people. For many years, I wondered why this was, and I've concluded that Yellow behavior is simply infectious.

If I say to my sister, *It looks like it is going to rain,* she simply replies, *I can't imagine that.* Pointing to the window, I say to her, *But look, it's actually raining. It's quite dark out there; we could have thunder before this is over.*

Sure, she says, *but the sun's shining somewhere!* Then she laughs—again. While the rain pours down outside, she sits on the sofa, unabashedly having fun. And I, along with everyone else, laugh along because there's really no sensible alternative.

5.2 THE MORE THE MERRIER

People with lots of Yellow in their behavior are focused on creating relationships. They are outgoing and can be extremely persuasive. They're easily captivated and overexcited and eager to share their emotions with others, including complete strangers.

And Yellows can talk to anyone. They're not at all shy, perceiving most people they meet as charming opportunities for a pleasant time. It can be on the bus, the train, waiting in line at the supermarket. Just about anywhere, in fact. Even in the elevator at the funeral home. They also regard strangers in a positive light—these are just friends they haven't gotten to know yet.

A regular observation is that Yellows are very positive since they're always laughing and smiling. That's undoubtedly one of a

Yellow's strengths. Their optimism is invincible. Comments from others about how everything is going to hell are often rejoindered with *But what a beautiful view we have!*

Just like Reds, Yellows have lots of energy. They find basically everything interesting, and Yellow individuals are the most inquisitive people you'll ever meet. Everything new is enjoyable, and a great deal of Yellow energy is spent on finding new ways of getting the job done.

Who do you think receives the most Christmas cards? Yellows. Who has the most contacts on their phone? You guessed right. Yellows. The most Instagram followers? Yes, Yellows. You seem to be getting the hang of this. They have friends absolutely everywhere, and they are excellent at keeping in touch with everyone in order to keep up-to-date. You see, Yellows want to know what's going on. They want to be at the center of the action, and they make sure they're at every party.

I can see you're already very much inspired, so why don't we take a closer look at the details?

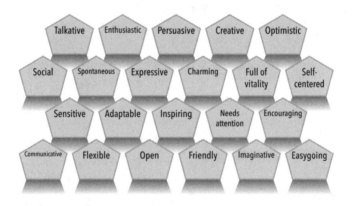

5.3 ISN'T IT AMAZING? I ABSOLUTELY LOOOOVE IT!

If there's anything that characterizes Yellow behavior, it's unlimited optimism and enthusiasm. Few things can keep their good mood at bay for long. A Yellow's entire being is concentrated on one thing—finding opportunities and solutions.

Hippocrates decided to call such people "sanguine" and the word has now become synonymous with optimism. For them, nothing is really a problem. Everything will work out. It's neither here nor there that the world is full of worries and hardships. With their incurably positive outlook on life, Yellow individuals bring joy to the people around them through their cheerful acclamations and entertaining jokes.

I have no idea where Yellows get their tremendous energy, but it's focused on having fun and devoting themselves to social cohesion. Everyone has to be involved, and a Yellow will not allow anyone to be down in the dumps. They can't have that. Should they spot someone who does not appear to be properly enjoying themselves at an event or at work, there is always a lively anecdote on hand to amuse the poor wretch.

Speaking of anecdotes . . . A good friend of mine is a Yellow, and his life has included more than its fair share of challenges. Micke's wife left him, his kids had issues in school, and on various occasions he's wound up laid off because his employers have gone bust.

I've lost count of how many car accidents he's been in, how many times his home has been burgled, or how many times he's been robbed. Sometimes I hardly dare to answer the phone when I see it's Micke calling. Quite honestly, he's the unluckiest person I've ever met.

But what's so curious about him is that none of this ever seems to bother him. Naturally, he's upset when misfortune strikes, but he doesn't seem able to stay miserable for long—for the most part he seems to be bubbly and effervescent.

I remember one occasion when we were both quite young. He had just bought an old Alfa Romeo. It was a two-seater with two doors. Painfully rusty, it was nothing short of a miracle that it even held together. Micke had the car for about a week before he wrapped it around a lamppost and couldn't get out on the driver's side. Afterward, I anxiously asked him what he'd done and whether he'd been hurt. His answer?

No problem! I just got out the other door!

5.4 THINK POSITIVE? HA! I WROTE
THE BOOK ON THAT!

Since Yellows are so positive and cheerful, they spread joy and warmth to those around them. Having an unyielding optimism, they demolish all opposition with the utmost efficiency. Isn't life wonderful?

Who can be upset when there's someone constantly pointing out the bright side? How could anyone fail to be inspired by a person who refuses to see half-empty glasses?

Emma used to be my neighbor and is the kind of person who sees the best in everything and everyone. She spreads joy wherever she goes—from the café on the corner to the annual family party. No one can stay morose in her company for long.

Who can be sad when they have someone pointing out the amusing aspects of every given situation? How can you help but laugh when—with a twinkle in her eye—she points out the absurdities of daily life that the rest of us may have overlooked? Emma refuses to see problems as obstacles. Instead, they are opportunities simply waiting to be explored. At what point does it click that this is not an Instagram meme but actually the way she functions?

Here's an example I heard years ago: On a camping trip with her best friends, Emma insisted that the persistent and doubtless ice-cold rain would only make their adventure much more memorable. While others were cursing the weather gods under their umbrellas, she had already broken into spontaneous song and started dancing around the campfire (in the aforementioned rain). Before long, she had the whole group on board and I doubt even they would be able to explain how it all came to pass. It just happened somehow.

A couple of days later when they got lost while hiking, instead of losing her nerve, Emma transformed the situation into an exciting treasure hunt. Using her phone and some old maps, she turned a potential disaster into an exciting challenge that not only boosted the group's spirits but also made a potentially stressful experience into one of playful discovery.

Emma has the unique ability to dial down the negatives and

replace them with an irresistibly exuberant mood that few can repel. She's that person who lights up a room simply by walking through the door, and her ability to get everyone feeling as if they're part of something fun and exciting is truly unparalleled. Every occasion (well, most of them) feels like a celebration, and you can't help but take your leave from her with a smile on your face. So how does this actually happen? How does it work? Well, I suppose that's one of the downsides of Yellow behavior. I don't think even she would be able to explain the underlying process. It simply comes to her naturally.

5.5 WHAT HAPPENS IF WE TURN EVERYTHING UPSIDE DOWN?

You won't find anyone more resourceful. If there is anything Yellows have an aptitude for, it's seeing solutions where others do not. Yellows have the unique ability to twist and turn things in order to progress. In short, they turn everything upside down and think outside the box. Call it what you want, but their thinking doesn't always follow a set pattern.

They move quickly: The Yellow's intellect is weirdly fast and astonishingly agile as it leaps and bounds from place to place in every conversation—it can be difficult to keep up, for sure. Often, they can find it difficult to explain their frequently wild ideas.

A good friend of mine likes to work on his home. Everything relating to interior design and garden design fascinates him. I suspect that Robban would secretly rather work in design on a full-time basis instead of his actual job.

I've seen this for myself, but I've also heard from his wife what happens. He walks around the garden, and she starts counting backward from ten. It never fails. On seven, Robban says, *Honey, I have an idea*.

There are a few reasons for this. Partly, it's because he finds it easy to think in images. He can simply "see" things in his mind's eye long before they become reality. And he has courage; he's not afraid to try new things. Or to talk about them. Usually, his mouth works in parallel to his mind as he unpacks these ideas. Once he's finished talking, the idea is fully formed.

I've worked with a Yellow who couldn't even cross the street without coming up with a few really thought-provoking business ideas—just by looking around. How does this work? It's hard to explain. For a long time, we asked him to write down his proposals. He thought that was a brilliant idea until he merrily forgot all about it and began to speculate on why salted licorice is only found in Scandinavia.

Something else that helps Yellows is they rarely feel any limitations. They really do dare to venture beyond the ordinary boundaries when they are being creative. Boundaries are usually a limiting factor, but Yellows rarely worry about such things. In fact, there's distinct evidence that Yellows don't even perceive the boundaries in the first place.

If you need help with a new project or idea, then go and find the most Yellow person you know. Bogged down in your own thoughts and needing a new angle on an old problem? Talk to a Yellow. There's no guarantee the ideas that emerge will be deliverable—realism still hasn't really made it onto the Yellow map—but one thing may lead to another, and before you know it, you might have something that actually works.

5.6 SELLING SNOW TO PENGUINS AND SAND TO BEDOUINS

With all their energy and optimism, Yellows are very, *very*, VERY persuasive. It's easy for them to get carried away, seeing opportunities and solutions where others only see a dead end.

It's often said that there is a difference between convincing and persuading, and many Yellows cross this boundary. But what they say sounds so good. With the help of language, they really are masters at winning people over to their side.

Regarding language: As I describe in my chapter on body language, most Yellows have a rich and varied way of gesticulating. This makes the whole experience very powerful indeed.

But it's more than just energy and willpower. Yellows have a unique way of expressing themselves that sways their listeners. They often describe images and are therefore able to influence more senses than merely hearing. That in turn creates impressions that can often be felt throughout the body.

Many Yellows are talented rhetoricians without being aware of it themselves. They know instinctively that their ethos, the message carrier, is just as important as the message itself. That's why they take care to reach out to you as an individual, usually by being informal and shaking hands. They'll chip in with personalized flattery. They make you feel important.

It's said the former US President Bill Clinton was phenomenal at this. Through his mere presence, he was able to make people feel extremely seen and appreciated. He had the kind of charisma that is naturally present in many Yellows—a noticeable interest in others, and the ability to ask exactly the right questions so others feel they are important.

5.7 I KNOW LOTS OF PEOPLE. ALL OF THEM, IN FACT.

If Yellows aren't allowed to cultivate their relationships, they will slowly wither and die. Okay, this may be somewhat exaggerated, but just think about it for a moment—the very definition of Yellow behavior revolves around their ability to build relationships.

The Yellow traits are inspirational. Yellows inspire those around them, and the best way to achieve this is through building relationships. A Yellow knows that by far the most important factor in business, for example, is relationships. If the person you're talking to—it doesn't matter what the topic is—doesn't feel positively about you, it will be difficult to make any headway.

Yellows know everyone. They have more acquaintances than everyone else. They like everyone. A Yellow doesn't need to know a person very well before calling them a friend.

To misquote the New Testament: "He that is not with me is against me." For Yellows, it's the reverse. Anyone who isn't actively against me is obviously with me. Anything else would be completely unreasonable. Remember that while Reds ask *what* is going to be done, Yellows immediately want to know *who* will do it. This question is crucial for their engagement. If the team or group doesn't function smoothly, a Yellow will feel unsettled. They need functioning relationships in order to do themselves justice.

5.8 SOME EXAMPLES FROM REALITY OF YELLOW BEHAVIOR

So tell me—have you ever met a genuine, bona fide Yellow? Famous examples include former US President George W. Bush—many try to describe him as a Red, but I don't think that's true at all. The multitude of blunders he committed during his career will go down in history, and all he did was speak from the heart—sometimes with no plan in sight. And who can forget the time at a summit of world leaders when, out of nowhere, he began to massage the shoulders of Angela Merkel, who is unfortunately a Blue through and through. That's what I call giving in to a spontaneous whim.

As for other Yellows? Well, Dolly Parton, Jim Carrey, and the almost unrealistically inspirational motivator Mel Robbins all spring to mind. And why not Han Solo from *Star Wars*, while we're at it? Cracking jokes while attacking the Death Star is something only a Yellow would do.

6

Green Behavior

6.1 THE REASON WHY IT'S SO DIFFICULT TO CHANGE THINGS—AND HOW TO GET AROUND IT

6.1.1 How Are We Going to Do This? It's Not Urgent, Right?

Green people are the most common. You'll meet them virtually everywhere. No matter where you look, be it in your neighborhood, in your local association, or at work, you can assume that there are Greens to be found all around you. How can I possibly know this? Statistically, Green behavior is quite simply the most common out there. Perhaps one in two people (allowing for some rounding) have Green traits of one kind or another.

What's the easiest way to explain who they are? Well, I would describe them as being the average of all the other colors. Please don't interpret that as something negative; keep in mind what this truly implies. While Reds are stressed performance seekers, Yellows are creative bons vivants, and Blues are perfectionist Knights of Excel Spreadsheets (see the next chapter), Greens are the most balanced. They counterbalance the other more extreme behavioral traits in an elegant way.

Hippocrates called them phlegmatic people. The Aztecs called them earth people. Passive, undemonstrative, unexcitable, placid, and tranquil are just some of the words you might find in the thesaurus.

It's just a matter of stating the facts—not everyone can or should be extreme; otherwise, we would never get anything done. If everyone were a driven leader, there would be no one left to be led. If everyone were an enthusiastic entertainer, there would be no one to amuse. And if everyone were a controlling perfectionist, then there would be nothing to control.

This means that Greens don't stick out in the same way others do and they often lend serenity to a situation. Where Reds and Yellows start off in top gear, Greens are significantly calmer. And where Blues get caught up in details, Greens try to feel their way to what is right.

If you have a Green friend, they'll never forget your birthday. They won't begrudge you your successes, and they won't drown you out at dinner by reeling off their own stories.

They won't try to outdo you and they won't pester you and stress you out by constantly making new and ever-increasing demands. Nor will they see you as a competitor if you're ever placed in a situation like that. They won't take command unless they have a mandate. And they won't. . . .

Wait a minute, please, you might be thinking. That's just a lot of things they *don't* do. What exactly do they do? Excellent question.

You can't ignore the fact that Greens are often regarded as more passive than others. They're not as driven as Reds, not as resourceful as Yellows, and not as orderly as Blues. Frankly, this describes most of the population.

For this very reason, they are easy to deal with. They let you be yourself. They don't demand much, and they never kick up a fuss unnecessarily.

Children with Green traits are usually described as being little angels. They eat when they're supposed to; they sleep when they're supposed to; they do their homework when they're supposed to.

But it's not just that. Greens will avoid causing offense if they can help it. They'd rather not offend anyone at all, and they won't talk back if their partner makes a strange decision. (At least, not to their face. When talking about it to a friend afterward, things may be somewhat different, but more on that later.)

They usually strive to fit in, which makes them more balanced people. They're ideal for calming down chaotic Yellows, for example. And they're excellent at warming up Blues, who can, on occasion, be a tad too cold.

My wife and I frequently hang out with a family in which the husband is almost unbelievably Yellow and likes to clown about and be at the center of attention—he comes up with funny games and will happily answer every single question himself. Everyone else is his audience, and he never steps out of the spotlight. And he *is* funny.

His wife is a Green, however: Calm, composed, and as laid-back as can be. While he jumps around and frolics (these may be middle-aged people, but I can think of no better way to describe it), she sits quietly on the sofa and smiles serenely. She's just as entertained as everyone else by his antics. I once asked her if she ever gets tired of her comical husband, and she quietly replied, *But he's having so much fun.*

This is a typical Green trait. They're very tolerant toward other people's singular behavior.

Is the picture becoming clearer? Greens are the people you might not think about—well, most of us don't.

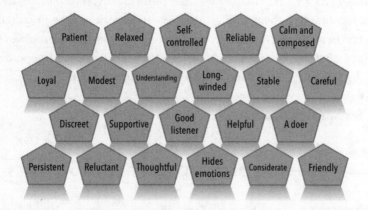

6.2 SOME SIMPLE BASICS

Green people are kindness personified. You can expect a helping hand whenever you need it. They are pronounced relational people who will do everything within their power to save their relationships. And they will invest lifelong. They will keep track of when your birthday is, when your partner's birthday is, when your kids' birthdays are, etc. It wouldn't surprise me if they even know when your cat first saw the light of day.

It's often said that Greens are the best listeners, and this is true. They actually listen to what you say—and they remember what you said. A Green will always be more interested in you than in themselves, and if perchance they happen to be interested in themselves, they would never dream of showing it.

You often find Greens in the public sector, where they help others, with no concern for personal gain.

They are also superb team players. The team, the group, the family always comes before the individual, and I would even say that societies consisting of Greens will always take care of the sick and the weak. They won't leave a friend in need; you can call them at any time. They always offer a shoulder to cry on.

One thing, though: Change isn't their greatest strength, even though change isn't completely alien to them. If you can justify the change and give them enough time, even a Green will be prepared to try new things. But a Green will remind you that you always know what you have, but you never know what you might end up with. The grass is not automatically greener on the other side, so to speak.

Sounds nice, right? Let's take a more detailed look at this.

6.3 THE BEST PAL IN THE WORLD

As I've already said, these are naturally friendly people. When they tell you they sincerely care about how you're doing, you can trust that they lie awake sleepless for your sake. Just like Yellows, Greens are relationship people and their interest in others is genuine and authentic.

If you ask a group of people if anyone is prepared to lend a hand and no one steps up to help, a Green won't jump in and shout, *Choose me!* However, they will look around and if no one else volunteers, then they will step up. Why? Because they don't want to leave you in the lurch. They know if you don't get any help, you'll feel bad, and although they can be passive, they're always prepared to help a friend.

I still remember a young woman I worked with at the turn of the millennium. Admittedly, Maja was certainly Blue as well, but above all, she was Green. Her problem was obvious: When someone asked for help, she always said yes. Every single time.

It was difficult to find her desk under the mass of work and papers stacked upon it, but she always got everything sorted in the end. We could always rely on her assistance in handling all the things the rest of us had simply forgotten about. Someone had assigned her to work in reception so her warm, friendly smile was the first thing new clients encountered. She never failed to serve coffee, straighten the cushions, keep track of how long clients had been waiting, or remind consultants at the ends of their tethers that they ought to tend to their clients a little better. Stuff like that.

What's more, Maja never forgot anyone's birthday or anniversary (or their wives' or children's, for that matter). She frequently sent short emails to all of us stressed-out consultants reminding us we had families who also needed to be looked after.

Granted, we could probably look after ourselves, but her kindness and consideration were sort of doing it for us by proxy. It was natural for her, and whenever we asked her to take it easy and to take care of herself for a change, she was borderline offended. She wanted to take care of us—it simply made her feel good. Of course, there were limits, and Maja constantly ran the risk of someone taking advantage of her huge heart. But when properly balanced, this selflessness is a beautiful quality.

Greens do this naturally. When having coffee, it's quite normal for them to ask the people with them if they would like a refill. While other colors would probably take their empty cups to the coffee-maker, Greens would fetch the jug and refill everyone's cups.

A Green wants to stay on good terms with everyone, so they'll even help people they don't really like that much. Otherwise, there might be some kind of hullabaloo, and that would be bad.

They see the best in most people and they're confident in others' abilities. Sometimes they do this so intensely it ends badly, but normally that's the fault of the other person, rather than that of the Green. They are so kindhearted that now and then others may take advantage of them.

Lasse, a good pal of mine, is a true friend like this. It makes no difference how much he has to do; if anyone needs a helping hand, Lasse is there, ready to step in. Sometimes in his eagerness to help with other people's work, he even forgets to do his own.

On weekends, he drives his own and others' children everywhere they want to go. He helps people move; he lends out his tools without people even needing to ask. He listens if you call to sound off about something. This all takes a huge amount of his time, and he gets far less done than he should, but he enjoys it.

6.4 WHEN THEY'VE FINALLY AGREED TO DO SOME-THING, YOU CAN REST ASSURED IT WILL BE DONE

If a Green says they will do something, you can be confident they'll do it. If it's in their power to deliver, they will. Whether it's a job that needs doing at work or something at home that's broken, they'll attempt to get it sorted. (The challenge is to make them say yes.)

It won't be done in the shortest amount of time possible, but it should be done roughly within the expected time frame. You see, they don't want to be caught out and unable to deliver on whatever it is, because they realize that might leave others in a bind.

And because they're good team players, they don't want to do anything that might cause problems for the team. Team comes before self, the team being the company, crew, sports team, or family. For the Green, it's natural to look after everyone else around them.

The reason why everyone works so well with Greens is a topic to debate. In some situations, it's simply because they don't like conflict. Mostly, however, it's because they're controlled by the desire to make those around them happy and satisfied. If they can please you with a job well done, they'll do it. The desire to please others verges on being a driving force for Greens. It comes naturally and requires no effort. And this selflessness is accompanied by an exalted serenity that lowers the stress level of those around them.

6.5 UNPLEASANT SURPRISES AND THE ICK

You can always count on a Green. If you've left them in the corner, then you can rely on them still being there when you come back. This is a work-related example, but I suspect it translates to relationships, too. Good or bad? I guess it depends.

In some organizations, it's essential to be able to rely on your coworkers. Creativity and ingenuity are not at the top of the wish list: You simply need people who understand the job and get it done without a lot of fuss or drama.

So you hire Greens. They constitute the stable core who will do as they're told. They don't have a problem taking orders—as long as the orders are formulated in an appealing fashion. Greens enjoy stability and a certain predictability in the workplace.

Or in the home. Or in their condo association. Or at their sports club.

Think about it. Whenever trouble is brewing—maybe due to a recession or when new managers take over—we see all kinds of interesting behavior in a group.

Reds never listen to the whole message and just rush off to do whatever they think should have been said at that protracted meeting. Unless, of course, they're busy yelling at the management because they don't agree with their decisions.

Yellows embark upon wild discussions without delay, speculating on what the message did and did not contain, as well as informing absolutely everyone about their take on what happened. Instead of working, they'll debate the news until it's time to leave the office.

Blues will return to their desks to concoct half a million questions to which no one yet knows the answers.

What do the Greens do in this situation? They just murmur. They try to be one with the wallpaper. If the management has avoided seriously sabotaging their sense of security, they'll trundle on without much grumbling. They keep their heads down. There's no point in making a lot of fuss and bother about it. Might as well keep doing what you were doing before.

This, in fact, makes things much easier. We'll get to how we help Greens to (eventually) change direction, but in the meantime, they're great at keeping calm and carrying on.

You'll always know how a Green will respond to some questions because they don't change their opinions with much frequency.

A few years ago, I coached Greger. He'd been the chairman of our condo association for a few years and his board was packed with nothing but Greens. Board meetings were always a calm and pleasant affair. He used to enjoy playing a little game when broaching new ideas to the building residents. He wrote little notes with the answers he thought he would get from each person. "No" from Anna. "Yes" from Stefan. "Maybe" from Bertil. Right every time! Greger knew them very well and knew how they would react to his proposals.

This wouldn't have been the case with Yellows. They don't even know themselves how they're going to respond when opportunities arise. Exciting, sure, but it's exhausting for those around them. With Green coworkers, however, you don't need to worry. You know exactly where you have them, even when you wish they were actually somewhere else.

6.6 WHO? ME? FORGET YOU EVEN SAW ME.

For every Green, the group will always come first. Team before self. Remember that. This is a fundamental truth for a Green, and it shouldn't be challenged too strongly. The working group, the team, the golf club, the neighborhood, the family—all these different groups are important for a Green. They often disregard their own needs, provided the group gets what it needs.

You may think that groups consist of people and if each individual is satisfied, the group as a whole will be content. This may be, but then the focus will be on the collective rather than the individual. The way a Green sees it, if the group feels good, every individual also feels good.

Here, the Green's thoughtfulness becomes apparent: They have infinite regard for those around them. This is partly the reason why it's—how should I put this?—challenging to get a straight answer from a Green. They're always trying to satisfy everyone else.

Allow me to share a rather vivid story with you. One Sunday a few years ago, a colleague I didn't know that well called me. I had only been working with Kristoffer for a few months, and I hadn't really figured the guy out yet. We'd not worked on any projects together and we'd never spoken outside working hours.

So when he called me one Sunday morning, I felt surprised as I picked up the phone. I saw who it was, but I had no idea what he might want from me at that time of day. Well. He greeted me cheerfully and asked what I was doing on a Sunday like this. (I had just bought a new house at that time and was busy renovating.)

Kristoffer asked what was on the agenda this particular Sunday, and I remember I said I was worried about the boiler. It was early winter. The temperature was just below freezing, and one of the circulation pumps wasn't really up to scratch. Because colder weather was definitely on the way, I was wondering if the pump could cope with a major cold snap.

Being a Green, Kristoffer asked a number of questions and gave me lots of good advice. He'd once had a boiler like it, and besides, he knew a plumber whom he might be able to ask to swing by and have a look—if I was interested. We chatted for a while, and I became increasingly puzzled about why he had actually called me. Surely he hadn't hit me up one Sunday morning to discuss my boiler—unless the man was psychic.

He asked me where I lived. I gave him the address, and he promised to make a note of it and pass it on to his plumber friend. We had by now been talking for a good five or six minutes. Then as a kind of "by the way," he asked me if I had any plans to go into town that day. I lived about fifteen miles from the office and hadn't intended to go to work that Sunday. I told Kristoffer this.

We chatted a little while longer, and in the end I finally asked him straight out what was on his mind. Then he revealed that he was standing outside the office downtown in a T-shirt because he had accidentally locked himself out when he'd popped out to fetch some lunch. I looked at the thermometer. Thirty degrees Fahrenheit and snowing gently. By now, we'd been talking for about fifteen minutes. I got into the car and saved him from freezing to the bone. Yes, this is a true story.

Everyone else is more important. A Green never asks for anything.

6.7 I KNOW EXACTLY WHAT YOU MEAN

Greens are—among other things—introverts. In other words, they are active in their inner world. This means they don't talk just for the sake of talking. When you're quieter than those around you, it's natural that you listen. And Greens want to listen—they're interested in you and your ideas.

They actually listen to what you say. Unlike Reds, who only listen when there is something to be gained from it, or Yellows, who usually don't listen at all (although they will normally deny this fact), Greens hear what you're actually saying. They have a genuine ear for human problems. They might not offer any suggestions or solutions, but they understand what you've told them. Don't assume that means they agree with you—but they are good listeners.

While reading this book, you've probably been trying to put the pieces together, dear reader. Where do the different colors fit in? What kind of job would be best for each of them? Who would work best with whom? What does the perfect relationship or marriage look like? These are good questions, even if there are no simple answers.

One observation that often arises when I work with these issues in different organizations is that Reds, and Yellows in particular, must be good salespeople. Granted, this is true. They're forward-thinking and relatively goal-focused. So, sure.

But Greens are often overlooked. If there's one thing salespeople ought to know, it's that there's value in talking less and listening more—something Greens do quite naturally.

Helena was a neighbor of mine who lived just down the street from me a few years back. She was a Green and very gentle in her manner. Most people around her couldn't fathom how she got by in this hard-as-nails world.

But I have a theory.

She once told me about the time when she was due to meet with a representative from the local council—apparently the bureaucrats were unhappy about the solar panels the family had just fitted on their roof. You weren't allowed to install them without a permit and this man was notorious for putting a stop to any and all projects that weren't to his liking, regardless of rational arguments for or against. Everyone in the local council had tremendous respect for this obstinate decision-maker. No one in the neighborhood had ever managed to persuade him to change his view—not even once. I suspect this had been the ulterior motive of whichever of Helena's neighbors had anonymously reported the solar panels in the first place.

But she pulled off one heck of a meeting. They bumped into each other in the car park outside the council offices where they were due to meet. The surly bureaucrat pulled into the car park in a beautifully preserved American classic car from the sixties. It was quite something. Helena said the only thing she could think of: *Wow!*

Do you like cars? he asked, before they had even greeted each other. Helena nodded, directing a smile at the car while saying nothing. Then he told her about the car, how much he had spent on restoring it, the paintwork and alloys, the engine.

He showed her what it looked like under the hood. Helena nodded and murmured approval and hoped he wouldn't ask her any questions, since she couldn't tell the difference between a Ford and a Toyota. But she didn't interrupt; she just listened.

The whole thing was a walkover after that. They sat down and he asked to see the plans for the solar panels that had already been installed. He said yes on the spot and signed the paperwork.

How did she do it? By doing nothing at all except one thing—she listened. And she kept her mouth shut.

6.8 SOME EXAMPLES FROM REALITY OF GREEN BEHAVIOR

Okay. Are there any Green members of your family? Most likely there are. As I said, one in two people on average have shades of Green in their profile.

Famous people known for their Green traits include Michelle Obama, Mahatma Gandhi, Luke Skywalker, and even our very own monarch here in Sweden, King Carl XVI Gustaf.

Maybe even Jesus Christ—that guy sure knew how to take one for the team.

7

Blue Behavior

7.1 HOW YOU KNOW THAT SOMEONE OUT THERE WILL ALWAYS CONSIDER YOU CARELESS

7.1.1 Why Are We Doing This? What's the Analysis Behind It?

The last of the four colors is an interesting fellow. Or lady. You've probably met them. They don't make much of a fuss, but they do keep tabs on what is happening around them. While a Green will just go with the flow, a Blue has all the right answers. In the background, they analyze, sort, evaluate, assess, rate.

You know you've met a Blue if you visit someone's home and everything is organized in a particular way. Clear labels and names on each hook so the children will know exactly where to hang up their jackets. Meal plans, divided into six-week cycles to ensure a balanced diet, stuck on the refrigerator door. Check their tools—be it in the kitchen or the garage—and you'll find that everything has its own spot and nothing is out of place.

Well, why not? A Blue DIYer or home cook always puts things back where they belong. They're also pessimists. Excuse me, of course what I mean is realists. They see errors, and they see risks. They're the melancholics who close our behavioral circle. Gloomy, sad, unhappy, depressed, and pessimistic. At least if we're to believe the thesaurus.

7.2 EXCUSE ME, BUT THAT'S NOT QUITE ACCURATE . . .

Well, maybe it's not quite that bad. But we all have a friend like that. Think about it: You're in a restaurant with your closest friends. You're discussing politics, sports, child-rearing, or space rockets. Someone throws out a random comment. It may be your Red friend who claims that Swedish astronaut Christer Fuglesang has been to space three times; it might be the Yellow who cheerfully claims that he lived on the same block as the aforementioned astronaut during his Växjö childhood.

Your Blue buddy clears their throat and gently informs you that Fuglesang has actually only been to space twice, and the second time he performed the heaviest lift ever in zero gravity (nearly eighteen hundred pounds, not that you asked), and that Christer was most definitely not born and raised in Växjö and not even in that corner of Sweden at all, since he was, in fact, raised in the Stockholm suburbs.

Furthermore, the good friend adds without a single expression revealing what he is really thinking, considering that Christer was no less than fifty-two years old when he made his second space trip in 2009, there will hardly be a third. The probability can actually be assessed as fairly low. Less than 5.74 percent. And we know this for sure, given that the coefficient . . .

You just have to give up, guys. This friend simply knows everything. They don't make a big deal about it, but their way of presenting facts makes it difficult for you to call them into question. They know where they found the info and could probably retrieve the book to prove their point.

That's the way it is with Blues. They know how things stand before they open their mouth. They've googled, read the owner's manual, and triple-checked five different YouTube channels—and afterward they present a report in full. With references and footnotes to boot. And heck, why not an unfathomable Excel spreadsheet, too?

But there's one important thing to note: If the question doesn't come up, it's unlikely your Blue pal will say anything on the subject. They have no need to tell everyone what they know. Of course, a Blue doesn't know everything; no one can. But you can usually bank on the fact that *what* they say is correct.

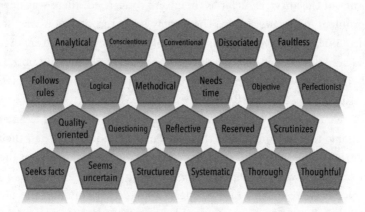

Did you notice anything about the art above? Of course you did. This time I listed the different characteristics in alphabetical order—something a Blue would certainly appreciate. However, I might get in trouble because I don't discuss each and every one of these characteristics individually on the subsequent pages. To all Blue individuals who are reading this—who have probably jotted down a little note in the margin to go to my website to look for possible explanations for this blunder—I just want to say I didn't mean to cause any strife.

Still here? Want some details? Read on!

7.3 IT'S NO BIG DEAL, I WAS JUST DOING MY JOB

A person who always knows best can be pretty unassuming, right? Of course, it's in the eye of the beholder, but isn't it modest not to make a fuss even though you have the answer to most things?

An out-and-out Blue rarely needs to be manning the barricades and beating the drum (or perhaps their own chest?) in order to make it clear to the world who the true expert is. It's often self-evident.

I don't consider this to be entirely positive. On more than one occasion, I've found myself in a group faced with a tangible problem we've tried to solve together. Two hours in, a Blue will appear and point out the answer. As far as they were concerned, there was never a problem in the first place. They knew what the situation was. But since Blues often overlook the bigger picture, they don't always act.

There have been times when I've wondered why they said nothing when they saw that we had a problem to solve. The answer on many occasions? *You didn't ask.*

It would be easy to feel aggravated by such a comment. But at the same time, I understand them. It's more my problem than theirs that they weren't invited to join the discussion. They knew that they knew the answer, and that was good enough.

Nor is there much cause to cheer, applaud, or summon the Blue to the podium once their charitable activity is a fait accompli and they have made some incredible contribution to the effort. Of course, it doesn't do any harm to celebrate. But they'll just nod, accept the praise and the prize, and then return to their desk, where they'll continue working on the next project. They may well wonder what the fuss was all about—after all, they were only doing their job.

7.4 WHERE DID YOU READ THAT? AND WHAT EDITION WAS IT?

A Blue can rarely get too many facts or have too many pages of fine print. People say the devil is in the details, and I can imagine it was a Blue who first said that.

No detail is too small to be noticed. Cutting corners is simply not an option for a Blue.

Hold up, you might say. *Not keeping track of every single tiny detail isn't really the same thing as cutting corners.*

If you ask a Blue, it is: Not having full control is the same thing as

not having any control at all. How do you put out a fire? One hundred percent, of course. Did you ever hear about a fire that was only
81 percent extinguished? Or just 46 percent? No. That's how careless
people handle a problem. One hundred percent is the only approach
that works. What do we get by cutting corners? How can you possibly justify it?

It doesn't work like that. Tell a Blue they can ignore the details
in the contract from the power company for their new-build house,
skip the last thirty paragraphs—there's nothing important in that
bit anyway—and they'll stare at you very attentively and question
your mental faculties. As usual, they won't necessarily say anything.
They'll just completely ignore what you just said. They would rather
burn the midnight oil checking all the facts than miss the slightest
detail.

A few years back, my friend Jonas was planning a big family gathering. It was going to be a reunion bringing together all sorts of people,
from his ancient great-grandmother to his distant third cousins. Among
our mutual friends, Jonas is renowned for his meticulousness and his
need for—ahem, how to put this?—detailed plans. He's the kind of person who spends hours reading product descriptions and user reviews
before ponying up for a new toaster.

When it came to this important reunion, Jonas had made up his
mind that it was going to be a picnic in the local park. The reason for
this idea was that he had read an article in a magazine at his barber's
about a similar picnic, and as far as he could tell, the participants
seemed to have been very satisfied.

He embarked upon the project by creating an extensive list of
specific details and instructions for the day. This list included everything from exact timings for each dish to be served to which games
would be played (and when) and what the options were. Some of
the picnickers were well past retirement age and could hardly be expected to play a round of softball.

He also drew up a playlist of background music for the event.
The music would be calmer during breaks for food, and more upbeat
during group activities. All artists and song titles were noted.

I stopped by his place one Sunday with some produce from my wife's vegetable patch to find him at the dining table in front of a huge spread of paperwork. Pretty quickly, I realized what his challenge was. He wanted to maintain full control of the day, but it was going to be difficult.

When I suggested that we might be a little more spontaneous and let the guests bring their own contributions to the food and beverages, Jonas's face clouded over. As far as he was concerned, you couldn't guarantee that everyone would get enough to eat if there wasn't a detailed plan in place, and what would my solution to that be? What was needed here was a carefully planned menu and associated schedule of mealtimes.

I laughed and pointed out that this was just a family picnic rather than a banquet to mark the award of a Nobel Prize. Surely it would all work out . . . ?

Jonas wasn't impressed. He needed more information, more details—lots more.

The challenges were innumerable. What if someone had allergies? What if the food ran out? Had I even considered a backup plan for bad weather? Can you barbecue in the rain? How can you be sure? Who can be trusted to know these key details?

So I sat down and helped him plan out every single detail of his picnic. We compiled lists of potential allergens in the proposed dishes, a backup plan if the heavens opened, and even a detailed seating chart in case people found themselves baffled when it came to sitting down.

On the day of the reunion, Jonas's wife tells me he was on tenterhooks. He was only satisfied once he'd seen that everything was going according to plan, down to the last letter. Once he realized that everyone was having a good time, even if they weren't always strictly following his plan, he was able to relax and enjoy himself a little more.

His need for detail and planning was apparent, and while it was sometimes overwhelming, it taught us all the value of being prepared. Perhaps a little too prepared.

7.5 I'M NOT IN HIBERNATION—BUT I NEED
TO SLEEP ON IT

The preceding example also illustrates another important characteristic of Blue behavior. They're generally very cautious. They often think: safety first. Where a Red or Yellow would take a wild chance, a Blue will hold off and consider everything one more time. There may be more factors to take into account, right? You need to get to the bottom of things before you act.

There's an old joke about who makes the best lawyer. It suggests it's the person without arms, because they can't hold up their hands and say *on the one hand* followed by *on the other hand*.

This cautiousness can manifest in many ways. It's a fact that for the Blue, the journey is more important than the destination—exactly the opposite of a Red. Obviously, this amount of caution can result in no decisions being made at all, and it also means that Blues rarely take any major risks.

As the old saying goes: "Decisions in progress."

Never taking any risks ensures a predictable life; we can probably agree on that. I'm not saying anything about how exciting and inspiring it would be; I'm just stating the facts.

Sometimes a Blue can completely refrain from starting something because they can't assess the risks. I once had a Blue acquaintance who had trained as an engineer, and whose motto for life was the best deal was often the one you didn't make.

Risk assessment is a complex thing, and who knows what dangers are lurking out there? A Blue generally solves everything by creating advanced systems that manage the possible risks that may arise. They set three alarm clocks. They leave two hours early when one would be enough. They check and recheck the kids' backpacks before school in the morning, even though they packed them the night before and no one has touched the backpacks during the night. They triple-check that the keys are in their pocket and, of course, they are.

Where else would they be?

The benefits of this are evident. Blues won't be taken aback by unexpected events in the same way others would be. And in the long run, they save a lot of time.

7.6 IT DOESN'T MATTER IF IT'S EASIER; IT'S STILL NOT RIGHT

Things can't be allowed to go wrong. That's all there is to it. Quality is all that matters.

When a Blue individual thinks their work runs the risk of being shoddy or of low quality, things come to a standstill. Everything must be checked out. Why has the quality declined?

At the risk of generalizing, I would say a fair number of engineers have distinct Blue traits: accurate, systematic, fact-oriented, and quality-conscious.

I can't know for certain, but I would imagine that Toyota, the Japanese car manufacturer, probably has a good proportion of Blue engineers in its workforce. They have an approach that involves always asking five questions to ensure quality. I would say this is a typical Blue approach (in addition to the Japanese mentality, which is very long term and rather Blue in expression).

So let's say someone discovers an oil stain on the floor. A Red approach might be to lambaste the person closest by and then order them to mop up the damn stain. A Yellow sees the stain and then forgets it but two days later is surprised to slip on it. The Green also sees the stain and has a bad feeling about it, because it really is a problem that someone ought to be addressing.

The outcome? Nothing. Nada. There the stain remains.

Now, the alternative. A Blue would probably deal with the stain personally since they consider themselves the master of these very stains, but they would also ask the following question: *Where did the stain come from?*

The answer may be that a gasket is leaking. This answer, of course, is unsatisfactory for a Blue.

Why is the gasket leaking? Because it's poor quality. Why do we have poor-quality gaskets in our factory? Because the purchasing de-partment was told to save money. We bought cheap gaskets instead of sealed gaskets. But who asked us to save money and compromise on quality? (Of course, there's always the risk that it will be down to the finance department in the end. . . .)

And so they continue. Maybe the problem will resolve itself. Maybe we'll get a report of what went wrong in the process but no actual suggestions on how to remedy it.

In the end, the solution might be to review our purchasing strat-egies instead of just mopping up the oil on the floor.

My point is this: A Blue is prepared to dive deep to get everything exactly 100 percent correct.

Blues argue that if they're going to do something, they must do it correctly. And vice versa—if a task isn't worth doing properly, then it's not worth doing at all.

Furthermore, because Blues usually find it difficult to lie, they will always point out the defects they uncover—even defects that may reflect poorly on themselves.

I clearly remember discussions my parents had when I was a child. We moved from time to time, and usually our house had to be sold, which involved a lot of work. Dad—the engineer—would, of course, do everything himself, plus he managed the viewings personally.

My mum was always upset that he began each viewing by point-ing out all the flaws and shortcomings of the house. It leaked here and there, and some paint had flaked off the wall behind the sofa.

"Why are you telling them that?" my mother wondered.

"Because these are the things that are wrong with the house," Dad said, oblivious.

"Sure, but do you have to tell that to the prospective buyers? Now they may not want to buy the house!"

He didn't understand the problem. You have to tell it like it is. As a very honorable and honest person, he couldn't hide the faults he knew were there. The shortcomings were there. He could live with the fact that we rarely made a huge profit on those deals. He'd been honest about the house, because that's how it should be done. And the disturbing statistics are there: Engineers are the worst sales reps. Too honest.

7.7 IF THE TERRAIN DOESN'T MATCH THE MAP, THEN THERE'S SOMETHING WRONG WITH THE TERRAIN

Logical and rational thinking are critical to Blues. Out with all the feelings (as much as possible) and in with logic.

Of course, Blues can't turn off their feelings completely—no one can—but they like to say they use rational grounds when making decisions. They value logical thinking highly, but they can very easily become depressed when things don't go their way. And depression (since we're talking about Blues, we need to add a caveat: I'm not talking about depression caused by chemical imbalances) has nothing whatsoever to do with logic—it's about emotion. Stress is a real condition but is very illogical for a Blue. It's real, but simultaneously irrational.

Few people can repeat the same steps in a process countless times, exactly the same each time, like a Blue. They have a unique ability to follow instructions down to the letter, without questioning them. That is, if they understood them and thought they were good in the first place.

How is it they can do this? Well, because it's rational. If it ain't broke, why fix it? While a Yellow or a Red would conceive of a new method mostly out of boredom, the Blue repeats the same thing over and over.

An interesting example of this is how they assemble IKEA furniture. If there's a manual, it must be read from cover to cover before work begins.

Reds—engrossed with the idea that they already know all this—will start turning screws and knocking pieces together without even checking what else is in the box. Any idiot can do this—let's roll!

Yellows decant everything from the packaging and spread it across half the house while telling anyone who will listen how great it will be to have the finished article in place. As we already know, they live in the future and can already clearly picture their new cabinet in its rightful place in the bedroom with their grandmother's old tablecloth draped over it and a lovely vase of tulips on top. Their approach to assembly is a little slipshod, but they don't struggle. Screws go in wherever it seems logical they should, and they skip one or two steps in the process.

A Green DIYer sets down the huge box by the wall and has a cup of coffee. There's no rush.

And what does our Blue IKEA customer do? They read through the instructions twice, examine every part, and make sure they match the pictures in the manual. Using a slightly damp (not too damp, 10 percent will do) cloth, they wipe everything down carefully to ensure no dust is present. The number of screws in the box is checked to ensure there are no unpleasant surprises down the line (and if there are parts left over, they may well dismantle the whole thing again). Naturally, the finest wood glue known to man is used, even though IKEA actually doesn't suggest you need any adhesive at all. But what do the people at IKEA know, anyway? Amateurs.

It may take a little extra time for a Blue to assemble their cabinet, but once it's in place, you can be sure it'll stand until the end of time.

7.8 THE DEVIL IS IN THE DETAILS

A few years ago, I wanted to redo the patio in my garden. Because I like working with my hands, in contrast to just talking each day, I thought I would do the job myself. Or at least part of it. My dad, well over seventy at the time, was going to help out because he knew I was pressed for time.

Easier said than done. To make sure we did a really good job, we were going to put down a layer of aggregate. Dad (who, as I've already revealed to you, was an engineer) showed up a few minutes ahead of a dump truck with all the gravel in the back. He had his own wheelbarrow with him, specially designed to maneuver gravel, and a special shovel that he always used for similar purposes. He didn't understand why I was standing there with my regular shovel. Everyone knew you had to use special shovels for things like this.

The truck came and dropped a hefty pile of gravel in the driveway. I imagined a few days of shoveling before me, and to be honest, it made me feel a little tired. But I was still ready to take on the challenge.

But my old man? He picked up a bit of gravel between his fingers, smelled it, felt it, and assessed its quality. After a grunt I interpreted as approval, he began to assess the pile itself.

He measured the height of the mound with his hand; he paced how large the circumference was. I asked him what he was doing. He didn't answer but mumbled numbers under his breath.

"One and eighty high, five meters in circumference, gradient . . . hmm . . ." After twenty seconds, he said there were between eight and three-quarters and nine and one-quarter cubic meters of gravel in the driveway.

I confided to him that it was actually nine cubic meters. On the dot.

Dad asked rather skeptically how I knew that. I pointed. "It says so on the truck," I said.

Dad was mildly impressed. I asked if he wanted to count each piece of gravel individually. He didn't deem that to be necessary.

For hours, he walked around the site and packed and pressed and raked the gravel, smoothing everything until he thought it was all in order. He used a level, plumb line, water, all the means at his disposal so nothing would go wrong.

The gravel needed to be laid at a ratio of exactly one centimeter per meter. Why? Such a dumb question. Because that's how you do it. Because he was a construction engineer, he knew what you were supposed to teach to people working on this kind of stuff day in, day out. One centimeter per meter. It had to be one centimeter. Exactly. Who knew what terrible consequences we would face if we got this wrong?

Please note the difference between one centimeter and a few centimeters. The former is exact, the latter very unclear. A few centimeters. It might be up to two centimeters if things went really badly. And an incline of a centimeter or two, well, that's a difference of no less than 100 percent. A colossal deviation.

(The funny thing about this story is not really the event itself, but what happened when Dad read about it in the first edition of this book. He argued that's not how it really happened. He corrected the story on several points and claimed that the truck had held twelve cubic meters—not nine. He also insists that he's not purely Blue, and there might be something in that.)

He's like that with everything. At home, if there are any technical questions about a television, a car, a microwave, or a mobile phone, out comes the manual. He always replies, *It says here that . . . Why do you think they wrote this stuff if it's not meant to be done that way?*

How do you answer that? How do you argue with the instruction manual? It's impossible to find arguments that a true Blue will accept. (My dad will also stop at a red light in the middle of the night, even if he is the only person within a ten-mile radius. Because that's the way you do it.)

The great value of this approach is obvious. He was never fooled; he always got what he paid for. It gave him an inner peace because he knew he had checked everything out very accurately.

If you know any Blues, I am sure you will agree with me. Under normal circumstances, they're very calm and balanced. Probably because they keep tabs on everything.

7.9 SILENCE IS GOLDEN

Introvert. Enough said. I could stop there. Many Blues I've met don't say a single word unnecessarily. That's just the way it is.

Does that mean they have nothing to say? That they don't have opinions about things? Not at all, they're just very, very introverted. Blues are calm and truly stable individuals. A curious example: The Aztecs equated this trait with the sea, the element of water.

Calm on the outside, but under the surface anything could be happening. "Introverted" doesn't mean silent; it means active in the inner world. But the effect of this is often silence.

In general, my advice is to listen attentively when Blues do actually talk, because they've usually thought through what they say.

So why are they so taciturn? Among other things, it's because they, unlike Yellows, don't feel the need to be heard. Sitting in a corner and not being seen or heard makes no difference to them. They are observers, spectators, more than central characters. They can find themselves at the edge of a group where they observe and record everything that is said.

And don't forget this: According to a Blue's values, being silent is something positive. If you don't have anything useful to say, then mum's the word.

7.10 SOME EXAMPLES FROM REALITY OF BLUE BEHAVIOR

Do you know everything there is to know about Blues now? Have you identified any in your life? Swedish tennis legend Björn Borg is undeniably a Blue. Kevin Costner and Barack Obama are probably mostly Blue, although there are other traits in both. Another that springs to mind is the researcher Marie Curie. Not to mention C-3PO in *Star Wars*. He's a real stickler—highly anxious and reluctant to step outside the box.

8

Who Gets Along and Why

8.1 DO WE ALL GET ALONG?

It's a widespread myth that everyone can get along if they just try hard enough. Whether this actually corresponds to reality is debatable, given that the vast majority of people make very little effort at all.

Social skills are more important than which colors you are. Regardless of what your profile looks like, the most important thing is to take your own traits to heart, develop your levels of self-awareness, and work to really absorb the nuances in your surroundings—rather than assume everyone else is like you.

Not that you would do that, but you and I both know, dear reader, that not everyone else is as sensible about these kinds of things as we are.

But sometimes looking at things in purely structural terms can be helpful, depending on what your constitution is. Are there any color combinations that work together better than others without much effort? Yes, as it happens. The diagram on the following page sets it out clearly.

As you can see, different colors work together with differing degrees of success. Again, there are plenty of exceptions, but let's say that none of the people involved have any real knowledge of their behavior patterns and therefore lack any real self-awareness. For instance, it's generally easier for two people to work together if they have the same

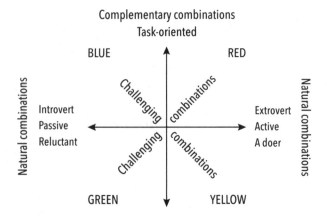

Complementary combinations
Task-oriented

sense of tempo and work at a similar speed. That's basically preaching to the choir. But there's more to be said on this matter.

8.2 NATURAL COMBINATIONS

If we look at the diagram above, we can see that Blue and Green could be an effective combination without much of an effort from either of them.

They would certainly recognize themselves in each other's ability to breathe calmly and think twice before doing something. Since both are introverts, each of them feels secure with the other. Neither of them will build castles in the air, because they prefer to keep both feet on the ground. They don't stress but allow themselves to dive deeply into things. Sure, they may find it difficult to make decisions, but the decisions they do make will probably be well thought out.

Similarly, Red and Yellow work smoothly together since they both want to shoot from the hip and keep moving forward. Both are powerful and outgoing, and because both are verbal, they can easily find the right words. Certainly, they'll have a different focus in the conversation, but the dialogue will still flow.

Both set high goals and think quickly. Say the homeowners' association has ordered everyone in the neighborhood to come out and clean the street. You divide the neighbors into different groups since that seems the logical way to do things. You probably end up doing it by door number. Big mistake.

A group of Yellows and Reds will set off at top speed with their rakes and shovels while being clear about what they want to achieve in the space of an afternoon; they'll also be motivating others in the neighborhood to do great things. The challenge probably lies in the fact that a Red can perceive a Yellow as being too talkative, but since neither of them is a world-class listener, they'll both just switch off when it suits them.

8.2.1 Complementary Combinations

It also works to look at the other axis and make pairings based on each color's focus. Both Blues and Reds are task-oriented.

Reds are certainly more interested in the result than in the process itself, and Blues are more concerned with the process and tend to ignore the result—but they're at least speaking the same language.

Both devote themselves to raking up leaves and spend very little time talking about sports or interior design—except during their coffee break (which for another group may be just as important as the main task at hand. More on that soon). They would complement each other in a good way. If we liken this to a car, a Red is the accelerator, while a Blue is the brake. Both are needed in order to drive successfully. The trick is not to push both pedals at the same time.

Similarly, there is some logic in placing a Green with a Yellow. The tempo at which they work will be different, but both of them will be curious about each other. Both believe people are interesting and important. While one likes to take it easy, the other likes having fun. They'll effortlessly find a similar focus. And they'll focus on chatting during the breaks—after all, it's nice to hang out, too!

The Green will allow the Yellow to take as much space as they want. One talks; the other listens. It can work out well. In addition, Greens are good at calming down the slightly hysterical Yellows, who sometimes have a hard time staying grounded. They'll never forget about the human being in the process.

Of course, there's a risk that they'll fail to devote sufficient time to the work itself, but they will have a very good time. People around them might feel they're only having a good time and not actually delivering anything. As both can find it difficult to say no, it might also be a good idea to avoid entrusting them with too much money.

8.2.2 Challenging Combinations

So far, so good. But there are also two very complicated combinations. This doesn't mean they won't be able to work together, but it definitely means there are obstacles to be considered. One possible solution is that both of them become more self-aware in the ways they work and interact with each other.

Take a look at this illustration:

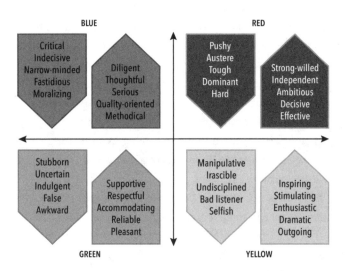

For each color, the right column shows the things a person sees in their own profile—the good and positive aspects. The left column shows how that person's *exact opposite* might perceive them in less favorable circumstances.

You've probably heard that a person was a real bore before you met them, only to discover a very interesting person with lots of exciting things to say.

Who's right and who's wrong? That's a very interesting question, and unfortunately, there's no good answer to it.

The problem lies in the interaction between each color and its exact opposite. The positive image expresses how each profile experiences themselves. The negative image is an expression of how they can be experienced by others. We all see different things.

8.2.3 And Then There Are Genuine Problems

It would be quite a challenge to put a Red and a Green together to solve a problem. If the task depends on effective cooperation, then issues will quickly arise. In the beginning, the Green is very passive, especially compared to the Red, who gets going even before they've heard the instructions. While the Green may find the task burdensome, the Red has already clattered off the starting line and over the horizon.

The Red will be dreadfully critical of the Green's constant moaning about the amount of work. At the same time, the Green will think the Red is an aggressive son of a bitch who never listens. Nevertheless, under favorable circumstances things may work out.

But why? In general, a Green is prepared to cooperate; that's their strength. They function well with many other people because they're more accommodating than demanding. So there can be a certain logic in setting a Red with a Green. A Red likes giving orders, and a Green is usually okay with receiving orders.

Based on DISC theory, the greatest challenge of all is to ask a Yellow and a Blue to work together. If neither of them is aware of how their personalities work, there will be friction from the outset.

The Yellow will dive into the task without the slightest idea of what to do or how to do it. They won't read any instructions, and they won't listen long enough to find out what the task is actually about. They'll speak at great length about what an exciting project they've been given. In the meantime, the Blue will start reading and researching all available materials. They won't say a word but will just sit there. They won't budge an inch while they think.

The Yellow, on the one hand, will consider this person to be the most uninspiring bore they have ever met. The Blue, on the other hand, will be disturbed by the Yellow's perpetual verbal barrage. They'll slowly begin to boil beneath the surface because of the incessant buzzing around them. They'll think the Yellow is a frivolous windbag, not deserving any attention whatsoever.

And when the Yellow finally realizes that they haven't won the Blue over to their side, they'll pull out all the stops and talk even more. In the worst case, they'll try to charm the Blue, which will end up in disaster. They'll withdraw into their own corners, with faces like they've tasted sour milk, both mad for completely different reasons.

Self-awareness, my friend, is the solution.

8.3 HOW TO ACT WHEN YOU DON'T KNOW WHO YOU'RE DEALING WITH? GO GREEN!

It's not easy to read and interpret everyone. If a person only has traits in one color, then they ought to pose no problems to you once you've finished reading this book. It'll be obvious what you should do. A person who is only Red or only Yellow is hard to miss. But even the genuine Greens or Blues are quite easy to detect if you know what to look for.

Statistically speaking only about 5 percent of the population has just one color that shows in their behavior. Around 80 percent have two, and the rest have three. No one has four, not with the tool I use.

It's also relatively easy to recognize people who have two colors. Two-color combinations normally follow any of the axes. So they are: Blue/Red, Red/Yellow, Yellow/Green, or Green/Blue.

It does happen, of course, that purely opposite qualities can be found in one and the same person. I've met lots of Yellow/Blue people. There's nothing wrong with that; it's just less common. But what's really unusual is distinctly Red/Green profiles. Why this is the case I don't know.

On one occasion, I met a woman who was a middle manager working for a company in the auto industry. She was determined and powerful in her manner, but at the same time she was extremely caring. Her care and attention for her employees was genuine, and it had some strange results.

Among other things, she could lose her temper very quickly. Her telling-offs were legendary. Once she realized this, however, she would do whatever she could to soften the effects of her actions and repair the damage. She felt genuinely bad for having been hard on various individuals, but in the heat of the moment she couldn't control herself.

This friction between the two conflicting colors in her behavior meant that she was very close to burnout.

People with three colors will always be more difficult to interpret. If someone is very difficult to place on the map, it may be because they have three colors. The situation will determine what behavior they exhibit.

The best advice I can give if you really can't analyze a person you meet is to shut your mouth and start listening. If in doubt, go Green.

People sometimes tell me that they can't understand someone because they don't do anything. But even a person who is very passive exhibits some form of behavior. And at this stage, you know what color is associated with someone who doesn't do much—that's a common Blue behavior.

The Other Side of the Coin

9.1 THE REASON WHY NOT EVERYTHING IS GOLDEN

Have you ever found yourself in a situation where you've been discussing the best form of housing, be it a house, an apartment, a condominium, or something else? Or which diet you should follow to live longer? Or maybe you've gotten stuck on which breed of dog you should get if you really don't want a cat. Although, have you considered a cat? After all, they're much easier than dogs. Right?

Or what about this one: Which type of weather is best? Which season do you prefer? And before you say "summer" and "warm," please be aware that far from everyone would agree. I would agree—I detest autumn and winter. I think the spring is nice, but only because it always leads to summer. But someone who goes skiing and likes cozy evenings in with a cup of tea and a good book might well prefer autumn and winter.

Speaking of good books . . . what are they? And according to whom?

How come? What is it that these people don't understand? I know I'm right while they're wrong, so what's the problem?

The interesting thing about this type of discussion is that all variants of the aforementioned subjects are to be found out there in the wild. If everyone wanted the same thing, there would only be one make of car, one dog breed, one food, one way to raise your kids, one religion, and so on and so forth.

Yet that isn't the case. Why?

Simple: Not all variants suit all people. We have different preferences and we have different requirements for this and that. But we may not always think that way. Instead, we think—when we encounter people who don't think like us and don't like the same things we do—that we're surrounded by idiots.

What the hell is wrong with that fool?

Admit it: You're still regularly overcome by the thought that a given person doesn't understand squat.

There are two ways of thinking here. The first is that if you truly understood the different patterns of thought that different people have, it would be easier to get along.

But the second is that the above rule only applies to other people. There's a huge number of different types of people, and the same thing happens to them, too.

You'll be discussing your new neighbor, or the coworker who just left their job, or Ellinor's new fiancé, or said fiancé's younger sister. *A pleasant, likable person*, you might say. *A deadbeat with a bad attitude*, someone else might say. All about the same individual.

For me, this has always been the allure of working with people—we have so many varied interpretations of the same person that we sometimes wonder whether we're even talking about the same person.

But perhaps that's okay. However, it can be worthwhile building on your knowledge of how people—not least yourself—may actually be perceived by people who aren't you, even if that perception might be wrong. A small deviation in core behavior is all it takes to make it work. If you're really different, then genuine conflict can arise out of thin air, and there's no guarantee anyone will be able to put their finger on why it happened.

So what does this mean for us? As the title of this book hints, there are people around us whom—in less favorable circumstances—we face certain challenges in understanding. There are others we simply don't understand, regardless of the situation. And the hardest to deal with are those who aren't like ourselves at all, since they're conspicuously behaving in the wrong way.

9.1.1 The Differences Begin to Become Clear

I'm guessing you can see the differences between the different colors, at least in broad strokes. The illustration below shows an example of how they differ. Some people are task-oriented, and others are relationship-oriented. While two of them are quick to act, the other two are reflective. And this is often the source of everyday misunderstandings, great and small. I'll come back to this point later, but I would like to take this opportunity to provide some nuances to the illustration of the different core behavior patterns that each color represents.

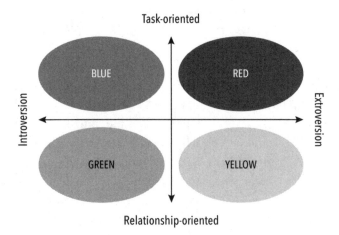

Obviously I'm not suggesting you would call people idiots—like Sture, who opened my eyes to all this in the first place, as related at the beginning of this book—but let's be honest, at one time or another, we've all been dumbfounded by encountering comments and behaviors that are the diametric opposite of what we would choose ourselves.

The point of departure for such reasoning is that *I'm always right*, but that means the other person in such cases must automatically be wrong. It's a tricky issue. But the truth is actually different.

Just because you're right doesn't necessarily mean I must be wrong.

We're actually very aware of the faults and shortcomings of certain people. Child psychologists claim we are most upset by the behaviors we observe in our children that we recognize from ourselves but wish weren't there. It's an intriguing thought, as well as a very annoying one.

Besides, who gets to decide what's right and wrong? You, or everyone else?

9.1.2 Time for a Real Cliché

No one is perfect. I know it's a cliché to say so. But really, there are no perfect human beings; no one is without faults or shortcomings. For a short while I thought it was me, but my friends quickly taught me otherwise. In my youth I was constantly looking for a role model who could become my mentor in life: a man or woman who was completely free from shortcomings and who knew just how to behave in every given situation. Someone who never lost their temper but always had an answer, no matter what was happening. A true role model who could show me the way forward through life.

I'm still looking. It would appear that no one has seen hide nor hair of them. And I guess that's how it is. We live with our shortcomings and make the best of things.

But are faults and shortcomings really what we're talking about each time we say someone is an idiot? Or is it just that we don't understand said individual? An attribute that may be useful in some situations is unsuitable in others. It's important to remember that communication usually takes place on the recipient's terms. Whatever people's perception of me may be, that is the way they perceive me. Regardless of what I really mean or intend.

A good way to approach this is to look at what the opposites would say about any given behavior. If we can coax the truth out of them, then we might be onto something useful. As always, it's all about self-awareness. Good qualities can become drawbacks in the wrong circumstances, no matter what those qualities are—and that's where the preceding model above can help.

9.1.3 A Quick Review of Core Behaviors

Reds are quick and more than happy to take command if needed. They make things happen. However, when they get going, they become control freaks and can be hopeless to deal with. And they repeatedly trample on people's toes.

Yellows can be amusing and creative, and elevate the mood regardless of who they're with. However, when they are given unlimited space, they will consume all the oxygen in the room, they won't allow anyone into a conversation, and their stories will reflect reality less and less.

The friendly Greens are easy to hang out with because they are so pleasant and genuinely care for others. Unfortunately, they can be wishy-washy and unclear. Anyone who never takes a stand eventually becomes difficult to handle. You don't know how they really feel, and indecision kills the energy in other people.

The analytical Blues are calm, levelheaded, and think before they speak. Their ability to keep a cool head is undoubtedly an enviable quality for all who aren't capable of doing that. However, Blues' critical thinking can easily turn to suspicion and questioning those around them. Everything can become suspect and sinister.

In the following chapters, I deal with how people might perceive the weaknesses of certain behaviors. Naturally, this is a sensitive area and can be easily misunderstood. Others prefer to see it as offering potential or development opportunities. Of course, the reality is that the greater your potential, the worse off you must be right now. You simply just don't know it.

When I coach individuals, this is usually where things can get messy. Why should we spoil the mood by talking about boring stuff like faults and shortcomings? Ick.

So as you read on, be aware that much is in the eye of the beholder. Who's right and who's wrong? The behavior patterns I'm talking about are described as other people may perceive them, even if the intention of the person who just made a fool of themselves might have been completely different.

One thing I know for sure regarding the different colors is that each one evaluates themselves differently.

Reds and Yellows tend to inflate their strengths and believe they have no weaknesses. Their self-confidence is often quite strong. They have powerful egos, and a great part of their success can probably be attributed to the fact that they don't get bogged down in faults and shortcomings but instead look for opportunities and good news. Clearly, this can't be endlessly maintained.

Conversely, Greens and Blues usually exaggerate their weaknesses and in certain cases even ignore their strengths. The consequences are clear. When you give positive feedback to a Green or a Blue, they sometimes appear to be immune to it and change the subject to something that went seriously wrong. Obviously, this is highly unproductive. Like I said, people are different.

10

How Others May Perceive Reds

10.1 WHEN STRAIGHTFORWARD ISN'T ALWAYS THE SOLUTION

If you ask other people about a Red, they may well paint a different picture of the Red from the one the Red would paint themselves. What a surprise!

Many people will agree with what you have read up to now about Reds, but I have also heard other comments.

Usually, these are expressed while the Reds are out of the room, because everyone else is afraid of their fiery temper. You've heard the Red say that they want to hear the truth. Over the years they've bellowed, *Say what you think!* into everyone's ears. But as soon as you do, you find yourself in the middle of a heated discussion with an angry Red about what is and isn't true, and before long you're the idiot. (Strictly between us, my own observations over the years would suggest that Reds are surrounded by more idiots than the rest of us.)

This means what you're going to read now will often be completely new for many Reds. Not many of us have ever been able to make these points to a Red before. It takes way too much energy.

It's logical when you think about it. Some people see Reds as

belligerent, arrogant, and egotistical. They are also seen as unyielding, impatient, and commanding. Not only that, but some would
even say they're high-handed, controlling, and aggressive.

I don't subscribe to this at all, but I've even heard people describe
Red behavior as being that of a despotic dictator. Suddenly the picture isn't as flattering: the born leader seen from their bad side.

First of all, let me say this: Nothing I've said previously would necessarily keep a Red up at night, because they are more task-oriented
than relationship-oriented. What everyone else thinks about Reds is
like water off a duck's back to them. Besides, everyone else is wrong.
But let's see what everyone else has to say.

10.2 WHY DOES EVERYTHING HAVE TO TAKE SO MUCH DARNED TIME? CAN'T YOU HURRY UP?

Well, what can you say? A person willing to step outside any frame-
work and across any boundary in order to get ahead is nothing if not
impatient. When the usual official channels take too long, a Red will
go up through a few levels of decision-makers and expeditiously look
for the person who really calls the shots.

The first example that comes to mind is the traffic in the beautiful
capital city of Sweden. Sure, many Stockholmers are in more of a
hurry than the national average when they're behind the wheel—
there's no doubt a survey out there to prove it. But since we're talking
about Red behavior, I'd like to tell you about a colleague I had a few
years ago.

Björn and I used a car as our principal means of transport, even in
the very heart of the city. It simply took too long to use public transport. Incidentally, Björn's driver's license is supended every now and
then, and the reason can undoubtedly be traced to his somewhat
liberal attitude toward speed limits. He lived far outside the city and
the journey into the office, about twenty miles away, could take about
forty minutes. That was on a good day; it could just as easily take an
hour and a half.

Björn rarely felt the need to adjust his driving according to the flow of traffic. After all, everyone else was driving so slowly. He felt there was no reason for him to obey every single rule of the road.

As far as he was concerned, posted speed limits were no more than recommendations—and that was only if you spotted the signs in the first place. They didn't apply to him. They were there for people who didn't really know how to drive a car!

On one occasion, a group of us colleagues were sipping coffee and discussing the situation on the roads of our fine capital city, which had reached critical status. Everyone was always complaining. Everything was at a constant standstill. Nothing seemed to work. It felt as if Stockholm were suffering from a vehicular infarction.

Björn didn't understand what we were talking about. He wasn't aware of this problem at all. On the contrary, he felt that the traffic hadn't been bad lately. When we questioned him a bit more, it turned out he usually drove in the bus lane. All the way. For over twenty miles. It was so much quicker that way. Björn even maintained that this was okay. You see, they apparently issued permits for the bus lane. He had one, and it only cost him some $200 a month.

I remember how it took me a few beats to realize what he was talking about.

Apparently the cops pulled him over about once a month, but it was worth it—he was saving so much time! The "permit" in question and its associated charges were, in fact, the fines he accrued. He actually thought it was a good deal. Time is money.

No, I'm not making this up—this is a real example. This story illustrates clearly how Red behavior works. They know just as well as everyone else that it's wrong to break the rules; however, since it's quicker that way, they do it anyway. Reds are notorious rule breakers. Once again, I would like to remind you of their intentions—to get the job done.

Reds have no problem taking one or two shortcuts. With such a generous approach to regulations and rules, you'll definitely arrive faster. I would even say that a Red is often so fast that if something were to go wrong, they would still manage to redo the project. At the same time, no one else ever really knows what's going to happen.

10.3 I'M NOT SCREAMING! I'M NOT ANGRY! AAARRRGHHHH!

There's no escaping this—their fiery temper. Because the way Reds communicate is so blunt and direct, many perceive them as downright aggressive. This is logical, but at the same time this perception varies depending on who becomes the victim of the Red's forceful point of view.

For instance, in Sweden it's not acceptable to behave in the kind of confrontational manner that would be fine in Germany or France. I'm not saying people quarrel more in those countries, but they have a slightly different approach to conflicts.

Think about it. In many workplaces people are encouraged to be candid and to have *open communication*. You'll have heard platitudes like this for decades. We have to communicate openly at work! Or in our motorcycle club. At home too, for that matter.

But what exactly does this mean? To tell the truth, it's easy to interpret this as meaning we should be honest with each other and speak our minds. Right? We want to have open and forthright dialogue. Nothing should stand in the way of the truth. Well, this is obviously excellent, open communication if the subject being communicated is important for achieving efficiency in an organization. I dare say you can see that yourself. So let's have open communication.

Who excels at frank communication? And can receive the same without getting cranky? Answer: basically no one.

Besides Reds, of course. For them, this is a nonissue. *Why are we even talking about telling the truth? It's obvious that you say what you think!* The whole discussion ends up being a complete waste of time. Many people find this stressful. Constantly having the truth pushed into your face can be burdensome if you have difficulty taking it.

My goal here isn't to define what's right or wrong; I only want to establish that all of us are different. I like open communication too—especially on home turf. My wife—an out-and-out Red—knows all about this, which means she doesn't bother to sugarcoat things unnecessarily whenever she has views on something I've done or not done. She knows to avoid a verbal uppercut, but she makes sure the message gets through.

That's one of the reasons why I love her so much. I know I can trust her words—and that means more than anything. Sure, I might grind my teeth occasionally, since I'm just like everyone else in that regard. Reality is what it is and I'm no better than anyone else at discussing my shortcomings. The truth stings. It simply has to be said, but damn, it hurts sometimes. And to all Reds reading this, you just need to be a bit more cautious from time to time.

So why do we sometimes perceive Red behavior as threatening and belligerent? Could it be because they don't give up in the first instance? Is it because Reds are happy to argue and debate even the small stuff if it's important to them? Is it because they don't hesitate to raise their voices, fix their gazes on people, or thump the table if that suits them? Is it because they sometimes have a tendency toward bluntness?

Imagine the following scenario:

You have a project, something you've spent a few days, or maybe even weeks, on. You begin to doubt yourself—have you been successful in your task? Is it as good as you wanted it to be? Would you dare show it to the client as it is now, or should you ask for feedback from someone you know will give you an honest answer?

Just then a Red comes sauntering by, and you take a chance. You are fully aware that this colleague—spouse, friend, cousin, neighbor—will be honest.

You ask for a frank opinion. With a degree of pride in your voice, you show them what you've accomplished, and you go through your process step by step. Without you noticing, the Red becomes impatient because they've already decided what their opinion is and they're getting tired of you withering away. Too many words.

With a wave of their hand that effectively silences you, the Red says, *It doesn't look that good. I don't really like what you've done there. Listen, it looks pretty shoddy. I'm amazed you didn't do better than this. I think you have to redo the whole thing from start to finish.*

Then they leave without thinking any more about it. You're left there feeling forlorn and crushed, regardless of what color you are.

Are you going to start over? Are you going to tear down the fence or rerun the budgetary process or whatever it is you were doing?

Am I exaggerating? Can this really happen in real life? Oh boy. At this stage, if you believe that such nasty people don't really exist, then you've never met a genuine Red. Or the Reds you have met have essentially learned how to be dishonest.

Think about it. What's the purpose of cutting a person down to size so completely? What was the Red's intention? It was to do exactly what you asked. You wanted an honest opinion!

Say exactly what you think, you said. It's possible you even added: *I won't be angry/sad/disappointed/suicidal.*

Dude, you better brace yourself for impact, thinks the Red. *It's coming for you.*

By asking for an honest opinion, you released a flood of brutal candor. You might get back up after being floored, but what about everyone else? How are they going to take it?

I long ago lost count of the number of times I've explained that when a Red goes all out on an issue that's important to them, an issue on which they don't intend to give up—well, the storm will be brutal.

If you're afraid of conflict, you shouldn't put yourself in that situation. A Red has no problem with conflict. Reds don't consciously create conflict, but a refreshing quarrel every now and then is never wrong, right? It's just another way to communicate.

A little tip: The worst thing you can do once you get into a conflict with a Red is to back off. That tactic can cause you serious difficulties. More on that later.

10.4 WHAT ARE YOU DOING OVER THERE? I CAN SEE WHAT YOU'RE (NOT) DOING!

Let's explore another fascinating phenomenon—the desire for control. What exactly are we dealing with here?

Simply put, it is where an individual needs to have power over a situation in which either groups or other individuals are present.

Those who have control needs often feel extremely uneasy about having to adapt themselves to a group or a situation and will eagerly come up with various strategies to avoid this.

A common form of behavior is to talk constantly, interrupting and ignoring others, in order to maintain control over the conversation.

Reds can probably be perceived as extremely overbearing, but it's important to note that they are interested in controlling those around them, but not in controlling every specific detail of a situation. (Attention to or control over detail isn't something we can accuse Reds of.) But it is important for a Red to feel they can influence what people do and how they intend to act on certain issues. Since they're convinced they know better, it's downright beastly for them to be forced to watch others running around like headless chickens.

What we're talking about here is a sense that they are actually better informed than everyone else. And because a Red feels they know best, they will keep tabs on everyone around them to ensure they all do the right thing. The advantage for Reds is they get everything done their way.

The disadvantage is obvious: Everyone else feels controlled. Some people think it's a good thing when someone else makes the decisions and holds the baton, but others feel constrained and just want to escape. There are even those who feel offended by it and turn to social media to express their frustration.

A few years ago, I helped organize a big family wedding, and my distant cousin Anna was a key mover and shaker in the planning process. Anna is a woman who really likes to signal her Red and Blue traits, which sometimes led to interesting situations during the wedding preparations.

She's incredibly quick and decisive thanks to her Red attributes. She had no problems delegating tasks (i.e., dumping them on others), even the more fun ones like selecting decorations or music, which many people struggle with.

However, her Red traits also meant she had a hard time waiting for others to perform their assigned tasks at their own pace. If she didn't see any immediate action, she was unable to stop herself from taking over and doing whatever job it was that was still outstanding.

This often led to other family members involved in the wedding feeling somewhat steamrolled. They would arrive at planning meetings to discover that things they had been preparing to grapple with had already been done—and what was more, they had been executed meticulously, thanks to Anna's Blue traits, which ensured high-quality outcomes with a focus on detail.

Although her intentions were good and the final results of her efforts were often excellent, I can reveal that her critical nature and lack of patience caused plenty of tension. She was quick to point out when something hadn't been done quickly or thoroughly enough, which wasn't always appreciated by the others, who didn't feel they had had the chance to do their bit for the shindig as a whole. She was looking for efficiency but missed the fact that there were a bunch of egos involved in that process. Some didn't like being sidelined.

In the end, the wedding was both beautiful and well organized, but the process left a lot to be desired in terms of family dynamics and cooperation.

I'd certainly be interested in you—if only you were a little more interesting. . . .

Have you ever met someone completely devoid of feelings? No, I thought not. Once again, Reds are not typical relationship people. There's nothing wrong with that, provided the person you're communicating with has a similar focus. But if a Red speaks to a pronounced relationship person (such as a Yellow or a Green), they can be perceived as very emotionally cold or even inhuman.

Let me illustrate what I mean with an example that happened to me.

I have a good friend whom I've always appreciated immensely (note how I'm starting with the positive so I don't give the erroneous impression that I dislike said individual—a very Swedish thing for me to do) and for whom I also have the utmost respect as a professional. Okay, fine. It's the notorious Björn again.

A few years ago, we were going through a rough spell in the company. The autumn had been hard going and exhausting: long days, late nights, and far too much work on the weekends. We'd worn ourselves out, we'd worn each other out, and we'd worn out our respective families. We were doing nothing but working. More or less everyone in the company was slightly burned out. We'd really earned a peaceful, restorative Christmas break.

To kick things off, our Green assistant had booked us in for what she thought was just the ticket—peace and quiet.

Thus, we found ourselves at this Japanese restaurant. We'd taken off our shoes and were settled on cushions on the floor, clutching our glasses of sake. Calm, soothing music was playing out of an invisible sound system. The servers were friendly, unobtrusive, and quiet. Everything happened in imperceptible whispers.

We played it very Swedish: Everyone scrutinized the menus while keeping half an eye on what everyone else was planning to order. You see, no one wanted to order anything that no one else was getting.

Except for Björn. He glanced quickly through the menu and declared what he had in mind. He was ready now and quickly grew weary of those of us who hadn't decided yet. Needing something to do, he started a conversation. At the time, my daughter had just changed schools, and Björn was inquisitive.

How did everything go with the new school? How's your little girl getting on?

Pleasantly surprised by his concern for my daughter and being a complete numbskull, I started to tell him. After about twenty seconds I noticed that Björn's eyes began to wander. He looked around the restaurant with a facial expression that said: *Why is he telling me this?*

He looked at me with a smile I interpreted as *You know me. You know how I function. I don't actually want to talk any more about that!* And he quickly began talking about something completely different.

Ordinarily, I should have been a little bit offended, maybe even insulted. How could anyone be so insensitive? Especially when I was talking about something I'd actually been asked to talk about.

Did this mean that Björn is coldhearted or that he cares nothing for other people? Not at all. He cares just as much as anyone else, but when he realized that everything was fine with my daughter, he simply lost interest. In his usual fashion, he signaled that the channel of communication was closed. Instead of sitting there hemming and hawing, pretending to be interested in various meaningless details, he said exactly what he felt through his actions.

Remember we're talking about interpretations and perceptions here. The intention behind a particular behavior is one thing; how we as recipients perceive it is another.

Personally, I was able to laugh the whole thing off because I know Björn very well. I know he would never dream of hurting anyone deliberately. When he tramples on people's toes from time to time, it's never intentional—it just happens. In reality, he is one of the warmest and most generous people I have ever met. It's just that you have to know him to understand this.

What would have been the correct answer to Björn's question about how my daughter was doing?

Great.

That would have been enough.

10.5 ALONE I'M STRONG, AND I'M THE STRONGEST OF YOU ALL

The word "egotistical" comes from the Latin word "ego," meaning "I." My I is, therefore, my ego. Linguistically, we have consequently chosen to suggest there is a correlation between people with big egos and being egotistical. Naturally, there are many people in our world who are selfish and egotistical. The world is teeming with them. Again, I want you to remember that we are speaking here about perceived behavior, rather than actual characteristics.

If we look at how a Red communicates, we can understand why many perceive them as egotistic. They might be a good friend of yours, or your older sister, a parent, or even a neighbor.

- *I think we should accept this proposal.*
- *I want that assignment.*
- *This is what I think about it.*
- *I have a good idea.*
- *Are we doing it my way or the wrong way?*

Add a sharp eye and distinctive body language and you'll see someone who will take whatever they want. They will fight for their interests. They will tell anyone who will listen that they've got this. Some people, especially Greens, find this "I" form of speaking to be unsettling. A Red's "I" message occupies their mind. (They share this trait with Yellows, who also have strong egos.)

But we've learned to take care of one another. We know that being solitary is not the same thing as being strong, that we need one another to survive. Cooperation is the model I have been preaching for more than two decades. That's why we think it's egotistical when Reds speak only about themselves. They make sure to help themselves before helping others. They are often willing to trample on someone else if they see an opportunity to advance their own interests. They may not do this consciously, but the effect is the same.

As a result, Reds often come out the winners in discussions. They see this as a natural part of a conversation. They always know best and will assert that everyone else is wrong. It suits their ego to behave this way.

Of course, consequences can include losing friends, people disliking them, and being cut off from information because no one wants them in the group. Once they've noticed this, they may well decide that everyone else is an idiot.

A couple of years ago, I was one of six people at a dinner. In some anguish, a man, Green/Blue, told me he was not feeling well. He couldn't live up to the responsibilities his new employer had burdened him with. He was struggling with his heavy workload and having difficulty sleeping.

This caused even more stress for him, because he knew that if he didn't get a good night's rest, it would be even harder for him to perform at work.

His wife, sitting beside him, tried to hide the fact that her eyes had become shiny with tears. The situation was truly uncomfortable for everyone in the room. Everyone at the table offered encouraging remarks along with cautious questions about how he might be able to turn around this tricky situation. We all expressed our support as much as we could.

The solitary Red male at the table had finally had enough and tore into the now practically distraught wretch before him.

His analysis was clear as day: *I think you complain too much. You're making money. I've never been sick, and I think people worry too much. I would never end up in your situation, and I really think you should pull yourself together.*

What a dinner that was. Suffice it to say, that statement didn't do much to improve the atmosphere for the remainder of the evening.

Let's cut to the chase—it's Reds who are the ones mostly surrounded by idiots.

How Others May Perceive Yellows

11.1 WHEN HUMOR FAILS TO SOLVE THE PROBLEM

Funny, entertaining, and almost divinely positive. Creative beyond the perception of ordinary people. Absolutely. Again—this is their own interpretation. If you ask other people about Yellows, you may well get a somewhat different picture. Many people will agree with what you have read up to now, but you will also hear other comments.

It's especially fun to ask the Blues.

They'll typically reel off a long list of adjectives, noting that Yellows are selfish, superficial, and much too confident. Some will say they talk too much and are bad listeners. Furthermore, they can be unfocused and careless. Suddenly the picture isn't as flattering.

When a Yellow hears these comments, one of two things can happen. Either they become deeply distressed and genuinely hurt, or it triggers a ferocious argument. It depends. The amusing part is that in the long run it doesn't really bother Yellows all that much. On the one hand, they're bad listeners, and on the other hand, they have what some might call a selective memory. They simply forget the difficult bits, and with their positive ethos they find it easy to tell themselves they don't have any faults or shortcomings. They don't remember any of that negative feedback. What was that all about? Not a clue.

Let's have a look at what Yellows struggle with—even if they don't always know it.

11.2 HELLO, EVERYONE! YOU WANT TO HEAR WHAT I'VE BEEN UP TO? HELLO? IS ANYONE THERE?

Yellows communicate a lot. I would like to repeat that now.

Yellows communicate a lot. With an emphasis on "a lot."

None of the other colors come close to the Yellows' ease in finding words, expressing themselves, and telling a story.

It comes to them so easily, so simply, so effortlessly that you can't help being impressed. (Some people call this "mouth diarrhea," but that doesn't have a particularly nice ring to it.) It's common knowledge that most people don't like speaking in front of others. They get heart palpitations and sweaty palms; they're terrified of making fools of themselves. This is totally alien to Yellows. Making fools of themselves isn't part of the deal, and if the improbable were to happen, they could always laugh it off with another amusing anecdote.

However, there can be too much of a good thing. Regardless of what you are good at, there is a limit, a time to break off. Yellows, especially those who lack self-awareness, don't have such a limit. It would never even occur to them to wrap up; if they have something to say, out it comes. The fact that no one else thinks it's important is neither here nor there.

A Yellow behaves exactly like most other people—they do what they're good at. And what they're good at is talking. There are countless examples of Yellows who completely dominate a conversation. Then add a hefty dose of poor listening and we find an interesting (aka one-sided) communication situation.

Many people become hugely frustrated by this limitless verbosity. The inability to shut up is often perceived as egocentrism. The expressions "windbag," "chatterbox," "all talk and no walk," and "the gift of gab" were probably all coined with Yellows in mind.

I've experienced the following example on countless occasions. Picture it: You're in a group of people sitting around the table at a meeting of the condo association board. Perhaps you're preparing for the annual general meeting, and you know you're going to have to increase the rates.

There's a number of people around that table. The chair expresses an idea; it can be about anything at all. When the time comes for comments, all the Yellows will reinforce the idea by repeating the exact same thing, possibly in their own words. (I would like to say to the women reading this that I am aware this behavior is more typical of males than females.)

Why do they do that? Well, first, it's important to signal when you are in agreement, and second, they can say it so much better.

A few years ago, I was embedded in a management team to study their group dynamics. This was at a major listed company in Europe whose management team had bagged more credits in institutions of higher education than they could ever practically put to use. Everyone was tremendously intelligent and experienced.

I had just purchased a mobile phone with a fun new feature: a stopwatch. Using this, I could time how long anyone in the group spoke for.

Interesting facts began to pile up. The room accommodated the CEO and his seven closest associates. Peter, the sales manager, was the Yellowest of them all. Out of nineteen items on the two-hour agenda, one item was assigned to Peter. Please note that ratio—1:19.

That represented around 5.3 percent of the agenda.

The CEO opened the meeting, but pretty soon a clear pattern emerged. Peter had opinions about every single item on the agenda. No matter who spoke at that table, he had something to add, reinforce, or simply babble on about.

I used my stopwatch and was fascinated by what I saw. He spoke 69 percent of the time. Yes. It's true. Thirty-one percent went to the other seven, including the CEO himself.

If you're Yellow, you may already have charged on ahead in this book, possibly because you recognized yourself and thought this was a very unfortunate and unfair example.

The rest of you are no doubt wondering how this is possible. It's possible because Yellows have no problem delivering opinions, views, and advice regardless of whether they know anything about the subject or not. You don't ever have to suffer through the uncertainty of knowing what a Yellow's understanding of any given issue is—and whether you've solicited that view is immaterial.

A Yellow has a generous approach to their own ability—when an idea pops into their head, they simply open their mouth.

People say that for Reds, thought and action are the same thing. For Yellows, I would suggest that thought and speech are interrelated. What Yellows tend to share is often completely unprocessed material that just tumbles out of that big opening on their faces.

Sure, it might be well thought out, but it's usually not. What's most deceptive is that, almost without exception, it sounds very good. Yellows know a thing or two about presenting an idea that sounds fantastic. If you're unfamiliar with this particular type of person, you may very well take everything they say as true—a serious mistake.

Very often a Yellow is both entertaining and rousing, and as I said, they can inspire people to take up new ideas. But should you get into a conversation with a Yellow, you need to be observant so that when they pause to catch their breath, you can quickly interject. Or quite simply bring the meeting to a close.

11.3 I KNOW IT LOOKS MESSY, BUT THERE'S A METHOD TO THE MADNESS!

A Yellow would hardly admit to being careless, but they have no natural way to keep track of things. They find working in a structured way boring. It means you have to fit the mold and follow the template. Those templates are often drawn up by someone else, which can cause ego-related issues for Yellows, just like it does for Reds. If there is anything Yellows want to avoid, it's feeling controlled by fixed systems.

The solution is to keep everything in your head, which doesn't work. It's not possible to remember everything. No one can.

So, inevitably, the Yellow forgets things, and those around them think they're careless. Missed appointments, forgotten deadlines, and half-finished projects pile up, because once their minds have finished the task, they don't go backward. They go forward. They leap onto the next project. They tinker with other things. They allow themselves to be distracted. They chat. They have a nice time.

Details. To complete a project, you usually need to be precise about details. There are a lot of opportunities for missteps here. Yellows don't like having to keep track of the details in a renovation project. I would even venture to say they're actively uninterested in details. They paint with broad strokes. Pun intended.

Generally, Yellows are great at getting things off the ground. They're resourceful, and with boundless creativity at their disposal, they can kick off various kinds of projects. But their follow-through to reach the finishing line isn't quite as good. There's a reason why some people's homes look the way they do.

Finishing something 100 percent takes a degree of concentration Yellows rarely possess. They get bored and move on, while the rest of us think they're careless. They think it's good enough. I mean, come on! Why does everyone get so hung up on the minor details? This turned out fine, after all! The fact that threads are hanging from the shirt or the document is full of spelling errors isn't as important as thinking up new things.

This is repeated in many different spheres. I have a couple of acquaintances who are hopeless at timekeeping. They're always pleased and excited to think things up, but they're incurable optimists when it comes to time. It makes absolutely no difference what hour you suggest; they will not be on time. Seven o'clock, half past seven, or eight. It's unimportant. They're late regardless.

And when they talk about it, they haggle down their late arrival from forty-five minutes to a little over fifteen minutes. After a while, they actually believe it themselves. But it doesn't matter—the rest of us wait patiently because their presence will be the highlight of the evening.

11.4 I'M GREAT AT JUGGLING LOTS OF BALLS—ALL THE BALLS, AS IT HAPPENS!

We need to talk a little about Yellows' inability to concentrate. They're always prepared for new experiences. But the downside to the incredible openness Yellows have for new things, ideas, and impressions is that there are so many new things!

And because "new" is synonymous with "good" for a Yellow, it's best if something new is happening all the time. Otherwise, our Yellow friend will lose focus. They can't be bothered listening to the whole story, the background, and all the details and facts that may actually be relevant. It's simply not of interest to them, and they will lose concentration.

So what do they do? Simple. Something else. They throw a new ball into the air to juggle. The problem with all these balls is that the Yellow might be able to keep them in the air for a while, but they can't get them all down into the right box at the right time. Instead, they leave the room and the juggled balls then whack someone else on the head.

In a conversation, the Yellow may very well start playing with their mobile phone or computer, or perhaps they'll start chatting to the person next to them. Softly at first, thinking no one will notice anything. It's not true, of course; everyone gets quite irritated.

But if no one says anything, they'll just continue. Here Yellows are like little children. They're good at testing limits. They continue until someone becomes too angry and puts their foot down.

And, of course, then the Yellow feels hurt. They just wanted to . . .

The way Yellows quickly get bored can have far greater consequences than a little disruptive behavior during meetings.

They're not good at trivial, everyday things like administration and follow-ups. As usual, most Yellows would contest what I just wrote. In their own eyes, they are the masters even here. But if we consider the ability to follow up, this could be a serious threat to the effective delivery of a project.

A new project? Great! Put together a new and dynamic team full of interesting people—check! Get everything going and develop ideas and concepts—are you kidding? Already done that!

Working like crazy at the beginning to really get things off the ground? Yup.

But then? Following up on what is actually happening or not happening in a project is extremely boring. That means looking backward; that's dull, and it won't happen. A Yellow can't maintain concentration long enough to follow through. They would much rather tell themselves that you have to show trust in people.

11.5 ME! ME!! ME!!!

Yellows aren't necessarily more selfish than others, but they quite often seem to be. How come? Mostly because of their dialogue, since they primarily talk about themselves. And when other people are not sufficiently interesting and exciting, a Yellow will interrupt and guide the topic toward something far more compelling—not infrequently themselves.

I remember a party I attended a couple of years ago where I met someone who reminded me very palpably of the Yellow stereotype. Let's call her Helen. Fantastically wonderful woman. Helen was a talkative person who always seemed to be at the center of attention. She dominated most conversations with stories about herself and her globe-trotting adventures, as if she viewed herself as the hostess for the evening rather than a mere guest among the masses.

Whenever others tried to contribute to the conversation, Helen would soon cut them off or raise her voice to drown them out. It became difficult for anyone else to get a word in edgewise, and there were other guests visibly exchanging desperate glances.

During the dinner, Helen chattered away uninterrupted, apparently not noticing that the others had lost interest in her. She continued to overstep the boundaries of what was appropriate to discuss at a social gathering, and I could see that many people were beginning to steer clear of her.

When I myself asked questions to the gentleman on her left and he wasn't quick enough on the trigger, Helen sort of leaned into the picture and answered on his behalf. Even though it seemed Helen thought she was well-liked and admired by everyone, the truth was everyone found her both intrusive and annoying.

In fact, the vast majority of people at that party hated the mere sound of her voice. They could hardly stand her.

11.6 YOU NEVER TOLD ME THAT—I WOULD HAVE REMEMBERED IF YOU HAD!

If Yellow people are one thing, it's that they're bad listeners. Really bad ones, even. Many yellow people I've met have of course claimed they're actually very good listeners—and of course have given entertaining examples of this undeniable fact—but it's really their memory that's at fault. They simply mean that they take everything in, but somewhere along the way to the brain's silos, whatever they heard simply goes . . . astray. Blink and you miss it!

No, it's not about memory. It's about how a Yellow is often uninterested in what others say, because they know they could say it so much better themselves. They fail to remain focused; they begin thinking about other things, begin doing other things. They don't want to listen—they want to talk.

They're also quite childish in that they only like doing things that are enjoyable. If a statement or story or just a plain old conversation is boring, they close their ears. And not all of them are entertaining to hear; that I can absolutely attest to.

Of course, there's a remedy. Take a course in entertaining rhetoric, then you may be able to keep your Yellow friend's, partner's, or colleague's attention. If you can present your message in a more amusing way, they'll at least remain seated a bit longer. Rhetoric is, in fact, not the art of talking but rather the art of getting others to listen.

If you have a good friend whom you have by now identified as Yellow, you know exactly what I'm talking about. You'll be mid-sentence when they open their mouth and start talking about something completely off topic. Poor memory? No, you were simply being tedious. But truly—add a poor memory into the equation and we really are in trouble.

Many truly successful people in society are better-than-average listeners. They prefer listening to talking. They already know what they know, and to learn more, they simply have to hush up and hear what others are saying. It's a way to absorb new knowledge. This is something Yellows need to understand better if they don't want to be perceived as completely hopeless—or stagnant in their personal development. They must, for example, listen to the message I have set out in this last section. If they refuse to take it in because it's a difficult and possibly boring message, they'll never learn anything.

How Others May Perceive Greens

12.1 WHEN AMBIGUITY BECOMES AN ART FORM

So what do others—other colors—think about Greens? The picture is ambivalent. Views differ. Beyond the fact that they're considered pleasant, friendly, caring, accommodating in listening to others' troubles, easygoing, and benevolent—well, people have views. A lot of them.

A person who says yes but means no—how do you handle someone like that? How are you supposed to know what they really think?

Reds and Yellows especially have issues with what I call the "silent resistance": remaining silent rather than speaking out. Certain Greens, however, tend to tell the truth behind the back of the person concerned. Therefore, others can perceive a Green as dishonest, even though their intention is only to avoid conflict.

In general, Greens always expect the worst and therefore tend to lie low. Then there's their inability to change. When a Green understands the need for change but still says, "No thanks," that leads those closest to them to think they are afraid of change, stubborn, unconcerned, or indifferent. Downright pigheaded, even.

As usual, we are talking about perceptions. If we ask Reds what they think about Greens, there will be no shortage of weighty opinions offered.

12.2 PIGHEADEDNESS WILL NEVER BE A VIRTUE

Riddle me this: What do you do with a person who never changes their views? Ever? Not even when the facts indicate it's time to take a different path? How do you handle someone whose resolve to continue on the present course is completely unshakable?

This is about an introverted profile, but the difference between Green and Blue is significant when it comes to change. A Blue puts off a decision while awaiting further facts, but Greens simply . . . put it off. And wait for it all to blow over.

They refuse to change their minds. They've made a decision about something and will not concede. Why? You tell me. Well, they've never done so before. They simply don't want to. That's just the way it is. Often they don't even know why themselves.

Think about it: It may have taken you your whole life to come to a particular opinion about the dangers of eating red meat, about the climate, or on Taylor Swift. Then this idiot comes along and says you should exchange your current opinion for theirs.

But you give as good as you get.

It's out of the question. It just doesn't feel right. Ignore the whole evidence thing and all that jazz.

The Green is waiting for the right "feeling" before they make any changes. If it doesn't happen, well . . . they're pretty patient. And it's easier to change nothing than it is to upend your whole worldview.

Let me tell you about a young man, the son of a family I've known very well for many years. This guy is reasonably good in school; his grades are okay. He has many friends.

At the outset, I would like to point out that when we speak about young people, in this case a teenager, we must be careful. This isn't a fully developed behavior profile or character. Young people still have things to learn about life in general. All impressions are not definitive.

So what's the problem?

This young man has his own ideas about what is true and false. And wild horses couldn't get him to change his mind. It may be something he heard from a friend or something he saw on television or something he picked up in school. Once this knowledge or idea, irrespective of its source, had been established in his consciousness, it couldn't be dislodged.

It makes no difference how often his parents point out the facts or how forcefully they present the evidence—his point of view is firm. It doesn't matter if they point out the danger in this or that way of thinking; he persists in his belief.

Think about it. You supply all the available facts, and the guy says he understands. He agrees it sounds logical. Other people could feasibly do it that way, with good results. But still, he's not prepared to change his point of view. Some people would call this pigheadedness.

What's the reason for this? Excellent question. It may stem from where he first got the information. If a friend says you can earn just as much money collecting trash as a newly qualified doctor, it doesn't really matter if it's true or not. If the same friend suggests you won't be arrested for drunk driving if you get behind the wheel after drinking three beers, then this becomes the truth, even if we, with all the facts at our disposal, know this is simply not the case.

If this guy is told that he'll get a terrific job if he just works a little harder at mathematics, it becomes true. If he got this info from his best mate, it simply has to be true. If a Green trusts a particular individual, that individual's word becomes law. This makes it easy to exploit Greens, because they can be a little naïve and gullible. And unfortunately, certain people take advantage of this fact.

Sometimes this obstinacy becomes a strength, no doubt about that. But when those around a Green perceive it as pure pigheadedness, it can create problems. And many people simply give up.

12.3 WHY BOTHER? NOTHING IS WORTH CARING ABOUT ANYWAY

Since it doesn't seem as if there is any great drive—there's even a degree of sluggishness, as well as the fact that Greens look around and wait to see what others do—you can easily get the impression that

Greens aren't all that interested in things. And often that's the case. They're more passive than active, and this has an impact on their behavior. Not much is going on there.

And what does it really matter? If you stay at home, nothing can really go wrong, right? What Greens fail to see is that most other people want to do things. They assume everyone thinks as they do and stays on the sofa. They're happy doing nothing. Anything that upsets this standpoint becomes a threat.

The result? Even more passivity. On one occasion, I heard a Red/ Yellow boss describe his employees as uninspired and uninterested in their work. It tormented him, because no matter how hard he tried to entice and insist, they never got out of the starting blocks.

He presented numerous ideas—some of which were quite interesting—but nothing happened. It can be like that with Greens. They recognize a good idea as quickly as anyone else. But, for example, while their Red colleagues sprint off with the baton, a Green just sits and waits. Often they're waiting for the right feeling to convince them of an idea's merit and if that doesn't happen, well . . . they didn't want to do anything anyway, so they don't.

This particular boss called in his employees and asked them how they viewed the business. He was worried about the apparent lack of discernible commitment. A couple of the men, who were in lower middle age, said straight out that they could think of absolutely nothing that was worth getting involved in. Nothing. The boss became extremely frustrated. He tried everything but got virtually zero reaction.

This can also happen in a marriage. There are stereotypes for everything. Like some women might be drawn to the strong, silent type, for example. Nothing wrong with that. But after they're married and she realizes this is all he is—strong and silent—she may not be as happy. And when she makes plans and he says he doesn't care, she gets frustrated. And so she makes even bigger plans. And he clutches the armrests on his favorite chair even harder.

This is the paradox. The bigger the plans, the less likely it is that a Green will commit. All they want is peace and quiet.

Here's an example: I've spent twenty years writing fiction and really hope to become a published novelist one day. Everyone in the family knows this. Not that I made a huge deal out of it, but I did not hide my ambitions, either. It had escaped no one that it had been my biggest dream ever since my teenage years.

I have a number of relatives who are superb at concealing their interest and engagement. One Green close to me understands how important it is for me to succeed. I have repeatedly spoken about my dream, explaining how it would make me feel if I succeeded as an author of fiction.

Yet this Green basically never asks how my writing is going. All I get out of them is a throwaway comment about once every five years that maybe I should lay off taking it so seriously since I'll only be disappointed. And when I say things like, *This year it will happen. Now is the time, damn it. I've got to work harder to succeed!* the response is, *Wow. That's a lot of work.*

Lots of work is a Green's greatest enemy, just because that's exactly what it is—work. They live in a mindset that everything should be easy.

This form of indifference and lack of commitment can kill the enthusiasm of even the most inspired person. I had to learn to rely on others to find the energy to struggle on with my writing. But a Green doesn't understand this. They don't want people to be invested, because that just makes them difficult. Instead, let's just sit here and do . . . nothing.

12.4 WHAT'S THOUGHT IN SECRET IS SAID IN SECRET

Greens are reluctant to take a position on sensitive issues. They most likely have just as many views and opinions as anyone else, but they don't like shouting them from the rooftops. The reason is simple—it can cause a fuss.

The consequence of this tendency is a rather abstruse manner of expressing themselves. Instead of saying *That's impossible*, they may respond with something like *It appears there are a few challenges in delivering that*. Sure, both statements mean the same thing: *We won't manage to do it in time.* But by using a less direct means of expression, they take fewer risks. If you take a clear stance on something, then you have to stand up for it. And that's hard. And liable to cause problems. You're much better off staying under the radar.

For a Green, it's better to be safe than sorry. By expressing themselves ambiguously, they avoid taking responsibility for the matter in question. They don't need to risk their good name if they're uncertain. If they haven't taken a position in support of something, that means they also haven't taken a position against it.

Some of you can hear how illogical this sounds, right? But if you're a Green, you know exactly what I mean. A woman I met once said that she believed what everyone else believed. But are Greens perceived as unclear just because they want to save a relationship? No, not at all. Greens just aren't as precise as the other colors. When someone says they absolutely hate listening to Lady Gaga, a Green would say that they can bring to mind better singers. When a Blue says they have lost five pounds since last Tuesday (late morning, since you ask), a Green says they've also most likely lost some weight lately.

This is because Greens are not as task-oriented as Reds and Blues. Greens don't speak about facts in the same way. They would rather speak about relationships and feelings, which makes it more difficult to be precise. Because how do you measure a feeling?

Saying *I love you* exactly 12 percent more than last month just isn't going to work.

What's thought in secret is said in secret.

12.5 CHANGE THAT? LET ME THINK IT OVER FOR A (LONG) WHILE

Here we have the biggest stumbling block. If you want to make changes in a group consisting of many Greens, I wish you the best of luck. If it's a major change, you should consider whether it's really worth the effort. If it's urgent, you can forget the whole thing. This is what happens in the mind of a Green:

- *I know what I have but not what I'll get.*
- *Things were better back in the day.*
- *This is how I've always done it.*
- *I've never done it like that before.*
- *The grass isn't always greener on the other side.*

Sound familiar? Sure, not all changes are for the better, but let's be reasonable! I'm not saying it's always wrong to express these sentiments, but when changes are really necessary, it can be very dangerous to take this stance.

A classic cliché—a little worn now, I know—is to consider how often you change where you sit at the breakfast table. I used to ask this question in the groups I met with. Many smiled and said they always sat where they usually sat because it just wound up that way. Sure, I do the same thing sometimes. But if someone were to point out that I was stuck in a rigid habit (or bad habit), I would do something about it. A Green, however, does not change their mind.

When you look at a Green's reaction to the question, you'll understand that we're faced with a problem. I've seen grown adults turn white as a sheet and mop their brows at the mere thought of sitting on the other side of the table. I've even worked with a man, Sune, who had such a meticulous lunchtime routine that if he couldn't follow it precisely, the rest of the day was shrouded in utter darkness. Sune had a favorite lunch spot beneath a painting. He sat there every day at lunchtime, week in, week out, month after month, and year after year. Always the same chair.

If he came into the dining room and saw that his spot was occupied, he would stop short. If he saw this quickly enough, he'd turn toward his backup location, not as good but still an acceptable spot, near a window. If he were forced to have his soup there, he would glare throughout the meal at whoever had taken *his* spot.

Of course, he never said anything. Instead, he just sulked for the rest of the day. This is another thing Greens often do—turn frustration inward and feel so awful that everyone notices it. If Sune's backup spot was also occupied, he would just go back into the kitchen, the rest of his day ruined.

Let me give you another example. My mother—sadly departed from this world and much missed; we'll never stop loving you, darling Mother—who was nothing if not Green, was always willing to help, and took care of her grandchildren whenever needed, especially when they were little. I remember one time when my wife and I were invited to dinner on a Friday night. Weeks in advance I had asked my mother to watch the kids because I knew she needed time to mentally prepare herself for it.

On the day the dinner was to take place, the hostess called: Her husband was sick, and the whole thing was called off.

I phoned my mum and explained to her what had happened. The dinner was off. We would be staying home that night. She became completely silent. I said that I still wanted her to come over, because the children were excited to see their grandma.

Mum was very hesitant. *What will happen now?* she asked. I said it would be just like we had planned originally—her bag was packed and the guest room was ready, so it would be a perfect opportunity to spend a little time together as a family. She hesitated. *It will be completely different now: You'll be at home.* She was flustered by the change, and she needed time to think about it. She promised to phone back.

What exactly was Mum's problem? Our change of plans necessitated no change for her at all. She was still going to stay at our house on Friday night. She could still see her grandchildren. She would, however, avoid having any responsibility for them. I tried to convince her that we could take care of her for once, instead of her taking care of us.

This was a completely new situation for her. We would still be there in the house. And that was the problem. My wife and I would be there. Maybe Mum had had her heart set on watching a particular show on television. Maybe she had thought about preparing a special meal for the children. Maybe one, maybe the other. I've no idea.

She never explained, so we can't know for sure. But the change was serious enough to warrant extra thinking time for her.

She came in the end. A nice little side story, quite possibly related to her generation: I fetched her at half past four. She asked why I had come so late. I replied that I had promised to be there at five o'clock and that I was actually half an hour early. Her response? She'd been ready since four o'clock.

12.6 I'VE NEVER BEEN SO UPSET, BUT FOR GOODNESS' SAKE, DON'T TELL ANYONE

This is the second major issue with Green behavior. They can't stand a squabble. This aversion to conflict causes many other challenges, such as stubbornness, ambiguity, and resistance to change. Because Greens are pronounced relational people, nothing is more important to them than keeping a relationship together. The problem is their method doesn't work.

You can look at conflicts in two ways.

The first way is called The Harmony Outlook, or striving for harmony. Everything depends on being on good terms with others. Reaching an agreement is an end in and of itself, even when it causes problems down the track. This means those who cause conflict are problematic troublemakers. Conflicts entail a bad mood, bad attitudes, bad communication, discord, and goodness knows what else. And so we smother conflict and pretend it doesn't exist. Because who wants to be involved with a troublemaker?

An acquaintance once used an interesting metaphor for this kind of behavior. She said it was like sitting at dinner staring at the rotting head of a moose in the center of the table. There are antlers and a giant tongue lolling out of its mouth, and there are blood and flies. The whole caboodle. Of course, everyone can see there's a moose head there, but no one says anything. You pass the potatoes between the antlers while pretending not to see them.

This may well persist for some time. Eventually, someone may give up and ask whether there is, in fact, a moose head lying in the center of the table.

It will be denied by all. Finally, someone at the table says, *We have to do something about this!* That person becomes an agitator, because we now have to deal with this unsavory severed moose head. Couldn't she just have kept quiet?

Nowadays, behavioral sciences know better. The aspiration of having everyone in agreement about everything all the time is an impossible utopia, not worth trying to achieve. It's stupid to even try. Eventually, someone will lift the lid off all that discord that was so effectively and hermetically sealed for such a long period of time—and what happens then?

Wouldn't you know it? There's a severed moose head there! It stinks from a long way off. In the end the Harmony Outlook inevitably leads to conflict.

The second way, and the opposite to the first, is called The Conflict Outlook. In short, this involves us accepting that there are conflicts in the world and they are hard to erase. It doesn't work that way. Some conflicts are even natural. No group exists where everyone is always in agreement about everything.

The whole point of The Conflict Outlook is to deal with every little dissentient opinion as soon as it rears its head. Reds, and also some Yellows, do this naturally. When they see something that doesn't work, they simply say it doesn't work. This means that problems can be resolved at an early stage. It means there's not much time for things to become horribly infected. But you have to deal with the issue before it begins to stink of rotting moose.

The Conflict Outlook usually creates harmony.

Sounds logical, right?

But, but, but . . . Greens will just turn a deaf ear to this. They'll do everything in their power to maintain that magical feeling that everyone is in agreement about everything. It's nicer when everyone agrees, isn't it? Wouldn't the world be so much better if there were no conflicts?

Consider a situation all of us have experienced at some point. We're in a meeting at work. There are maybe ten people present in the room. Add or subtract from this so you recognize the situation. Someone—the boss or anyone at all—has just completed their presentation and now asks what everyone thinks. Full of expectation, they look around, awaiting feedback.

If there are any Reds or Yellows in the room, they will speak their minds on what they've just seen and heard. The Reds will love it or loathe it. Either way, you'll know immediately what they think. The Yellows will speak about their own reflections on the proposal. One or two Blues might have a few questions.

What do the Greens do? Absolutely nothing. They'll slump down in their chair, trying to merge into the furniture itself. They say nothing at all unless asked a direct question by the boss. They look anxiously around, hoping someone will say this proposal is, in fact, an incomprehensible mess. The group is too large for them to trot out any dissenting opinions. To say something truly dramatic or negative would mean everyone's eyes would be on them, and there's no way that's going to happen. If they say what they are really thinking, a heated debate will erupt, and since a Green doesn't want to take part in heated debates—they don't even want to be in the same room as one—they simply stay silent.

How will the speaker respond? They'll assume everyone is in agreement, right? What they don't realize is that half the people in the room think it was the stupidest thing they have ever heard. When the truth creeps out—as it has to, sooner or later—guess what happens then? Got it in one.

The Harmony Outlook inevitably leads to conflict.

12.7 PASSIVE AGGRESSION

And that brings us to the final issue with Green behavior. Because you can be 100 percent sure of what will be said by the people standing by the coffee maker or lingering in the smoking area: the truth.

Imagine the internal pressure that must form in someone who chooses to keep their real thoughts and opinions to themselves. Let's ignore for the moment the reason why Greens choose to stay quiet. The consequence of this is the pressure has to be released somewhere. And since they don't really have the courage to confront their partner, their boss, their kids, or their rude neighbors, something else has to happen. The truth must come out somewhere.

What Greens do when they need to ease that pressure is talk behind your back. When in small groups of two or three people, they

are more than happy to vent their dissatisfaction. And they're surprisingly good at it, too.

As long as they think they're out from under your treacher-
ous gaze, they'll slander you in ways you would never expect of a
Green. . . .

This is passive aggression in its most unpleasant form. Greens
would probably deny that this ever happens, but in my experience
this is exactly what happens.

Being passive-aggressive entails, among other things, never having to apologize. It is someone who applies mental violence to suppress every desire to say what they're thinking. This is an individual
with clenched fists and gritted teeth who claims not to be angry at
all. Someone who is completely incapable of doing things they don't
want to do; someone who has made nonaction an art form. The human form of a stone.

Passive aggression can be found everywhere and is primarily
characterized by passive hostility and the avoidance of direct communication. It's a kind of direct resistance while also embodying a
remarkable absence of actual confrontation. And it's an area in which
many Greens have developed exceptional levels of expertise. Funnily
enough, they're not only unaware of their own inner aggression, but
they actually think they're always very nice.

"Passive-aggressive" was coined during World War II to describe
soldiers who refused to join the ranks but didn't want to show this
openly. Instead, they signaled this through sulkiness and procrasti-
nation. Like most phenomena, this strange phenomenon has probably existed since the very beginnings of humankind.

When you meet a passive-aggressive person (regardless of color,
because this is not a trait totally exclusive to Greens), they do not
seem to be interested in anything at all. They're lifeless, blasé, un-
perturbed. All you get from them is a weighty *hmm*. In some cases,
they seem so blank and shut down they can't even bring themselves
to shrug.

The passive-aggressive person is very likely not fantasizing about
going to that function you've been invited to but eventually under-
takes to come along anyway. However, they spend so much time on

vague preparations that by the time they have gotten ready (after much effort), the party is already over. It was easier than simply saying, "No thanks" from the start, but it was also a way of punishing you.

Punishing you for what, you may ask? And that's a great question. It can be any perceived injustice at all, but you've probably made a fool of yourself somehow. Where a Red would have given you a resounding scolding and told you where to stick it, a Green doesn't dare speak up. Nonetheless, they're still mad at you for something you said (or didn't say) and this is your punishment.

Their entire behavior toward others is defined by a resistance to demands.

For example, if a passive-aggressive person has agreed to wash the car before the end of the weekend, they'll start the job so late on Sunday it'll be pitch black outside before it's done. What's more, they'll blame it on the sun for having the temerity to set just as usual, but they won't say a word about the fact that it was their own poor planning that gave rise to the situation in the first place.

At the same time, to fail in the car-washing endeavor will have been the plan all along. This is a peculiar paradox, and I'm not sure that Greens who engage in this behavior even understand themselves what they're doing.

At the same time, passive-aggressive people tend to be demanding, dependent, and afraid of being on their own, and not infrequently they suffer from relatively low levels of self-confidence. In some cases, they are deeply miserable and often downright bitter. In their own eyes, however, they're utterly incapable of making mistakes. In addition to this, they also refrain from taking responsibility for their own actions. They excuse themselves to escape all blame, even in situations where it would be downright absurd to try. When the you-know-what hits the fan—and it will—they'll immediately lay the blame elsewhere.

Do I need to point out how frustrating this is to absolutely everyone around them?

Normally, when people are annoyed by something going on, they give a hint as to what that is. While they may try to keep a lid on it out of politeness, it rarely lasts. Eventually, they have to say something about what's caused the frustration. Reds blurt out what they think when the incident in question is barely over; Yellows try to keep it contained but can't quite pull it off. And Blues draw up a critical list of perceived mistakes.

But this isn't how passive-aggressive people go about it. Oh no. They bottle it up and act as if nothing happened in the first place. It's as if they haven't noticed anything at all. The oil remains there on the waves, as if eternal.

The passive-aggressive person's internal well-being, however, is in a state of total dissolution. Anger rages beneath the surface, and sometimes it can even be spotted via their spasmodic, suppressed body language. Many psychologists even claim that passive-aggressive people are, in fact, always filled with rage.

The problem is they never empty the bag or relieve the pressure or open the valve. Pick any metaphor you like—the consequence is still the same.

How Others May Perceive Blues

13.1 WHEN YOU GET DOWN TO IT, THE DEVIL IS MOST DEFINITELY NOT IN THE DETAILS

Even perfectionist Blues are subject to criticism from those around them. It can be because they are perceived as evasive, defensive, perfectionist, reserved, fastidious, meticulous, hesitant, conservative, lacking independence, questioning, suspicious, tedious, aloof, and coldhearted. Oof! The list of shortcomings found in these bastions of bureaucracy tends to be quite long.

But mainly, Blues find it difficult to begin anything new because they want to prepare very thoroughly. Everything involves risk, and Blues can be almost obsessed with details. Never place too many Blues in the same group. They'll plan into the next century without ever putting a shovel to the ground.

Furthermore, many Blues are perceived as highly critical and almost suspicious. They miss nothing, and they have a tendency to deliver their observations in an insensitive fashion.

They create quality work, but their hair-splitting, critical approach to almost everything reduces the morale of those around them to dangerously low levels. These are people who consider themselves to be realists. In fact, in everyone else's eyes they are pessimists.

Pretend you're looking at the world through the lens of a Yellow, just for a while. Let's see what that might entail.

13.2 RIGHT HAS TO BE EXACTLY RIGHT; OTHERWISE, IT'S JUST WRONG

Let's be honest from the start. All this keeping track of facts and focusing on details can go too far. There are limits to when it's reasonable to keep researching.

Blues want to have all the information on everything, and this can lead to problems with those around them. People who would be satisfied with "good enough" simply can't cope with hearing all those questions and witnessing all this relentless poking into details. A Blue believes that "good enough" is never really, well, good enough.

I enjoy working around the house—changing the decor, hanging wallpaper every now and then. A few years ago, we renovated our kitchen, and even though I got tremendous help from my family, I did quite a lot myself. I'd say I've got a reasonable knack for these kinds of things: I'm not naturally gifted, but I'm not completely hopeless, either. I worked and toiled and was quite happy when it was finished. For a DIYer, I thought I managed it quite well.

Hans, a good friend of mine, came by. We've known each other for many years, and he's very much on the ball. He knew I'd worked very hard and that I felt quite pleased with myself. When he came into my kitchen, he looked around and said quietly, *New kitchen? Looks good. That cupboard door is crooked.*

Okay, so maybe it wasn't nice to hear that. But for Hans, it was the highest form of logic. He observed a mistake and his sense of perfection meant he couldn't ignore it. What's more, he's not much of a relationship person, so he didn't give any thought to whether it would be appropriate or even necessary to tell me about it. He wasn't directly criticizing me, only something I had done. Namely, not fitting the cupboard door straight.

Fastidiousness can be expressed in various ways: It can be the person who can't cope with papers that aren't perfectly aligned on a desk, who rewrites an email about fifteen times to get it truly perfect, or who works for hours on a simple Excel spreadsheet or PowerPoint presentation, just giving it the finishing touches.

They never seem to finish anything—there's always more to be done.

Once, I was delivering a training course on behavioral science to a group of people who all worked in the same office. The group consisted of about twenty people. The first afternoon, I handed out the results of the behavior analysis each of them had undergone earlier. Everyone read about themselves with increasing fascination, and most of them seemed very satisfied.

Except for one lady. She was extremely upset by her analysis. You see, it was marred by so many errors she could barely bring herself to list them all. After confirming with her that it was okay to discuss it in front of the whole group, I asked what she was displeased with.

She told us there was too much that didn't accord with the way she perceived herself. For example, the analysis revealed that she could be a perfectionist. She wasn't like that at all. I noticed people in the room starting to smile ever so slightly. Apparently, her colleagues knew something she didn't.

I asked her why she thought the analysis maintained that she was a perfectionist. She had no idea. The whole thing was a complete mystery. It was a totally useless tool.

Realizing the woman was a Blue, I was careful not to argue too much. She wouldn't take me at my word. I was just some random consultant who had been working with this tool for a measly twenty years. What did I know?

Instead, I asked her to give an example showing that she was *not* a perfectionist.

No problem, she had lots of evidence for this thesis. For example, she had three children, each of whom had three best friends. When she came home in the evenings, there were so many shoes piled up inside the front door she practically had to do the high jump to get in. She began by shaking the dirt off the doormat and putting the shoes in order. She confided to me that she used to put the size tens at the back, as those guys went home last, so it seemed most logical. She placed the smaller sizes closest to the door in neat rows.

Then she went into the kitchen. What did she see there? Crumbs everywhere. All these youngsters had been eating sandwiches, and the kitchen looked like a war zone. It took her twenty minutes to clean up, put everything back in place, sweep, wipe the tables and worktops. Only then could she take off her coat and relax a little.

A perfectionist? Her? Not on her life.

Her colleagues were in stitches. The woman looked around, not understanding what the hilarity was all about. That any of this could be remotely obsessive was beyond her. Her house was so untidy— that was her point.

The funny thing about this story is that a few years later I met the same woman but in a totally different context. She gave me a big hug and said the analysis of her behavior was 100 percent correct.

Stunned, I wondered how she had arrived at that conclusion. It turned out she had kept the behavior profile in her purse for a while; the analysis had a list of behaviors and qualities, and every time she found herself doing one she ticked it off on the sheet. In the end, she had ticked them all. She was so Blue it almost hurt.

She liked the analysis. An amazing tool, on the whole.

13.3 I DON'T REALLY KNOW YOU, SO KEEP YOUR DISTANCE

You've done it. I've done it. We've all done it. Gone up to a person who seems to be a decent sort and started talking about this and that, thinking you're going to have a nice chat.

After a while, you realize you're the one doing all the talking. If you have Yellow traits in your behavior, you may notice that there are strange pauses in the dialogue of a Blue person. That is, if there's any dialogue at all. You may notice the other person is fidgeting a bit, signaling that they don't want to be part of this conversation.

What's going on? We're just talking about the game yesterday, or about what the family did last summer, or where you're going on holiday. Do we have a problem, or what?

Yes, in fact, we do, because this person doesn't willingly speak with strangers.

Wait a minute, you may say. *We've been working together for three months, and by now it should be perfectly okay to ask what his dog's name is.*

But this guy requires a lot of personal space, both physically and psychologically. He needs to know a person extremely well before opening up. Not like a Red, who says whatever they currently feel like saying; not like a Yellow, who reveals their darkest secrets because they assume everyone is interested; or like a Green, who can be personal, but only in small groups and in a controlled environment.

A Blue doesn't need small talk. They can easily give the impression that they don't care about other people, because they don't cultivate any relationships. Sure, they care, but their needs are of a different type from everyone else's. They like being in their own company and with immediate family.

The result is obvious for those around them: Others find them coldhearted and distant. That personal bubble is obvious, and it can be very chilly, particularly for Yellows and Greens. And so they call their Blue friend a drag. Blues can easily make us feel ill at ease.

Why is he so cold and dismissive? Doesn't he care about me at all?

13.4 BETTER SAFE THAN SORRY—PREFERABLY THREE TIMES

A good family friend couldn't leave her house without first checking to see if her keys were really in her handbag, even though placing them there was the last thing she had done before going to the front door. It's called being a control freak.

Here is an ancient example I still can't get out of my head. Back in the eighties when people still used cash, I worked as a teller in a bank, where I served people who had queued for thirty minutes for one single reason: to check that the balance printed on the ATM receipt really was correct.

Much anticipation. The same computer. The same balance.

But you never know. Best to check. And double-check. If a triple check had been possible, they would have done it. Unfortunately for them, the internet was yet to be invented.

Where does this need for control come from? Why can't Blues trust what other people say, or just accept the information they hear?

Answer: They can, of course. But if they also check themselves, then all the risks will be eliminated, right? The fact remains that they don't trust others. Everything has to be confirmed. And recorded, and documented properly.

Remember, we're talking here about behavior as perceived by others. A Blue checks everything one extra time because it's possible to check everything one extra time. When everything has been confirmed, then you just have to make a decision.

I have a good friend who uses Excel diligently. But not like the rest of us. This guy has a special method. He writes a formula and inserts all the data. Then, before he saves and closes the spreadsheet, he double-checks all the figures using a pocket calculator.

Did you ever hear anything that stupid?! If you were to explain this to a Red, they would declare the guy an absolute idiot. Explain it to a Yellow and they would laugh themselves to death. Tell a Green and they'd file an anonymous report with the authorities to note their concerns for the welfare of said individual. Any Blue would understand the whole thing immediately. There is a theoretical possibility that there could be errors in Excel. Even though he typed the formula himself, something might still go wrong.

Better to be on the safe side.

How do others perceive this? Read on!

13.5 THE ONLY THINGS YOU CAN TRUST ARE YOURSELF AND YOUR OWN EYES

Of course, the guy who questions Excel has a problem explaining himself. Many people around him have their own views about his method of always having to double-check and triple-check everything he does himself and everything everyone else does. They get furious when he shows through his actions that he doesn't trust them.

The other tiny little problem is that everything takes a terribly long time. Of course, this can be managed by working more hours. What's more problematic is the way relationships can suffer because of this habit. How demoralizing is it when you try to tell someone about a possible breakthrough and the first thing the person does is isolate all the different components and call into question every single point?

Of course, if everyone looks long enough, they will find mistakes.

Nor is it even sufficient to be right. You have to prove yourself to a Blue. If they consider you an authority in a particular field, they'll be better at listening to you. The road, however, can be tricky.

I've delivered many training courses and given many lectures on this subject, and if there are people who ask complicated questions, they're usually engineers, technical sales staff, or financial controllers. Maybe the occasional tax lawyer. They're often Blues, and they're not impressed with me.

Just because I have made my living doing this for more than twenty years doesn't mean I know what I'm talking about. (Remember the woman who was accused of being a perfectionist.) The only thing you can do is accept that among these people, the standard of proof will be much higher. As we know, the fact remains that if I have prepared well enough, I can prove that what I am saying is true. In time, they will trust me.

13.6 SUMMARY

Well, I seem to have upset you all. Nonetheless, I think it was worth it. You see, sometimes we have to bring ourselves to face the truth.

The American psychologist and researcher Tasha Eurich has conducted some fascinating research into self-awareness. Her 2019 TED Talk is well worth a listen for the full details, but the short version is that she did a meta-study on research about self-awareness and concluded that self-awareness is a fairly unusual phenomenon.

Generally, when you ask people about it, around 95 percent state they are above average in this respect.

Yes, you read that right. I'll repeat it: 95 percent of people say they are above average. (It's like asking men about our car-driving skills. We're all above average.)

Anyway. Then you ask them to describe themselves.

Yet when you conduct a so-called 360-degree analysis—i.e., you ask people close to the subject about their characteristics and then compare these answers with the subject's own perceptions—it turns out that the proportion of people with high levels of self-awareness is actually closer to 10 or 15 percent.

That's a pretty big deviation. On a good day, we might say there's an awful lot of potential there—but on a regular day, we'd have to admit there's a problem.

Of course, a natural question is as follows: If someone claims not to be a perfectionist but others say they are, who is right and who is wrong?

This isn't just a philosophical question. As I've previously touched upon, communication takes place on the recipient's terms. If you think I seem like a hopeless perfectionist, then I assume that's how you see me. It doesn't necessarily mean I'm a long way up the international perfectionist scale; it just means I'm evidently more of a perfectionist than you are. Or more of a perfectionist than I think I am. Or more of a perfectionist than you're willing to put up with. Or something else entirely.

This kind of thing very quickly leads to impossible meta-discussions and before you know it, you've lost track of which way is up and which way is down.

In a nutshell, the problem is that if I behave in a way that seems to annoy those around me, it can be smart to take notes. If a lot of people around me are bugged by my behaviors, then eventually that becomes my problem, too. That's just how it is.

I'm not sure it's possible to exaggerate the value of this challenge.

When I coach people, usually the hardest thing is accepting this discrepancy in outlook. Someone thinks their approach in area X is completely right, yet they keep encountering resistance. Does that mean they should raise their voice and demand that others fall into line? Or might it be a good idea to open dialogue with the affected parties, whether you're at work or at home?

My vote goes to the latter.

When the brown stuff hits the fan, I'd argue that while there may be factual issues underlying the situation, 90 percent of it boils down to poor communication.

And that's an area in which we can all contribute.

14

What Really Pisses Them Off?

14.1 A PERSON'S TEMPERAMENT CAN REVEAL A LOT ABOUT THEM

We touched on the subject of aggression, albeit in passive form, in the section on Greens. How about we take a look at the more immediate form of anger?

Since time immemorial, humankind has sought to come to grips with that burning feeling that compels us to clench our fists and erupt into stinging tirades when someone helps themselves to the last pastry in the break room. Not that you wanted that last pastry, but who does she think she is, helping herself to it without asking? Outrageous, to say the least. If she had asked, obviously you'd have said no thanks, but that's not the point here.

Anger, the spice of a fiery temper, has long driven us crazy and fascinated researchers the world over.

But where does anger come from? Why do we even have it as an internal resource? Not infrequently, it causes trouble for both us and those around us.

If you dig down into your primal instincts, you'll find anger lodged somewhere close to your survival strategies like fight or flight. This explosive little feeling isn't just a biological reaction, it's also something that can come to life when someone transgresses our social norms and personal boundaries.

For a long time, it was considered bad manners to exhibit anger—you simply weren't supposed to behave like that. And I guess it's never going to be regarded as polite to blow your top in a meeting. But there is a far greater understanding of anger today, and you're unlikely to be institutionalized for public shows of madness or hysteria.

Research on anger really has taken a number of fascinating turns over the years. Early studies in the field regarded anger as a primal mechanism for dealing with threats—essentially part of the fight-or-flight response that helped our ancestors survive in a perilous world.

These early theories laid the foundation for our understanding of anger as a basic sense of survival, where our quick response to threats could be the difference between life and death.

But in recent decades, psychologists and neurologists have come to look at anger as something much more complex than just an impulsive reaction. Studies using modern technology such as functional magnetic resonance imaging (fMRI) have provided insights into how anger affects different parts of the brain.

For example, we know that activity in the amygdala (the part of the brain associated with emotional processing) increases when people feel anger. At the same time, studies have also identified connections between the frontal lobe (responsible for decision-making and impulse regulation) and our ability to manage anger. This is all very simplified—my point is that progress has been made.

In addition, sociological and psychological studies have explored how anger functions within social interactions and its role in shaping social hierarchies and norms. Some researchers believe that anger can have a communicative function that signals dissatisfaction and injustice, which can lead to change and adaptation in social groups (aka Red behavior).

The researchers' interest also extends to how anger affects political processes. Electoral behavior can often be driven by emotional factors, and anger has been specifically shown to be a powerful motivator for political engagement. For instance, studies have shown that anger over political issues can increase voter turnout and support for specific politicians who appear in response to whatever caused the anger in the first place.

Take a look at social media and you'll quickly get the impression that people are pissed off more or less all the time, but I doubt things are really that bad. As a rule, I don't think it's good to suppress your anger— you should do something with it. And I firmly maintain that anger isn't always a bad thing. It's baked into our biology. There must be a reason why nature created us like this.

Overall, the field has evolved from a simple understanding of a reactive emotion to a deeper insight into its complexity and manifold impact on everything from personal relationships to how we choose to view large-scale events in the world around us.

However, it is not just the scientists who have examined the concept of anger.

Philosophers have long speculated upon this intriguing emotion's role in shaping our ethical and moral landscape. From the dialogues of Plato to Nietzsche's fiery elements, anger has often been regarded as an emotional catalyst that can summon up all sorts of things.

Don't forget our old friend Socrates, who was always bludgeoning Athenian politicians with his incessant questions. His method, which often infuriated his opponents until they were probably boiling with rage, was actually an ingenious way of revealing moral truths and creating philosophical insight. It's a very smart tactic that I've deployed in negotiations myself. What is really upsetting the other person? Once you know that, the rest is as easy as pie.

Or what about the eternally brooding Hamlet whose *to be or not to be* can be interpreted as an internal philosophical debate? His anger toward the injustice and betrayal at the Danish court eventually precipitated a full-blown tragedy. Hamlet shows how anger can bring a person to the brink of moral decisions where each step is just as charged with passion as it is with danger.

Modern philosophers like Martha Nussbaum have also grappled with anger—with a twist. Nussbaum suggests that while anger may feel justified and perfectly acceptable, it's often counterproductive in the pursuit of a better society. She has even expressed the idea that a world without anger might be fairer and more ethical. I really don't know about that.

Whatever the case, there's one thing we know for sure: Anger plays a big role in life and it always has.

The next time you feel your blood boiling because someone else grabbed your parking spot, think about how angry it's reasonable for you to be.

The next time you're pissed off because your kids aren't listening to you, consider releasing a dose of anger to see whether it makes them listen better.

Let's be serious: It's possible to draw conclusions about someone's behavior based on their temperament. By "temper" or "temperament" I don't just mean what frustrates a person, but rather how they react when something happens. Another way of saying this might be to talk about a person's disposition: how they react to changing circumstances and what sort of energy they have.

But yes, anger is a good and exciting gauge by which to judge a person's color. Moreover, it's situational. What upsets one person may not upset someone else at all. By observing how someone reacts when things go wrong, you can get some important clues, which will help you quickly and easily assess them.

Let me give you an example of a quick diagnosis.

14.2 RED: WHAT THE HELL?!

For the sake of simplicity, let's compare different temperaments to different types of drinking glasses. I would suggest a shot glass for a Red temperament. *But*, you might say, *that little glass doesn't hold much.*

Indeed it doesn't, and many Reds function like that, too. It doesn't take much for them to lose their temper and erupt. I'm certain you've experienced this. It could be about traffic jams, missed phone calls, someone moving too slowly on the escalator. Not getting their own way. Someone just being generally dense. Remember that of all the colors, they are the ones most often surrounded by idiots.

For a Red, there are many reasons to be irritated. A Red's strength is that when they explode, they rid themselves of any anger or irritation they've been feeling.

They erupt briefly, but it doesn't last. They drain the shot glass, which doesn't take long since it's not that big in the first place. (I'm not referring to how those around a Red perceive things.)

The advantage is that, for all their raging, the anger usually subsides quickly. A Red can rarely manage to be angry for long. It's just too much hard work to be in a constant state of anger. They blurt out what they want to say, and then move on.

Sure, they might leave many confused people around them, but why should the Red care? They're done with the incident in question. Then something deeply upsetting happens again, and again they erupt. And again. And again.

Imagine you pick up the shot glass and pour it out over your desk. Not very helpful, but quite manageable. You can easily clean it up.

That's the whole point. But remember the shot glass fills up just as quickly as it was emptied. It will happen again.

Many perceive a Red's temperament as totally unpredictable. It can erupt at any time. Yet I don't think it's quite that bad. If you know the person in question, you probably also know what triggers their anger.

However, it's important to know that a Red doesn't consider themselves to be an angry person. All they've done is give someone a piece of their mind or perhaps raise their voice. Again, it's just a way of communicating.

But to a Green, it might seem that a Red is angry even when they're just sharing their opinion. So much is in the eye of the beholder. It's common for people to simply back off, to avoid confronting the Red and triggering their anger. But by letting their anger get the best of them all the time, Reds miss out on a lot of feedback.

14.3 YELLOW: DAMN IT, I REALLY AM
VERY UPSET!

Even the cheerful Yellow loses his temper: Don't let anyone tell you otherwise. Although Yellows generally have a sunny, optimistic disposition, they have a temper as well. Like Reds, they are active, perceptive people and take in many impressions. This means they have a lot to react to most of the time.

And if you're quick-thinking and your tongue sometimes runs away with you, well, things can happen. What comes out of your face's front door isn't always well thought out. Because Yellows are expressive and emotional at the same time, you'll know in advance when the mercury starts rising.

An observant person won't have any problem noticing that a Yellow is working their way up to bursting. The look in their eyes intensifies; their gestures become impetuous; their voice is raised. All this happens, but it happens gradually.

If the Red temperament is like a shot glass, we can liken the Yellow temperament to an everyday drinking glass. It holds more and it's easier to see when it's full. The level rises a little at a time, and if you're paying attention, you'll have no problem observing this as it happens.

Now, if we take that glass and pour its contents all over your dining table, what's the result?

It will be a lot messier and much soggier than when we poured out the shot glass, right? The tablecloth will be ruined, the napkins soaked through, the hitherto great atmosphere down the drain. And it will take more than a single paper towel to mop it all up again.

But we can still handle the situation. Even this temperamental outburst can be managed without too many serious complications. If nothing else, you will learn a variety of imaginative insults.

There are also advantages in a Yellow's temperament. No, really, I mean it. They'll feel guilty that they laid into someone close to them: a spouse, a family member, a neighbor, or maybe even you. So they'll make an extra effort to be nice the next time you meet.

They will have a bad conscience, something a Red person would rarely worry about. If a person happens to be a combination of Red and Yellow, things can get difficult. In this case, there's a lot of ego in the room, and you won't quite know what's happening. Depending on the driving forces and motivational factors the individual may have, they can assert their own position almost to the point of absurdity.

Genuine Yellows can let their egos get in the way most of the time. The good thing, however, is that due to their poor memory, they don't hold grudges for long. Rather like Reds, being angry for a long time just isn't for them. As we've already established, life is generally a game for Yellows, which means anger is usually a negative for them.

They quickly forget there were any problems, an ability that can make Greens and Blues find Yellows a little bit too exciting.

14.4 GREEN: BEWARE THE FURY OF A PATIENT MAN

I dare say the person who coined this old saying crossed paths with more than their fair share of Greens. In fact, it wouldn't surprise me if you've never seen a Green lose their temper. It may be that your good friend, the amiable and gentle pal you've never had a serious argument with, hasn't ever shown the tiniest shred of bad temper.

Does that mean Greens can't get angry? Not at all. It means that instead of turning their temper outward, it's oriented in another direction. Inward.

I would liken a Green's temperament to a fifty-gallon beer barrel. Can you imagine how many shot glasses it would take to fill it? We could fill, fill, and fill some more before we even started covering the bottom of it.

Many Greens function like that. They receive and accept life's injustices without objecting. This is very much connected to their desire to avoid conflict but also to their inability to say no. They simply agree because it's easier that way.

Does this mean that Greens don't have any opinions of their own? Not at all; they have as many opinions about things as anyone else. They just don't talk about them. And this can be a problem.

They fill the barrel. Week in and week out, a Green accepts one perceived injustice after the other—note that I said "perceived"—without the barrel audibly creaking. But the rest of us keep filling them up.

It may take several years before the barrel is full. But the law of nature is that it must eventually start brimming over.

Now take this barrel, lift it up, and pour the contents out over your dining table.

What happens? Everything will be washed away. The water in the barrel will not only wash away everything on your dining table; even the table itself and you along with it will be carried away by the flood.

There's no stopping it. It all has to come out.

You're saying that I didn't show you enough appreciation? Really? Really?! Last week I said the food tasted good. Let me tell you something . . . Three years ago you promised we'd go to Denmark and it still hasn't happened. And when we moved in together in 1997, it was supposed to be like this, and let me tell you . . .

All the wrongs are stored within easy reach for all eternity and none of them will ever be forgotten. Everything has to come out. Just take care that you're not the spark that sets it all off.

The problem is large-scale. Greens don't release any anger or frustration; they control their emotions so as not to create trouble or stand out. But they feel and experience just as much as everyone else. They simply lack the natural tools to release everything.

But we can help by becoming facilitators. We can ask questions, engage with them, and look for signals.

Look at their body language to detect any signs of disapproval. Create a healthy environment around a Green so they become comfortable enough to say what they think and don't have to continually compromise their position. Otherwise, they'll turn all their frustration inward. And we know what this kind of stress can do to a person.

I have my own private theory, which I certainly cannot prove scientifically, but I suspect this may be the main reason why Greens suffer burnout. They carry anxiety, anguish, and even anger for so long that it eventually makes them ill. It's a noticeable problem that should be taken seriously.

14.5 BLUE: VISIBLY SHAKEN. TO ABOUT 76.5 PERCENT, AS IT HAPPENS . . .

During an extremely stressful period in my earlier career in the banking sector, I once heard a thought-provoking comment about Blues. All of us were working day and night, and many of us were exhibiting signs of stress. The air was thick with frustration.

Our credit controller was in the middle of the whole thing. Nothing got to her. She never even acted stressed. Her face was absolutely inscrutable, and her gestures were as constrained and moderate as always. While the rest of us ate our lunch on the go, she took her full sixty minutes and ate in peace and quiet. . . . It was as if nothing could disturb her peace.

Then one of my Yellow/Red colleagues said, *She's not normal. She doesn't have any feelings in her body.*

It sounded logical—what a robot! But now that I think about it, that can't be right. Everyone has emotions and everyone is largely governed by their emotions. They just look very different.

Blues have less need to communicate than Greens or Yellows. So they simply don't do it. They continue to sit quietly. Some things are turned inward even for Blues.

Those who are quick thinkers may wonder if Blues run the risk of burnout just as much as Greens do.

Actually, no. They have a system to keep stress under control.

Metaphorically speaking, Blues have as big a beer barrel as Greens have, but there is one crucial difference: At the bottom of the barrel, there's a handy little tap. This tap gives the Blue a valve to release part of the contents of the barrel. They can regulate the pressure whenever they wish. And they most definitely want to.

Moreover, the tap unfortunately leaks. It's not tight enough to create a perfect seal, and small drops drip out most of the time.

A Blue's dissatisfaction comes out in the form of tiny grumblings.

Oh come on, now someone's gone and lost the ruler.

Typical. Now I'm going to have to finish up on my own. As usual, I get the most boring task.

There's no structure here. Typical. If only people put things back where they found them. Sigh.

And so they continue. Their pinpricks affect those around them, but what they hear is no more than sullen muttering. The embers never flare up into a real fire.

The rest of us interpret this as endless whining about stuff that shouldn't really matter one way or the other, but there's an underlying and genuine dissatisfaction there.

And because a Blue isn't sufficiently active to instigate something, they'll argue about things rather than doing something about them. It might be that others ought to see what they can see, or that they don't have a mandate to act, or that they are in a foul mood.

But for them, this is a great way of keeping the pressure under control. So the barrel will never need to be emptied out over somebody's table, and serious catastrophes are avoided.

The way to manage this nagging is to ask counterquestions. Ask for concrete examples. Ask for suggestions for improvement. It may, in fact, be the case that the Blue has solved the problem that is plaguing them, but they need a straight question in order to step forward and suggest a solution.

Be there and listen. You're the one who has the most to gain from the situation.

14.6 WHAT CAN YOU DO ABOUT THE FACT THAT PEOPLE DON'T EVEN GET PISSED OFF IN THE SAME WAY?

With these simple observations in mind, you can quickly form an idea of what type of person you're dealing with. Pay attention to how they react under stress and pressure, as it can reveal a lot about their true character. Many of us show our true selves in such situations. A person who maintains their composure or can laugh off a stressful situation may be more emotionally robust—i.e., they have greater self-control than someone who quickly loses their temper or becomes defensive. How they cope always says something about the person in question.

But, at the same time, remember that no system is perfect. These are only indications, and they apply only to individual colors. Besides, as I wrote previously, different situations can give rise to completely different forms of behavior.

Generally speaking, the more important a particular thing is for a certain person, the stronger their reaction will be. This insight is perfectly logical, but it is also fundamental when you are attempting to understand what drives people and how they deal with conflict and challenges.

If someone insults your neighbor, you may think it's unfair but it's hardly going to put you on the warpath. On the other hand, if someone were to insult your wife, you'd be bloody furious. That's just an example, but there's an intriguing gradient of differences for us to consider here.

Another example plucked from daily life: Reflect how different people react to the same stress factor, like getting stuck in traffic. Some people may be incredibly annoyed by the morning rush hour and will rant and rave uninterrupted, while others may see it as their chance to listen to their favorite tunes and chill out. After all, it's the only moment of peace and quiet they get all day. . . . Reactions like these can also provide us with valuable clues as to personality types. The first person may be more impulsive and fixated on immediate results (like arriving on time) while the second may be more patient and flexible (we'll get there when we get there).

It's also important to remember that cultural, social, and personal factors can affect the way a person reacts to different situations. What may seem like an overreaction in one culture may be an entirely normal response in another. Understanding these subtleties can provide a more nuanced understanding of someone's behavior and help you navigate social interactions more deftly.

By studying these behaviors and reactions, not only can you learn more about others, but you can also gain insights into yourself and how you react in similar situations.

It's nothing to be unsettled by, if you ask me.

Body Language and Its Secret Signals

15.1 WHY THE WAY WE LOOK REALLY MATTERS

The first impression in any rendezvous with a new acquaintance will always be more crucial to how the relationship will unfold than any subsequent impression. One factor is what the body language of different colors looks like. Among other things, you display a certain body language to other people, and this is potentially a very useful thing. This body language will then be interpreted. But that gives rise to a question: Can you present yourself as someone you aren't? Science is not entirely in agreement.

Let's take a closer look at body language.

"Body language" refers to all forms of nonverbal communication, conscious as well as unconscious. Differences in body language vary both between individuals and between different groups of people. Our body language also functions as a social and cultural marker, even if there are common biological foundations.

The modern English language contains about one hundred and seventy thousand words, of which five thousand are used regularly. Of those, we might use a vocabulary somewhere in the region of one thousand words in our day-to-day. In comparison, according to certain scholars, body language contains almost seven hundred thousand signals. We could debate the exact numbers, but that's not the point. Just be aware that there is an immense number of signals, more than we are conscious of.

I'm not going to examine all these signals, but it's still interesting to see the differences between different behavior profiles. The same thing can mean different things depending on who it originates with. Just remember, our state of mind, our situation, and whether we feel safe or unsafe can have a crucial influence on our body language.

15.1.1 Posture

If you have a relaxed, natural but not slack posture, other people often see you as exuding self-confidence. If on the other hand you have a shrunken posture, it can be interpreted as resignation and disappointment.

If you have an erect, somewhat wooden posture, people can believe this is a signal of dominance; in other words, you demand respect from those around you. However, it could also be an indication that you were trained at a military academy.

What about folded arms? Is it true this indicates dissociation?

Well, yes and no. Not everyone who sits or stands with their arms folded over their chest is being negative. Sometimes it's just a comfortable position to adopt. But this is the interesting thing: When that posture appears, at what point did the change actually occur? What did you say that made them fold their arms? It may be worth keeping track of.

15.1.2 Gaze

We use our gaze in many different ways. Shifty eyes generally suggest the person in question would rather be somewhere else. Other people meet your gaze steadily, without even blinking. This creates a totally different impression.

It's said that liars can't look you in the eye and they often shift their gaze to the side, with the side in question depending on whether they are right- or left-handed. This is a myth that has proven very difficult to kill off, and it just so happens that the reality is the exact opposite.

But since this is commonly known even among liars, the worst rogues have learned to stare you straight in the eyes when they are lying. So nothing is that obvious. (Someone repeatedly touching their neck is more often an indicator of a liar. Give it a try and see. If someone asks you whether you enjoyed the meal, try scratching your neck and telling them it was delicious. Take note of their reaction.)

When something is awful or unpleasant, many cover their faces. And when you need to think, you often close your eyes for a while. There are lots of small signals you can look out for—if you're interested in that kind of thing.

15.1.3 Head and Face

When speaking, we usually either nod or shake our heads, depending on whether we agree or not. When we listen extra carefully to a discussion, we may tilt our heads to one side. This signals compassion and empathy.

Hanging your head or furrowing your brow can signal sadness or depression. When we're amazed at something, we often raise our eyebrows, while we wrinkle our noses at things we don't like. The face alone has twenty-four different muscles that can be used in countless combinations.

There are also theories pertaining to micro-expressions—these are very small muscular twitches—but science has not reached a consensus on how these should be interpreted.

15.1.4 Hands

The handshake. Yes, this is a true classic. The good old handshake can tell us a lot about a person. Just how hard should you grasp the hand of the person you're greeting? Limp and feeble handshakes often indicate submissive behavior, so if you have a handshake like that, it might be a good idea to press a little harder.

If a handshake is firm, it probably suggests that person is

determined. Anyone who squeezes way too hard probably belongs to the first category I mentioned before but would like to belong to the latter.

Clenched fists rarely mean good news; usually they indicate aggressiveness. Not to mention how that's taken by those around them.

Certain nervous people pick at their clothes, removing hairs or threads. This often indicates they would rather focus their attention on other things. Holding your hands clasped behind your back often expresses power and security.

Pointing at someone with an open hand and your palm toward the ceiling is an open gesture that is perceived to be both positive and encouraging. If you opt to do the opposite, this is effectively like asking the other person to shut their trap.

Remember what I said about lies? A more effective way to spot a liar is to notice if they put the palm of their hand on their chest—preferably their right hand over their heart—and sigh indignantly when accused of lying. *Would I lie? How can you say that about me?*

This gesture is intended to strengthen their honest intentions, but it immediately puts those around them on their guard, because it is so unnecessary and over the top. There's definitely something fishy going on there.

15.1.5 Territory

It's very important that everyone has their own personal territory, because everyone needs a space of their own. Among other things, this territory can be the distance you maintain from people when you're speaking to them.

The personal zone is generally a few feet and the social zone is three to ten feet. By the "personal zone," we mean the space when two people who know each other are communicating. The "social zone" refers to the space between strangers who are communicating. You generally won't mind having close friends within a few feet, while strangers typically need to be kept at more of a distance. This might originate from ancient times when a stranger could just as easily be a mortal enemy seeking to take your life—so you stayed a club or knife's length away from them.

But this is also very much contingent on which culture we're looking at. In my beloved Scandinavia, the personal zone is definitely bigger than it is in the Mediterranean. Which is preferable? Not a clue. It all depends on who you ask.

15.2 SO WHAT DO WE DO ABOUT ALL THIS?

That was a crash course in the basics of body language. What variations are there in this behavior? It's obvious that some "well-known" facts about body language don't apply to every single person. Someone glancing to the left might sometimes be lying—but they might also be trying to recall something from memory.

In my corner of the world, an axis of time begins on the left and continues to the right. That means if I'm thinking about the past, my focus will be drawn . . . to the left. And sometimes my eyes can't help but follow.

Another example is how people deal with uncertainty. A Green who is unsure leans backward. They're afraid of potentially aggressive situations and possible conflict. A Red who is unsure leans forward, as their way of dealing with this uncertainty is to try to dominate the conversation. And thus they signal aggression.

On the following pages, I've listed further examples of the differences. Try observing people in real life to see if you can pick out any of the following forms of behavior. But remember, body language is very individual.

Sure, there are the general expressions that apply throughout the entire world and among all people—a contemptuous stare, for example, looks similar in every country—but there are so many differences that you'll have to study your fellow mortals to sharpen your ability.

The following short sections are intended to serve as a simple guide.

15.3 RED BEHAVIOR

Some simple basics to keep in mind are that Reds:

- keep their distance from others
- often have powerful handshakes
- like to lean forward
- use direct eye contact
- use controlling gestures

As I mentioned previously, Reds often have a clear and distinctive body language. You can usually recognize a Red from a distance.

When you walk through large crowds, you'll see people swarming around, standing still, conversing with others, or just looking to see what all the fuss is about.

Let's say you're looking at a town square teeming with people. If you look really closely, you'll see a person crossing the square at a brisk pace, completely disregarding the people standing in their way. Their gaze is fixed on a point way ahead and the Red speeds up and crosses the square without any problem. They don't give way but make others move aside. Their gait is decisive and powerful. They expect the rest of us to get out of their way.

The first time you meet a Red, they usually maintain a certain distance. Their handshake won't be hearty, but it will be powerful. Expect that the Red—be it a man or woman—will grip a little bit harder to show who's boss. (Some people consider this alpha male behavior, but it also occurs in women. A Red has a need to demonstrate they are someone to be reckoned with.)

Forget overexuberant smiles. Their face can be downright grim, especially if you're attending a business meeting. But even in social settings, Reds maintain some reserve. A Red won't give you a big bear hug (well, not while they're sober; under the influence of alcohol, anything can happen).

When things start getting tense—which usually happens rather quickly when Reds are involved—they will lean across the table and argue their case forcefully. Eye contact will be very direct, their gaze fixed on you. When it comes to the language of power, Reds have their finger on the trigger right from the start. Be prepared for that.

Also be prepared for a relatively limited use of gestures, but those gestures that do surface can be controlling and aggressive.

Reds point at people very readily. The notion that it is rude to point at people isn't something that worries them. They'll either use a single finger, or they may even point using their entire hand. It's also common that Reds point at you by stretching out their hand toward you with the palm facing down. If you want to give this a try, ask someone to point at you that way, and then think about how it feels.

You can also clearly see that Reds—of course, they are not alone in this—are more than willing to interrupt you. They draw breath continuously, hoping to find gaps in the conversation. If they have to wait too long to speak, they'll throw themselves into the conversation with a loud voice and simply take over.

15.3.1 Voice

What about a Red's tone of voice? It's often strong. We hear these people clearly because they think nothing of raising their voices to make themselves heard—as loud as it takes. Of course, even Reds can be nervous and worried about things, but usually you won't hear it. Their voices rarely waver or tremble.

This is one of the secrets Reds have. No matter what's happening behind the facade, Reds will sound convincing. No stammer, no hesitation. Finger on the trigger. If we don't listen, they'll say it again, but louder. In the end, they always get through.

15.3.2 Speed in Speech and Deed

As I mentioned earlier, Reds are always in a hurry. Quick equals good. Generally, this applies to both speech and actions. Everything happens at a furious pace. Because speed is the factor many Reds measure success by, it will be all go. With a couple of sharp changes of direction when required.

15.4 YELLOW BEHAVIOR

Some simple basics to keep in mind are that Yellows:

- are tactile
- are relaxed and jocular
- show friendly eye contact
- use expressive gestures
- often come physically close to others

A Yellow's body language is often very open and inviting. Smiles appear constantly, even when there's not much to smile about. Yellows often joke and will appear lively and energetic while not being overly wide-eyed. They're often very relaxed when in company.

Yellows may semi-recline on the sofa when paying a visit to a neighbor they don't, in fact, know very well at all. But this is typical for Yellows. When a Yellow feels secure in any given situation, you can see it. They're an open book.

The similarity with Red behavior lies primarily in the tempo. Yellows move quickly and distinctively. They often radiate a strong self-confidence.

Personal space is a relative thing for Yellows. While some colors don't like having people sit too close to them, Yellows will willingly move up very close. Yellows can spontaneously start hugging everyone around them. Man or woman, it doesn't really matter. It depends on what the feeling and the mood are like that day.

It's not uncommon for others to recoil when this happens, and Yellows find this very tiresome. But it's not just hugging that Yellows like. It can be any simple form of physical contact. A hand placed on an arm, a pat on the leg—it doesn't have to mean anything except that the Yellow wants to reinforce whatever it is they've just said. What a Yellow understands to be a natural and spontaneous manner may be perceived by others as a solicitation of . . . well, who knows what? And of course, it can all end in tears.

In general, with Yellows there will be jokes and countless smiles all around.

Eye contact is no problem; it's intense, cheerful, and friendly.

15.4.1 Voice

A Yellow's tone of voice radiates a strong commitment from start to finish. Yellows can be very engaging. (And if they don't feel like doing a certain activity, then that charm won't be forthcoming.) You can hear it from afar: laughter, fun, intensity, enthusiasm, joy, energy.

Generally speaking, Yellows show empathy very clearly. They're with you either 100 percent or not at all. And this can be heard in their voice. It goes up and down; it changes in tempo, vigor, and intensity. Yellows often have a powerful melody in their way of speaking.

No matter what emotion has seized the Yellow at any given moment, it will be noticeable in their voice.

15.4.2 Speed in Speech and Deed

Tempo. Not quite the same rate of action as Reds, but a decidedly fast pace. Have you ever met anyone who, when in a hurry to say something, kind of stumbles over their words? Only half of them really come out as they should. You can surmise what is being said, but sometimes it's incomprehensible. These are Yellows whose mouths simply can't keep up with everything they have to say. Their thoughts are running too fast—even for them. But above all, you may experience them as mercurial. They're quite simply entertainers who are good at keeping people captivated.

15.5 GREEN BEHAVIOR

Some simple basics to keep in mind are that Greens:

- look relaxed and like to be in physical proximity to people who know them well
- act methodically
- tend to lean backward
- use very friendly eye contact
- prefer small-scale gestures

Greens are often—but not always—slow and gentle in their body movements. When they're feeling completely in harmony, they have a relaxed body language that exudes calm and confidence. No impetuous movements, no sudden tossing of their heads or hands. Nice and easy.

Their gestures are often less flamboyant than other colors' and are well suited for smaller groups. Greens don't feel at ease in larger groups, so they become more closed and will appear reserved. Greens often have body language that gives them away. They try to hide their true feelings but don't always succeed. If they're out of balance or feel uncomfortable, it will be visible—usually through their folded arms.

When sitting around a table, you can expect Greens will tend to lean backward. This is something of a paradox, as they don't really have a problem getting close to people. Just like Yellows, they like to touch others. It's fine as long as they know the person they are touching.

Beware, however, of touching a Green who hasn't given a clear sign that they know you well enough. It's easy to cross the line. They can be protective of their personal space.

You often notice when a Red walks across a room. Since Greens are the complete opposite of Reds in many things, one might say that Greens make discretion a point of honor. It's not uncommon that they try to make themselves invisible.

The reason? They don't want to be the center of attention. Attention is usually bad news.

Greens almost always have friendly faces. If not, then they're quite neutral. Don't expect any exaggerated smiles or overexuberant greetings. Hesitant reserve is the name of the game. But the difference will be huge if a Green knows you. If they think you're good friends, they can be very intimate and friendly. But if they feel as if you have only just met each other, well then, you'll have to be patient.

Let Greens come to you. Don't force yourself on them. In time, when they trust you, they'll relax and become more natural.

15.5.1 Voice

A Green's voice will never be strong; it's not likely they will drown out the group. You'll have to make a little bit more effort to hear them. Even when Greens speak in front of a larger group (they may do this if they don't have any choice), they'll speak as if there were only three of you sitting around the table. Sometimes it may appear that Greens don't see the other hundred people in the room. The volume is generally low, and it can be difficult to hear what they say.

But their voice will always be soft and radiate warmth. The pace will be slower and the variation in tone not at all like when a Yellow speaks.

15.5.2 Speed in Speech and Deed

Generally, Greens have a slower pace than Reds and Yellows but not quite as slow as Blues. Speed has no value in itself. If a heightened tempo risks destroying the cooperation in the group, Greens will reduce the speed. It doesn't matter what the deadline is. The most important thing is always going to be how people feel.

15.6 BLUE BEHAVIOR

Some simple basics to keep in mind are that Blues:

- prefer to keep others at a physical distance
- either stand or sit still

- often have closed body language
- use direct eye contact
- speak without gestures

The easiest way to describe a Blue's body language is to say they don't have any.

Okay, maybe that's a little too simplistic. What I mean is there's not that much to interpret in a Blue. Neither their face nor their body gives much away. Whenever I talk about body language and Blue behavior, people tell me how impossible some people are to interpret. When I ask if these are people who sit almost perfectly still without moving so much as a muscle in their faces, they usually nod and think this is remarkable.

They're probably talking about Blues. But a person who doesn't exhibit much movement or even temperament reveals nothing. In this case, it's the lack of distinctive body language that tells us what we need to know.

Many Blues can make very dramatic statements with an expressionless face. I once heard a Blue manager announce that the whole department was to close and that we had to draw up redundancy plans for three hundred employees. Not a muscle in his face moved unnecessarily.

This is what gives people the idea that Blues lack feelings, but this is, naturally, untrue. Let me remind you again that a Blue is an introvert, which is to say, most of their emotions simply operate beneath the surface.

It also works the other way. Once, many years ago, I saw a lady win half a million dollars on a Swedish game show. Behind the camera her husband could be heard screaming for joy, while the lady herself sat very still with a cool smile. It was almost eerie.

The host was smiling and waving his arms around, and for a while you had to wonder who had actually won. But the lady herself uttered nothing more than *This is so nice, thank you*. She hardly budged an inch. I don't think it was because she was already a millionaire; it was because she was Blue. This is simply the way it works.

Beneath the surface, I assume she was relatively satisfied with the outcome. One of these days, I must call the channel and ask if they still have the recording, because it's such a vivid illustration.

When you see Blues speaking in front of larger groups, this tendency becomes very evident. Just like Greens, they have no need to be the center of attention. The difference, however, is that while a Green would like to be swallowed up by the floor, a Blue will firmly remain standing. They'll try to whip up the masses while remaining completely motionless with a fixed face.

Another clue is that Blues require a relatively large amount of private space around them. They often feel more comfortable keeping others at a distance. Naturally, it depends on how well they know each other, but this zone is significantly larger than it is for Yellows, for instance.

If others come too close, Blues' body language becomes closed. Both arms and legs will be crossed, indicating they're keeping their distance.

As I mentioned earlier, Blues move less than others. When they stand, they stand still. There's not that much swaying and walking about. They can very easily stand in the same spot for a whole hour while giving a lecture. When they sit down, they remain seated more or less in the same position all the time. Stillness is an apt word for what we observe.

This also means there's very little gesticulation. Imagine a Yellow—a really outgoing, positive figure—and now imagine the opposite. Take away all the movements that aren't needed (most of them, according to Blues) and you begin to get the picture. Stony-faced, as someone once described it.

However, one thing Blues do—that others may struggle with—is look you straight in the eye. You see, they have no problem with eye contact.

15.6.1 Voice

Though not exactly weak, a Blue's voice is restrained and subdued. They don't make much of a fuss about themselves. They tend to give a controlled impression. It's common for them to sound very pensive, as if weighing every word before it's allowed to see the light of day.

Generally, there's little or no variation in a Blue's voice. They sound more or less the same all the time—whether they're reading that day's TV listings or thanking the nation after winning a general election. Without much rhythm or melody, they just continue to say what's in the script.

Musicians tend to have difficulties with this. They think everything a Blue says flows badly.

15.6.2 Speed in Speech and Deed

Slow. At least if we compare it to others' speech. If we take a Red or even a Yellow, they'll speak at the speed of sound. A Blue has a completely different pace. It will take as long as it takes. Speed is of no interest. Don't expect any major variations in tempo or intensity.

Not long ago, I met a very Blue young man who told me that everything he did took a long time to complete. He didn't make a big deal out of it; instead, he simply stated it as fact.

15.7 SUMMARY

Well, there we have it. As you can see, there are differences and it can pay to keep track of what they are. A furrowed brow may well mean very different things depending on whether it belongs to a Red or a Blue. In a Red, it means you're pissing said individual off. In a Blue, that same wrinkled forehead indicates focus and concentration. Apparently you're a subject of interest.

The easiest way to decipher someone's body language is always to start by establishing the baseline—how does this particular individual normally behave?

And sometimes things change. New movements emerge. Faces alter. And when that happens, you'd be well advised to pause for thought. *Why has this changed and might it have anything to do with me?*

Good luck!

16

Adaptation—How to Handle Everyone Else

16.1 HOW TO HANDLE EVERYONE WHO ISN'T LIKE YOU—THE IDIOTS

A question put to me regularly when I'm training people of all four colors is which color is best suited to adapting to others. Which color has the best social skills, when you boil it down?

The problem is you can't answer the question like that. The four colors only exhibit their natural behaviors. They don't show any tendencies toward different abilities or skills. Adapting to your surroundings in the right way is simply a matter of social skills.

Why would anyone want to learn a specific thing, regardless of what it is? For example, what makes someone work on their skills at dealing with different types of people? Interest? Need? The desire to solve a problem? Or is it perhaps because they're taken with the subject itself?

All this is more clearly linked to circumstances and driving forces than it is to which color we are. I've met people of all colors and combinations who have made enormous strides forward in terms of their adaptability and social skills. I've also met Reds, Yellows, Greens, and Blues who said all the right things but showed through their actions that they hadn't taken in anything whatsoever.

So personal interest and possibly whether any reason compelling enough has ever arisen seem to be crucial to the outcome. Really good leaders are always working on their social skills and their ability to hone their communication, but that's the case regardless of their color.

A man once said (admittedly with an ironic smile on his face, but still) that the test of intelligence is simple: *If you agree with me, then you're intelligent. However, if you don't agree with me, then you are clearly and undoubtedly an idiot.*

I assume you're intelligent enough to interpret this message correctly. But seriously—all of us have wondered why some people don't understand anything. How is it that seemingly intelligent people are also simultaneously capable of being such complete and utter idiots? This was a problem I encountered when I was a young man. They didn't see what I saw. Some people delicately say that such individuals lack the right "intellectual elasticity," but that's only because they're too well bred to let the word "idiot" come out of their mouths.

16.1.1 If Everyone Were the Same

It's hard to disagree with the assertion that diversity enriches us all. Imagine a world in which there was only one type of everything. A world in which everyone lived in identical houses that were all the same size with the same lawn in front and the shrubs lining the garden in exactly the same way. On the driveways of these identical houses you'd always find the same make of car—the same model too, and more or less the same color.

Inside the houses, the floor plan and decor would be practically indistinguishable. All families would be the same size. Everyone would dress the same and sit down to breakfast at identical dining tables taking up the same positions and eating the same foods as their neighbors.

I'm sure some will think that sounds like a perfect world—just think how straightforward everything would be! You'd be off the hook for having to make any decisions, since every time you went to the shops there'd only be one type of food in each category to buy.

One kind of milk. One kind of bread. One kind of breakfast cereal. Only one flavor of potato chips. And so on.

If you cared to stop by the clothing store, you'd quickly find out that all shirts came in more or less the same color. There would be one type of trousers and all shoes would be effectively identical. How easy life would be! You wouldn't have to make a new decision ever again.

However. Most of us instinctively feel our stomachs turn at the thought of this imagined world. Because just think about the prospect of arriving at work in identical cars, dressed the same, with the same haircuts and all doing . . . the same jobs? It would end up feeling like China under Chairman Mao.

If you ask me, this sounds like hell on Earth.

And I dare say you realize this is nothing more than a stupid example.

I know, and I agree. But now imagine that everyone was basically the same on the outside and inside. Pick any appearance you like. All over the planet, everyone would have the same skin tone, be of the same height and weight, and everyone would think and say basically the same stuff.

It's impossible to contemplate a world like that.

What am I trying to get at with this point? Well, I want to draw attention to the obvious: The fact that people are different in their manner and nature is perfectly logical. It's also a good thing, given that the alternative is horrible. Not to mention impossible.

When you find yourself occasionally sighing over the fact that you can't wrap your head around people and how it seems as if they don't understand you, either, and thinking how it would be easier if everyone was the same, remind yourself that the alternative would be worse.

Naturally we have to make an effort with each other. To deny this fact would be naïve. But we'll always be different to one degree or another, so the trick is to find the similarities and do something positive with what we find—an endeavor that is far from hopeless.

By practicing your own ability to analyze and interpret human behavior, you will be spared many a headache. Once you understand an individual, all you have to do is find out how you should act when faced with said person. Regardless of which colors you think apply to you so far, I hope you feel that things are getting interesting and that you can put this knowledge to good use. Let's delve a bit further.

16.1.2 So . . . Apparently People Are Different

What can we do about the fact that people are so different? That they react and function in completely different ways? And is it possible to adapt to every kind of personality? What does the fact that a room is full of all sorts of people at the same time mean for us? It's a thought-provoking question. Here's another—if it were possible to be a complete chameleon in any given situation, would it be wise to try?

It's natural for us humans to be who we are—we all have our core behaviors. But there is a plethora of reasons why we may feel the need to adapt to our surroundings.

It's often suggested that we need to be flexible and adaptable in order to deal with all the different situations and people we may encounter. There's even a name for this concept: emotional intelligence. Or social skills. In order to cope with this constant adaptation, it's important we're aware that adaptation takes effort and in some cases a great deal of energy, too.

Our natural condition is to use our core behavior—what we really are without any external influences.

Our "unnatural" behavior is to continually adapt to others and be "right" for the situation, but this requires ability, training, and energy.

If we're uncertain as to what is "right" in a situation, if we're unskilled or lack sufficient energy to cope with the role we currently believe is the right one, we will be frightened, hesitant, and often stressed. That results in us being drained of even more energy, with the consequence that our core behavior becomes ever more visible. We will be exhibiting more and more of our true self, and that may not be our best side.

It may even be a big surprise to those around us who are used to us behaving in a certain way.

16.2 IN A PERFECT WORLD

In the best of worlds, everyone can be themselves and everything functions well from the word "go." Everyone agrees at all times and conflicts don't exist at all. The days go by smoothly. We take each other's views into account on those rare occasions when there is debate. Everyone looks out for everyone else's well-being, and if something goes wrong, we all pitch in to help.

This place is said to exist, and it's called Utopia. But if you think you can change everyone else, you're in for a real disappointment. It would surprise me if you could change anyone at all.

No matter who you are—Red, Yellow, Green, or Blue, or a combination of multiple colors—you will always be in the minority. Most of the people you encounter will be different from you. No matter how well balanced you are, you can't be all the types at the same time.

So you have to adapt to the people you meet. Good communication is often a matter of adapting to others.

But wait a minute, you may be thinking. *That isn't true. I can be myself. In fact, I never adapt myself for anyone, at any time, and that works perfectly well. It's brought me this far in life.*

Sure thing.

Of course, everyone can start with themselves. But don't expect to get through to other people with the message you're trying to share. If you can live with the knowledge that most people you meet won't buy what you say, well, you don't have a problem.

And no matter how you've made it to the present day, who knows how far you might have gotten if you *had* adapted yourself to the people you met along the way?

16.2.1 You Already Do This, Even If You Don't Think You Do

Besides, you already adapt your behavior, even if you don't realize it. We all adapt to one another all the time. It's part of the social game, the visible and invisible communication that is constantly in progress. The majority of people know roughly when they should be quiet, when they should talk, and when it might be a good idea to laugh along. Most of us are also well aware that it would be socially inept to tell dirty jokes at a funeral.

Sometimes there's a conscious reaction behind the adaptation we make, but more often than not it will be something we do instinctively. Sometimes it works out; sometimes it doesn't.

I'm proposing a more reliable system. You don't have to gamble or guess. You can make the right adjustment from the beginning. Please note: usually. No system is perfect.

Some people I meet don't like the idea of deliberately adapting to others. They consider it dishonest and manipulative. *It's my right to be myself!* Sure thing. You don't have to do this. It's completely up to you. But the following are my suggestions as to how we can deal with different types of behavior.

16.2.2 An Example of How Difficult It Can Be to Accept Reality

Before taking the plunge, I'd like to share with you a true story about a man I met during a training conference many years ago, a likable and very popular entrepreneur who had achieved great success in his field. This man—let's call him Adriano (mostly because that's actually his name and it makes this so much easier)—was extremely Yellow, a real visionary with ambitious plans that were only occasionally put into effect.

Adriano had never thought about or reflected on how he behaved as a person or how he was perceived by others. There had never been any reason to. It was a complete nonissue. Someone had persuaded him to come to this conference, and he didn't really know what he was getting himself into.

The topic that day was the same as this book; it was a full-day workshop where we worked on how to understand different behavior profiles. After the lunch break, I saw that something was troubling Adriano. His face was serious, and his body language had become very closed. When I started talking again and explaining the various profiles, he sank deeper and deeper into his chair, and it was obvious to me that he was thinking about something else entirely.

I asked what was troubling him.

An explosion followed. He exclaimed, *This is wrong! It's bugging me so much!*

How could I categorize people like that? Put people into a theoretical grid system?

It turned out that he didn't like the idea of adapting to other types of people, but not because he thought everyone should adapt to him. No, what worried him was that he saw it as a way to manipulate others and he didn't like it. Didn't like it at all, in fact.

By now, everyone in the room—including me—wondered what the real problem was. Adriano argued forcefully that you couldn't categorize people this way. That using a bunch of models was just wrong. He thought it was highly dangerous not to go on pure feeling.

Someone in the group made it clear to him that he of all people should listen, since he was the one constantly attracting conflict. The debate was soon in full swing, and after thirty minutes I had to call a time-out.

I could understand Adriano's concern, and I respected the fact that he raised the issue in the first place. What worried him was that it wouldn't work: If everyone adapted to one another, no one would be themselves any longer. To his way of thinking, that would be the greatest deception—not to be yourself.

There's undeniable value in what he said. At the same time, of course, the choice is always yours. The more you learn about other people, the easier it becomes for you to make decisions. Join in the game, or go your own way. The decision will always be yours.

Furthermore, Adriano was also deeply resentful that I, as a specialist in the field, could describe him in quite some detail and give examples of how I thought he was wired. When he looked at the assessment tool that describes such an individual, he went completely silent. He'd realized that I knew more about him than he did, even though we'd only just met, and he was fuming.

Fortunately, once we'd sat down and talked it through, there was a happy ending to this story. What I learned from that encounter was that I had to be careful with how I use this knowledge.

16.3 HOW OFTEN DO WE FOLLOW A SYSTEM WITHOUT KNOWING IF IT WORKS?

No system is perfect. There are always exceptions. Like I said in the introduction to this book, this is just one piece in the jigsaw puzzle of human life. It's certainly a large and important piece, but it's far from the whole picture. Once we've explored how to adapt, I'll go into further depth in certain areas, which will probably leave you with more questions. But let's finish with the colors first.

I've divided up the sections on adaptation into two parts for each color. The first part deals with what you need to do to interact meaningfully with another person—when you really want to get through to them and get them in a cheerful mood and make them feel understood. In sports management, this is what is known as "pacing." You simply meet the other person wherever they happen to be. Instead of yelling across the town square, you cross over to the other side.

The second part deals with how you get people to take your side. What a particular profile wants in a situation isn't necessarily the best thing to do to make progress. This is the important part—leading. Once you've crossed the square and you're in the same half of the pitch, how do you successfully bring the person with you to your desired destination?

You can do a great deal of good—if you choose to.

Adapting to Red Behavior

17.1 WHAT A RED EXPECTS OF YOU

17.1.1 Do What I Asked of You, as Quickly as Possible—Preferably Even Faster than That

If you ask a Red, they'll agree that most people are too slow. They speak too slowly, they have trouble coming to the point, and they work ineffectively. In a Red's world, everything simply takes way too long. And you and I are both too slow by half.

Remember what I told you about impatience in Red behavior, about their constant pursuit of (ultrafast) results. When other people turn things over in their minds from morning to night, it drives a Red crazy.

Thought and action are one. Things need to be done quickly. If there's anything Reds dislike, it's endless discussion. It makes them flip out.

17.1.2 What You Should Do

If you want to adapt to a Red's tempo—hurry up! On the double! Speak and act more quickly. Much more quickly. If you can wrap up a meeting in half the allotted time—well, what are you waiting for?! If you have a Red with you in the car, they won't be upset if you drive a little bit over the speed limit. (If you drive too slowly, your Red passenger might insist on taking the steering wheel.) Speed limits are really just recommendations, after all. If you're prepared to pay a little extra, then you can really speed things up.

Up the ante! Do everything faster. Move more quickly. Look at the clock often, because that's what a Red does. What elements can be removed from any given task, whether at home or at work?

The same rules should apply whether you're doing your job or tidying your garage. What can be streamlined? Throw your rubbish straight into the dumpster without sorting it and save yourself precious minutes. Is it really necessary to do everything perfectly or are you prepared to embark upon tasks without knowing exactly how they'll work out? When an idea strikes like a bolt from the blue, shock yourself into action. Stand up and get to work!

17.2 DO YOU WANT SOMETHING? COME ON! OUT WITH IT!

As you now know, Reds are very much to the point, and they enjoy being with other people who have the ability to tell them what they want—quickly. If you have a tendency to go around in circles before getting to the crux of the matter, you'll have difficulty getting through to a Red. They'll tire of you if you waste words for no reason. And they know when they're dealing with a chatterbox.

It's very common for people to provide some background to a problem before describing the problem itself. And maybe even some more background to the possible solution of the problem. References, proof, a bunch of technical explanations—all at a high level to demonstrate that they really know their stuff.

Forget it. It won't work.

17.2.1 What You Should Do

If you want to have a Red's full attention, cut the small talk. It's vital that you're clear and straightforward. Determine the most essential point of your message and start there.

Don't use a single word unnecessarily. But make sure you've done your homework when it comes to the background. Questions may come up. If a Red senses you're uncertain, you'll be grilled on the facts.

Written materials should be concise and, above all, well laid out. No endless dissertations written by someone who loves to see their own words in print. (And you can actually write contracts or rather big business deals on the back of a napkin. That's a trick I've deployed more than once.)

Think about how few words you could use to express yourself. Is it possible to be more to the point? Consider cutting to the chase, and check whether a Red actually needs to know the background. Keep information sparse at first and see whether they ask for more details.

Say you're going to tell a Red about an idea you've just had. Share your final point first—that's what the Red is sitting there waiting for, anyway. Then you can get into the details.

It'll work splendidly. If you want to hold their attention for a longer spell, start with powerful words like "disaster," "chaos," or "serious mistake." That should make them prick their ears.

17.3 I DON'T GIVE A DAMN WHAT YOU DID ON HOLIDAY

Reds live in the present. Everything that happens is happening here and now. They have a unique ability to focus on what's on the agenda *right now*. Therefore, you need to stick to the topic when you speak to a Red. They have no problem with creativity or new ideas; those are always appreciated as long as they move the conversation forward. But when a Red feels you've departed from the agenda altogether and are beginning to fiddle-faddle, you can be sure conflict isn't far off.

The most effective method for a Red is to establish what the problem is and then just get to work. Simple, isn't it?

17.3.1 What You Should Do

Stick to the topic! The easiest way is to prepare your case very precisely before going into a meeting with a Red. If, in the middle of an interesting discussion, another thought pops into your head, write it down and ask at the end of the meeting if it's okay to raise the issue.

If someone with lots of Red in their behavior asks what time it is, answer the question with the exact time. *It's half past ten.* Don't say there's plenty of time. They'll decide that for themselves.

Don't describe how the clock was made, either. And once again— don't forget to keep up the pace. For a Red, "speed" will be synonymous with "efficiency."

This is probably most important for you if you have Yellow traits in your profile. If your mind tends to wander, then simply refrain from telling a Red everything you think. If you're talking about holidays with your spouse, avoid babbling about what your neighbor's plans are. Dull.

If you're discussing the week ahead with your Red spouse, stick to the plan. Say you wanted to do some gardening—don't bring up all the things you wish you'd gotten around to the week before. Dull. What your spouse actually wants to know is what you're going to do now.

Remind yourself that most Reds have learned to sit quietly and nod along, but they will interrupt you and ask you to zip it if you go too far off topic.

17.4 WE'RE TALKING BUSINESS NOW—AND DON'T YOU FORGET IT

Being businesslike in business doesn't really sound like a novel idea, but think about it. If you're in sales, you've probably attended countless training courses where you have learned that you have to build up a relationship with the customer. Get to know them. Win them over to your side. This is good advice. Do it. Build relationships as much as you deem necessary.

Just don't do it with Reds. For example, if you begin a meeting with a Red whom you've never met before, nothing could be worse than asking where they live, where they last went on holiday, or what they thought about the game last night. They don't care. They're not there to chat or to make friends. They've come to do business. Deeply Red individuals become downright irritated and aggressive when they notice that someone is trying to be buddies with them.

A Red is not here to be your pal. They're here for one reason and one reason alone. To do business. We can't rule out the idea that they might even throw you out—figuratively speaking—if they perceive your attempts to be friendly as ingratiation or fawning. They wouldn't dream of doing this themselves and nor should you.

And don't flatter a Red if you don't know them well. For the love of God, leave the compliments at home. Note that this also applies outside the workplace.

17.4.1 What You Should Do

Paradoxically, Reds are the easiest color to persuade. If you want to convince a Red of something specific, all you have to do is present your proposal and request a response. To hell with the game last night. Never mind that you saw them in the supermarket last week. They didn't see you anyway.

When a Red trusts you and has decided you're a decent person who can be advantageous to them . . . well, you may find they start discussing cars, boats, or the latest political developments with you. And when they do, play ball. But then and only then. And don't be surprised if the meeting ends mid-sentence. Once they have satisfied their need to socialize, they will wrap up that instant. It has nothing to do with you. They're just done with the conversation.

I don't care whether it's a new neighbor, a colleague, a client, the friend of a friend at a garden party—keep your nose out of their personal life. Keep it superficial. It's fine to say things like *Was it you who came in that Porsche?* but it is not okay to ask said individual where their spouse is. That's much too personal if you don't know each other.

Stick to safe areas that don't relate to the individual. The weather, global affairs, traffic, and the state of the economy are all much safer ground.

17.5 YOU DON'T ACTUALLY KNOW? THEN WHY AM I WASTING MY TIME ON YOU?

It may sound like a contradiction, but a Red would also like you to be determined and direct. Although they often demand that they get to make all the important decisions, they strongly dislike dealing with vacillating people. Dancing the hesitation waltz does not instill trust. Comments like *It's hard to say, It depends,* or *I don't really know what to say* just frustrate Reds.

If you have an opinion, out with it. Reds judge you and form their view of you based on how distinctive you are. You should listen to them, of course, but you must have an opinion of your own. Otherwise, you're weak, and that's not a quality that will win you any points.

Keep in mind that we all like people in whom we can recognize ourselves. A Red won't meet other Reds every day, so when they actually do, they're pleasantly surprised. *An equal! Wonderful!* I have met Reds who have rubbed their hands in glee before starting a heated debate.

17.5.1 What You Should Do

Never sell yourself cheaply. Deliver your views without batting an eyelid. Reds can definitely make a noise and clatter about and stamp their feet—not to mention raise their voices and clench their fists. A not uncommon reaction is to back down when faced with behavior like this. It's not a nice feeling to be browbeaten, is it?

Take a clear stand. If you agree, then say so up front. Say: *You're completely right!* Feel free to add, *The fact that not everyone can see this is unfathomable.* Now you've got something in common—you're surrounded by idiots.

If you disagree, say so right away. Do not play along. Do not pretend.

But do not say: *You are wrong*. What you can say is: *My experience differs*.

I've said it before and it merits being said again: The worst thing you can do is back away and let them walk all over you. If you let a Red walk all over you, you lose something very important in their eyes—respect. If they don't respect you, they'll eat you alive. And walk over you again and again and again until you become completely and utterly marginalized. You won't be someone to be reckoned with in the future. A complete doormat.

The best thing you can do is place yourself in the eye of the storm, indicating to them they're wrong. When a Red discovers that you won't give in, they'll turn in an instant. If you know what you are talking about, that is.

Most important—don't hesitate. A firm, swift answer is better than drawn-out shilly-shallying. You can always say you've changed your mind later on without any issues—after all, Reds are constantly changing their minds. It simply demonstrates that you have an agile intellect. Advantage you.

17.6 YOU CAN SLEEP WHEN YOU'RE DEAD

Reds will usually work hard—perhaps harder than any other people you have met. They will have many irons in the fire at once, and they'll have complete control over everything that's happening.

A Red can live with the fact that everything won't be right the first time. But remaining active will definitely be a clear wish for them—if not a downright requirement. When at work, it's all about working hard. In a relationship, it's about not getting marooned on the sofa or glued to a screen for too long.

You've got to be diligent and do your bit. I wouldn't go so far as to claim that Reds can't accept a lower tempo on occasion. They're very digital in this respect: They're either on or off. But activity is preferable. Efficiency—even in their personal lives—is also desirable.

17.6.1 What You Should Do

Be willing to take the initiative. Offer suggestions the Red didn't ask for. As usual, get ready for a fight, but they will like that you are driven.

Please note the wording in the preceding sentence. It doesn't say that they'll like *you* because you are driven. It says they will like that you are *driven*. A Red may very well like you—that's sometimes the case—but don't expect lots of glowing praise.

Remind yourself to avoid comments like *Can't we just do nothing this weekend?* Be sure to chip in promptly when ideas are floated. Say things like *Sounds good, let's go right away.* Set aside time for yourself to think up activities so your Red partner or friend doesn't start to think it's all incumbent on them.

And sometimes tag along to stuff you're not interested in doing—it'll work wonders for your relationship. Compromise doesn't have to be a bad thing. Life is full of compromise and sometimes it's well worth negotiating a little. When dealing with a Red significant other, there's one thing to be aware of: Just because you gave in last time doesn't mean they feel they have to return the compliment next time. They want to win every negotiation. How you handle that challenge will vary from case to case. But you need to be prepared for the fact that you will always be starting from scratch. You might like to remind your partner that having agreed to a holiday in Kuala Lumpur last time, perhaps you could take a trip to Iceland this time. But expect to encounter the same tussle all over again.

In fact, even if a Red husband or wife explicitly promises that if they get their way on occasion A, then they'll give in on occasion B, you can't be completely sure they'll keep their word.

Why not?

Well, Reds never follow the rules of the game. In their world, they think of it as *deciding all over again*.

17.7 WHAT YOU ALSO NEED TO DO WHEN YOU MEET REDS

I'm afraid it's not simply a case of adapting to how the Red wants you to behave, since that would entail prostrating yourself before them. There are several other things you need to keep an eye on in order to get anywhere. Because Reds have their faults and failings but often turn a blind eye to them, you can help them achieve a better result—so long as you know how.

That brings us to the part known as "leading," where you've gained the confidence of the Red by using pacing; what follows are a few things you ought to bear in mind when seeking to get your Red onside.

17.8 DETAILS . . . BOOOOORING . . .

Essentially, Reds dislike getting into details. It's boring and takes time away from more important things. Thus, Reds tend to be expensively careless about the small stuff. You can accuse Reds of many things, but meticulousness isn't typically one of them.

For them, the destination will always be more important than the journey, so Reds will do just about anything to achieve the desired results. Reds won't naturally stop to consider the small things or analyze their method.

17.8.1 What You Should Do

If you really want to help Reds do better work, try to demonstrate the benefits of keeping an eye on the details. Explain that the results will be better and profits larger if they consider a couple of small but crucial elements of the project.

Be prepared for them to huff and puff and exhibit a general unwillingness to act on your advice. But if you're good at arguing, your advice will be followed. As we know, Reds are good at pushing themselves to the limit, as long as they make headway.

Remind your Red spouse or colleague that the profit is often to be found in the details. You may have to assume the role of checker, but don't let the Red rush too far ahead without checking certain things in advance.

One way to get them to listen is to emphasize that the result will be better if you find out how much timber you're going to need, when the Nilsson family are going to be in town, or exactly how far it is to that restaurant.

17.9 QUICK AND OFTEN FRIGHTFULLY WRONG

As I have described several times before, everything in a Red's world tends to be terribly, terribly urgent. You can imagine the risks this entails. Putting the pedal to the metal may seem like a good idea, but only when everything else, and most of all everyone else, is on the same train. Normally, Reds rush ahead of the group, only to get annoyed when others can't keep pace.

A Red needs someone who can get them to pause and realize that not everyone has grasped the situation as quickly as they have. They'll never be able to carry out all the phases of a project on their own—even if they believe they can and probably attempt to. They still need to have others on board with them. That's true whether it's an assignment at work or a home renovation project.

You've probably heard the expression "quick and wrong." There's a real risk of that here.

17.9.1 What You Should Do

Say things like *Your focus is impressive, but sometimes things go wrong. Let's reflect a bit on this here and now and save time in the future.*

This is a smart approach since time is a vital resource to a Red. Of course, they know this already, but they may need reminding. Simply point out that it takes a long time when things have to be redone, and that the best time to pause for thought is before getting started.

Give examples of instances where time was lost by being too

hasty. Point out the risks involved in hurrying too much. Explain that others can't keep up, and point out that it would be great if everyone knew what the project was about. Don't give in. Assert that not even they can manage everything themselves. Force the Red to wait for others.

Afterward, try to discuss the event and show clearly and distinctly what was gained and how much the Red has profited by taking things a bit more slowly.

You need to keep your wits about you at this juncture, since it's a very unpopular message to impart, but if you stand firm in your beliefs, then you can do it.

17.10 LET'S TRY A FEW COMPLETELY UNTESTED IDEAS AND SEE HOW IT GOES

Or should we? Red individuals aren't anxious about risk. Many Reds actively search for risky situations just for the thrill of it. In fact, what others might perceive as dangerous behavior a Red wouldn't even think of as risky.

However, Reds do need someone who can weigh the advantages against the disadvantages. Disadvantages are boring, of course, so a Red individual will often simply ignore them. Since the answer to what risks you take often lies in the details, your approach should be similar to the one outlined in the example above.

17.10.1 What You Should Do

Help the Red calculate the risks by always looking at the facts. Facts are something they understand. Since Reds prefer not to look backward—old and boring!—and focus on the present and the future instead, a plain and honest exchange of experiences may be called for.

Give examples of situations that historically were shown to be dangerous. Those might be health risks, going downhill skiing without a helmet, or calling your mother-in-law an idiot. Prove your point with facts and demand your Red think twice before deciding to take on a new project without first having checked the conditions.

As usual: You're right—stick to your guns and don't give in.

17.11 I'M NOT HERE TO BE YOUR PAL. OR ANYONE ELSE'S, FOR THAT MATTER.

As you've probably realized by now, relationships aren't really front and center of Red minds. As you also know, this isn't true of all people. A Red's way of cultivating relationships may vary, but a common criticism will be that it happens on their terms, even in their personal life.

People around Reds frequently feel they're being steamrolled. It's rarely the Red's real intention; it's just something that happens. You can't make an omelet without breaking eggs and all that.

Reds may not understand that others are avoiding them because they would rather avoid conflict. A lot of people shun conflict like the plague. This means that Reds can be excluded from important information. Not being invited out for a beer on a Friday is unlikely to trouble them, but feeling excluded from important decisions will. In the worst case, this can lead them to suspect the people around them are deliberately withholding important information. The power struggle is just moments away.

17.11.1 What You Should Do

Reds need to understand that the road to full transparency is to adapt to others. That thought may never have crossed their minds; they're mostly focused on themselves and their own thing. But by realizing that no one can manage everything alone, they can be prevailed upon to pause and actually care about other people.

Once a Red understands that many people think it's important to chat about their child's first tooth, the furnishings in the cabin they rented on their last holiday, and the boat they're dreaming of buying, that Red is able to listen actively and contribute to the discussion. Once a Red understands what all this small talk is about, the door is open. You may even learn something about them, too.

Simply outline how you can best be repaid in order to be as helpful as possible.

17.12 WHAT KIND OF WEAKLING ARE YOU? JUST HANDLE IT!

They will simply be pissed off—it couldn't be said more clearly. Their temperament is such that it detonates every now and then, causing everyone around them a fair share of grief. They don't notice it happening themselves; yelling a little bit is just another way to communicate.

No one likes a bully, but not everyone is willing to say so. When a Red tramples on someone's toes, you must tell them nicely that it doesn't work like that. They'll assume an innocent face and pretend they don't understand what you're talking about. Secretly, they'll be thinking that if some people are scared of them, well, that's actually kind of cool.

17.12.1 What You Should Do

You should confront this behavior immediately. At once. The very instant it occurs. Okay? No nonsense is to be permitted. Clearly declare that you will not tolerate any attacks, nasty comments, or uncalled-for outbursts of anger. Demand adult behavior, and if they lose their temper again, just leave the room. It's important that you never let them get their way just by barking their head off.

The most important thing you need to remember is that this is a technique Reds use and it has been working for them for years. Acting out and quarreling have been serving them well since they were a young child. In their experience, they've been able to argue their way to whatever it is they want from their surroundings. You can't rule out that their family have had to put up with a series of outbursts down the years. And I can promise you they have found ways to avoid triggering the fire alarm unnecessarily.

It's worth bearing in mind that very few people have confronted them about this, meaning a demand for calmer conversations will probably only lead to even wilder discussions. And here's a well-intentioned warning: Don't use expressions like *You need to lower your voice*. It'll just make matters worse.

I don't necessarily think this is the most endearing approach, but it may get Reds to listen better.

18

Adapting to Yellow Behavior

18.1 WHAT A YELLOW EXPECTS OF YOU

18.1.1 Isn't It Nice Being Here All Together?

In essence, Yellows are not necessarily afraid of conflict. If something goes wrong, they can blow a gasket, but if possible, they prefer a pleasant and cozy atmosphere. Yellows are at their best when everyone is friends and the sun is shining.

A Yellow, however, can be very sensitive to whether people are in good spirits or not. If the people in a group are in bad spirits and aggression is pouring down like a cloudburst, they won't be happy at all. A bad mood and negative vibes are not the best conditions for them.

This also means they may feign deafness in the face of any negativity or bad news. In layman's terms: They pretend it's not happening.

18.1.2 What You Should Do

A Yellow functions best when they are happy and content. That means their creativity is at its zenith and all their positive energy is flowing. You should strive to create a warm and friendly atmosphere around them.

Smile a lot, have fun, and laugh. Tell funny stories. Try to be an entertainer yourself. Distract them from possible negative impacts. You should also listen to their crazy jokes, laugh along at all their childish remarks, and kindle an easygoing and happy-go-lucky atmosphere.

If you do that, they'll feel better about you and listen to you more, which is always a good thing. A Yellow in a bad mood is not much fun to be with—they can become noticeably grumpy when nothing is going their way. And none of us want that.

18.2 I ASKED SOMEONE TO FIX THAT TINY DETAIL— IT'S JUST THAT I CAN'T REMEMBER WHO

Keeping a Yellow's interest is, in all honesty, not the easiest thing to do. There are many things that bore the socks off a Yellow employee, customer, friend, or neighbor.

A foolproof method to put a Yellow to sleep quickly and efficiently is to bring up lots of details. Please, don't do that. A Yellow simply can't cope with details. It just gets tiresome.

Not only will they forget what you're talking about, but they'll also decide they don't need any of those details. Their strength lies in the broad brushstrokes. Feel free to ask a Yellow to draw up a vision for the next ten years and you'll see a veritable fireworks display of ideas you wouldn't have ever thought of yourself, even if you live to be a hundred years old.

But don't ask them to explain how to make it happen, because that would be a real challenge.

18.2.1 What You Should Do

If you want to keep a Yellow's attention, strip away as much of the minutiae as you possibly can. Always start with the big questions. It's perfectly fine that you know how to install the latest surround-sound system, but don't bore your Yellow friend with these details. It's not for them. They just want to know how to get the music started.

It's just like with Reds, only worse.

Yellows don't care about how things work, only that they do work.

Help them. Unburden them. Handle the boring stuff on their behalf. Don't ask a Yellow to take notes in a meeting. They won't get down half of what's said since the minutes taker will think it's all so self-evident there's no need to commit it to paper.

But remember they don't care how things work—just that they do work. Don't bother getting out the instruction manual, because it won't get read.

Explain in loose terms that you'll handle all the boring stuff and let them get on with doing what they're good at.

18.3 FOLLOW YOUR GUT—IT WORKS EVERY TIME

If I had a dollar for every time a Yellow has explained a totally crazy decision by saying it felt right, I'd be dining out at a fancy restaurant every single day of the week. There's even a study that shows some people make better decisions if they go on gut feeling. Yellows love to cite that particular study. Whatever you do, never mention it to your Yellow friend if they haven't already heard about it.

It has to feel right. They have to be able to taste it. Feel it. A Yellow can readily ignore the actual facts so long as it feels right.

Don't misunderstand this: A Yellow understands perfectly well that some people look at facts and that this is important. They're not stupid. It's just that they're not interested. They want to feel their way through life because that's more inspiring.

18.3.1 What You Should Do

Accept that Yellows feel their way through life. Don't try to force rational Excel spreadsheets onto them.

Do you want to get a Yellow to make a decision? Put the Excel spreadsheets aside, lean forward, and say with a broad smile, *How does this feel?*

They will get it right away. And you'll get an answer.

Yellows have a fairly big safety zone and they're not unduly afraid of risk. Adapt to it. You can get through to them by showing that you too follow your gut. No matter how wrong this might feel to you, this is the way to a Yellow's heart. They'll recognize themselves in you. You'll become the best of friends. The sun will shine on you.

Say that you admire their ability to dare to listen to their inner emotions. Show that you appreciate this trait in them.

18.4 NO ONE'S EVER DONE THIS BEFORE? NICE!

While a Red focuses on speed, a Yellow focuses on the latest and greatest. "New" is synonymous with "good." All Yellows know that. And why not? Without creativity and new inventions, all development would simply grind to a halt, right?

Everyone likes having a little excitement in their everyday life. The difference lies in how we define "exciting." For a Yellow, "new" means "exciting." Yellows are so-called early adopters—the very first to try out new things.

Check out who is wearing the latest fashion, or who is the first to drive a new and preferably unusual model of car. Who has the latest iPhone and who knows what restaurant will be the newest sensation in a few months' time?

How can they keep track of all this? Don't ask me. They probably devote some of their working time to keeping up to speed on all things new and interesting. But they're also early adopters when it comes to implementing new work methods and new concepts. It's just great fun.

18.4.1 What You Should Do

The most stupid thing you can do is try to counteract this urge. Allow a Yellow to devote themselves to the latest thing and you will find you have a Yellow who is in a splendid mood. If you want to convince a Yellow of something, use expressions like "state of the art," "newly developed," and "never before used." "Unique," "cutting edge," and "untested" may achieve similar results. Your Yellow will really get into gear.

No one else has ever tried this? I have to have it!

They'll like you because you're so exciting and so interesting and, above all, innovative. Equip yourself with lots of energy, because it can be challenging to keep up-to-date. What an excellent contact you'll be! Yellows will adore you. However, be prepared to be replaced rather quickly if they find someone else who is even more knowledgeable about newer things.

18.5 YOU SEEM INTERESTING. WANT TO KNOW WHO I AM?

By now we've established that Yellows like other people. They function best if they surround themselves with a crowd. Of course, Yellows don't adore everyone they meet, but they will give the majority a decent chance.

You need to show a Yellow you are just as open and friendly as they are. If you're too closed and private, they'll feel unwelcome.

Why didn't you reply when they spoke to you? Why didn't you laugh at that funny story about their dog? Why don't they know anything about you? What are your dreams? Who are you, really?

Insufficient personal connection can result in a strong sense of insecurity, and your relationship won't develop in a positive direction. If you're Red or Blue, you need to think carefully about how to get this to work.

If you want to, of course.

18.5.1 What You Should Do

Share yourself. Prepare personal anecdotes that describe who you are. You don't need to reveal your innermost desires or greatest fears in life, but you do need to demonstrate that you're a flesh-and-blood human being.

Show that you're approachable: Smile a lot and ensure your body language is open. When a Yellow wonders where you grew up, don't just respond with Sundsvall. Tell them you lived in Stenstaden, that you used to run the trail around Södra Berget, that you once got hammered in the bar at Hotel Knaust, that you know the bank manager and the lady of the manor.

It may seem a bit unnecessary, but you should definitely show interest in the Yellow as a person. Admittedly, it won't be difficult to find out things about them because they'll freely tell you a great deal. But be sure to show you are curious and interested.

And remember that Yellows are very susceptible to flattery. If you really want to get into their good books, stroke their egos as much as you can bear.

18.6 WHAT YOU ALSO NEED TO DO WHEN YOU MEET YELLOWS

To keep a Yellow in good spirits, you need to rub them the right way. The problem will become obvious after a while. They won't get that much work done.

I've watched a group of Yellows who were trying to solve a problem. They all spoke at once and had a great time, and when you asked them how things were going, they said, *Fantastic!* But nothing got written down. And to be honest, it doesn't much matter whether this social stuff happens during working hours or during leisure time.

To really make headway with Yellows, you need to do more than just create a great atmosphere. But once you've tuned into their frequency, you need to do the following.

18.7 THE DIFFERENCE BETWEEN LOOKING LIKE YOU'RE LISTENING AND ACTUALLY DOING IT

I'm just going to tell it like it is—Yellows are, beyond a shadow of a doubt, the worst listeners. They'll generally never admit it, since you can tell from the very term "bad listener" that it's negative. Many

Yellows really see themselves as good listeners. They're listening to stuff all the time, apparently.

Who knows where they got that idea? It's simply not true. Of course, there are Yellows who listen—when it suits them. Or when they've already got what they wanted out of a conversation. But in most cases, forget about it. It's a button they consciously have to press, otherwise nothing will happen.

They don't want to listen. They would much rather talk. Most Yellows simply think they can express everything far better than you and I. The problem is they neglect to listen to what anyone else is saying.

18.7.1 What You Should Do

How do we solve this? When you're dealing with Yellows, there are certain things you need to do. It doesn't matter if you're speaking to your partner about your summer holiday or to a colleague about an ongoing project, you need a plan of action. You need to have prepared yourself carefully. You have to know what your message is and exactly what response you need from them.

You must persuade the happy Yellow person to answer your questions very concretely, and hear them say, *Yes, I will be there at four just as I promised*, or *Of course I'll let Mum know exactly what we have agreed to.*

But—big but—be prepared to follow up if it's important, because the Yellow didn't write any of it down. Yellows think they'll remember everything without taking any notes. Unless you managed to persuade them to write it on their calendar, of course. That would be the best way. But in all other contexts, you should expect that what you've said has gone in one ear and out the other.

What you can do is hand over a piece of paper and pen and then issue the following order: *Write down the following:* The party is on Saturday in two weeks' time (give the date here). *We're due at this address at X o'clock, and if you forget, then you'll never be invited back. Capiche?*

18.8 NO PROBLEM—THAT WON'T TAKE LONG!

Yellows are time optimists; that's just the way it is. Sure, things can be done quickly, but rarely as quickly as a Yellow thinks. This is to do with the fact that they simply can't plan or structure their lives.

I've personally worked with people who legitimately believed they could manage eight meetings per day, who thought it only took two days to renovate an entire kitchen, and that it is possible to walk across Stockholm city center in thirty minutes—on a bitingly cold Monday morning in April. These are typical manifestations of a Yellow's optimism.

The problem is obvious. It's impossible to accomplish everything a Yellow wants to do, particularly because they don't actually know how long anything takes.

And even if they do ask someone how long it takes, they won't listen to what that person says, because what they're saying is wrong. After all, the Yellow believes they probably know best.

The other problem is they won't get into gear when they should.

Do you know anyone who has taken a day off to paint the bedroom and at three o'clock in the afternoon hasn't opened the can of paint yet? *I'll just do this first.*

There's nothing nasty about this; it's just a total inability to have a realistic sense of time. And a genuine belief that this commodity is inexhaustible.

I remember a dinner I went to with a few Yellow friends. When reserving a table at this particular pub, patrons were told that tables were needed back after ninety minutes, which meant that if you got there twenty-five minutes late, there wouldn't be time for a starter or a dessert. The kitchen wouldn't be able to manage it. My wife and I arrived fifteen minutes early. We headed straight for our table and sat down to wait for the others. Time passed. Forty minutes later, twenty-five minutes late, the others arrived, joyfully joking about how they had lost track of time because of this and that.

We had just enough time to order a main course, eat it, and quickly pay for it before the next booking arrived. The strange thing was that when we spoke about the incident afterward, their recollection was that they were just a few minutes late. They had simply repressed the fact that they missed 30 percent of the dinner.

18.8.1 What You Should Do

Coordinate all appointments properly with Yellows. Synchronize your watches. Explain very clearly that the plane takes off at 8:00 P.M. and if they don't show up by then, they'll be left standing at the gate.

If the dinner is due to start at 7:00 P.M., invite everyone else for that time, but make it 6:30 for your Yellow friends. They'll arrive last anyway. They'll come with very well-worded and entertaining excuses. Be prepared for very colorful stories. But also be aware that Yellows will emphatically deny that they are optimists about time. They'll insist they most certainly kept an eye on the clock. It was just that something happened on the way.

But dare to make demands when it really matters. Tell it like it is: If they aren't sitting in the car with the engine running, ready to leave two hours before takeoff, you'll die of a heart attack. Explain that you'll be deeply upset with the Yellow and that your very friendship may be damaged by this eternal messing up of plans.

This argument really hits home with Yellows.

18.9 IT LOOKS LIKE A HAND GRENADE
WENT OFF IN HERE

The most cluttered desks I have ever seen have all belonged to Yellows. They're the ones with computer screens with so many Post-it Notes stuck to them you can barely see the display. The most topsy-turvy garages and the most overloaded attics belong to Yellows as well. But this is only the visible part.

You should see my good friend Christian's bedroom—he's turned out to be a dapper British gent, but his room looks like the aftermath of the Dresden bombings. There's no need to be alarmed. You'll come across all sorts of oddities, and if you have Blue traits, then you'll also receive various explanations for why things are occasionally all over the place when you ask why. And this is still only the purely physical.

Meetings are moved or forgotten, things disappear, whole cars are lost in parking lots. Keys of all sorts are gone without a trace.

Furthermore, many Yellows have no ability to plan their day. They can go to the supermarket five times in a row and buy three things at a time because they didn't write down what they needed.

This can be because they don't know what they want until they get there or because they're sure they'll be able to recall the nineteen things they need to buy. (Yellows have a very generous view of their own abilities. They'll tell anyone who'll listen that they have the best memory in the world.)

18.9.1 What You Should Do

If you really want to help a Yellow get organized, make sure they get some structure in their life. Help out by creating a simple list. If you're going shopping, write things down. Your partner or pal will forget half the items. Afterward, show them the success that imposing order brought about. Point out that you didn't forget even one small thing, and it was all thanks to the list you wrote.

Create a structure for the Yellow. What you have to remember is that the people who most need structure in the form of schedules and lists are Yellows. Paradoxically, they hate all of that. They won't let themselves be "shoehorned" into a system not of their own choosing. Be diplomatic. If you press too hard, you can get some powerful reactions:

Why does everything have to be micromanaged? Are we living in a fascist state, or what?

But don't give in. Demand adult responsibility.

18.10 THE MOST IMPORTANT THING IS TO LOOK GOOD. ALL THE TIME.

Look over here!

Me, me, me. Yellows have strong egos, just like Reds, no doubt about that. They like getting attention; they throw themselves into the center of things faster than anyone else.

They enjoy themselves most when they're in the middle of the action. Your Yellow friend is a ray of sunshine, talking more loudly and much faster than everyone else and lighting up the room with their behavior.

Shine the spotlight on me. See me, hear me, like me.

The flip side is obvious. No one else gets any space. Many conversations end up with the Yellow individual loudly and resonantly speaking about their experience or their opinion. No matter what you are talking about—war, starvation, dieting, cars, executives, gardens—a Yellow will bring up a story in which they themselves are the protagonist. If they don't have any story, they'll make one up.

Their thoughts often begin with the word "I." *I want, I think, I can, I know, I will.* It's quite natural. They like other people, but there is one thing they like even more: themselves.

18.10.1 What You Should Do

Yellow people cannot be allowed to consume all the oxygen. They need to hear—from someone with courage and perseverance—that they have to let others join in the conversation or whatever it may be.

It's impossible to explain this in the midst of a conversation with others present. It won't fall on fertile ground. A Yellow can be very offended by such criticism (beyond sensitive), especially if there are others listening. You may struggle to imagine anyone who would appreciate being publicly humiliated, and indeed, there aren't many people who would, but Yellows see this as a bigger and more extensive problem. Receiving criticism is always difficult, but when there are other people listening to this tale of woe, it affects a Yellow's entire being. It doesn't look good, and what are people going to say?

They'll think things like, *Everyone else just thinks of themselves*, or *I'm the only one who looks out for me*.

This type of feedback must be given discreetly and in a positive way. It depends a little bit on how Yellow the person is, so you will probably need a plan.

Make sure you're well prepared with examples and demonstrate that you're there for them.

And there's another thing to be prepared for: You may very well become enemies in the process. You're definitely taking a risk here. Hearing you are egocentric and self-centered is extremely unflattering. Yellows will understand this; they're not stupid. But they will argue your analysis is wrong. So you'll have to work hard here.

Or swap pals.

18.11 ALL TALK, NO WALK

As I mentioned earlier, Yellows spend more time talking than they do getting stuff done. They have a penchant for talking about everything they need to do rather than actually doing anything. This applies regardless of whether it's ironing all those shirts ahead of a trip or doing the weekly clean of the house.

I've mentioned it several times before, and if you know a Yellow, then you'll know what I'm talking about.

Okay, so many people have trouble getting motivated to work, especially with boring tasks. That is not unique. But Yellows find it particularly hard to leave the starting block when faced with uncomfortable tasks.

It may be having to call a dissatisfied customer, or finishing building the deck in the garden, or going to the pharmacy. If it's dull and uninspiring, it won't happen. Their excuses for avoiding these tasks will be numerous and imaginative.

Because a Yellow's perspective on time is based in the future, they spend more time talking about the future than dedicating their energy to getting there. Seldom have so many crazy plans been drawn up or so many insane goals been set as is done by Yellows. Because they think aloud, people around them believe these fantasies are going to happen: *Wow! It sounds amazing!*

18.11.1 What You Should Do

To help your Yellow friend, you need to make sure they put their shovel in the ground and start digging. Push them, but push gently. Treat them a little bit like you would treat a child.

Be kind but clear. If they notice you're becoming their taskmaster, things may become difficult. Yellows hate feeling controlled. They need the most help to get into gear, but that doesn't mean they like it. They are free souls and don't obey anyone.

So you need to be diplomatic. Softly and gently explain the value of actually doing the job itself, now that they know what needs to be done.

Take a moment to explain to a Yellow how the great popularity they already enjoy can actually be increased if they just get this over the line. Everyone will love them for it, and so they will be more beloved than ever.

Does that sound simple? It is simple. All you need to do is overcome your resistance to inflating someone's ego in such an obvious way. But it will work.

18.12 IMMUNE TO CRITICISM

This could very well be a subtitle to a section on bad listeners, because these things are connected to each other.

Let's be up front about this. All of us make mistakes. And even when we're not dealing with downright mistakes, there's hardly anything or anyone in the world that can't be improved in some way.

This is obvious to everyone, even to a Yellow. When talking about tangible issues, Yellows can get on board with the idea that others really do need to pull their socks up, get it together, and start over.

They may even admit that there are no perfect people. So far, so good.

The problems arise when we try to make a particular Yellow understand that they too may need to improve. This creates a conflict, especially if the criticism is expressed in public.

Yellow people find it difficult to cope with criticism. They don't like it because it doesn't look good. Imagine, there's someone who doesn't like everything they do and everything they say!

I have individually sat down with Yellows and given them personal feedback on their profiles. Everything goes fine until we get to the page with the heading "Areas of Improvement," which is to say, weaknesses.

Even if we're on good terms, the temperature in the room gets significantly cooler. Defensive walls pop up quicker than you can say *poor self-awareness*. Deep down, the Yellow individual knows that he has weaknesses; he just won't consider talking about them.

18.12.1 What You Should Do

If you wish to get through to a Yellow with negative feedback, you need to be persistent. Create a friendly atmosphere in the room and find the right tone so your criticism lands where it should.

You can always thump your fist onto the table as hard as you can to really shake said Yellow. Go hard on them and mete out as much as they can take. You may sometimes have to resort to this, especially if you've exhausted all other avenues. Pursue the conflict and see how it unfolds.

I don't recommend this. Better to work slowly and consistently, repeating the same feedback.

Clarity is key. Ensure you are extremely well prepared, with all possible facts to substantiate your claims. Yellows have a gift that surpasses all else: They're bloody good manipulators.

If they notice you're being serious in your criticism and you really are going to follow up on the issue, they'll switch into top gear and try to lead you astray. They're good at putting up smoke screens. Make sure you don't get lost in the fog.

Also be sure to get real answers to your questions, and be sure they understand the message. Insist they write down what you have said. Ask them to repeat your feedback. Yes, this is true even of your spouse.

But—you have to set up an action plan. Why not do it the next time you sit down to breakfast? Right now you've probably got as far as you can with them. They're grumpy and don't want to absorb any more. The risk is they'll completely run out of energy if you keep going.

Oh, and there's one more thing. None of the aforementioned happens in the case of positive feedback. In that case, your happy loved one will absorb 100 percent of everything you say. Even broadcast it on TV, if possible.

19

Adapting to Green Behavior

19.1 WHAT A GREEN EXPECTS OF YOU

This may be the most important chapter in the entire book, given that Green is the most common color out there.

How about a quick refresher? Security will always be important to a Green. A Green worries about everything that may happen. They don't like insecurity and deal with it by hiding under the covers. If you don't see it, then it's not there. They don't want to be anywhere that feels too insecure. They strive for stability and don't even want to think about wild gambles.

Now, I hear what you're thinking. *The world is a pretty dangerous place. There's an infinite number of dangers out there. Absolutely anything can go wrong. My relationship may fall apart; I might get sick; my husband or wife could leave me; my children might think I am an idiot. Not to mention my boss may start agreeing with my children. I might lose my job. I could end up in conflict with a lot of people. On the way to work, I could have a car accident. And did you know that a tiny fish bone caught in your throat can kill you?*

All these things make life scary. Anything can happen.

19.2. IT HAS TO FEEL GOOD; OTHERWISE, IT ENDS UP FEELING . . . BAD . . .

Many Greens I've known over the years in my role as a coach have said that all these potential dangers paralyze them. They become overwhelmed with thoughts about these risks and dangers. They become completely powerless to act. And since they're not particularly motivated to get out there into the wider world, it becomes easier to just stay at home, nice and safe by the fire.

19.2.1 What You Should Do

So what can we actually do about this? We can easily end up stuck in a dead end. Accept that this person simply doesn't think like you do. Accept that they are driven as much by fear as anything else—perhaps even more.

Show you're prepared to listen to what they're anxious about. Don't say things like: *There's nothing to be afraid of.*

It doesn't work, because the fear itself is real. And it's also not true. There are many things to be afraid of. We all have things we're anxious about; a Green just has more of them.

Instead, help your Green friend face their fear of the unknown. Encourage them to brave things that feel scary and still move ahead. Just as we learned to swim as children, despite the fact that the water looked cold and dangerous, you can give support through small, gentle nudges forward.

When your friend says the grass only looks greener on the other side, simply take a deep breath and keep at it. Eventually, you'll prove that it really is greener after all.

19.3 NOTHING HAPPENED. TWICE.

I'm sure you'll recall I mentioned the Green's passivity. Nothing is too big to be ignored. Being proactive and driven, having an active lifestyle—all these things disturb tranquility. And that won't be appreciated.

Greens won't be happy if you're constantly coming up with new things to do. They feel at their best when they don't have to be active all the time. Or even half the time. They come home on a Friday evening so completely exhausted from spending the week trying to accomplish as little as possible that they now need to have a good rest.

I've met Greens whose efforts to avoid work cost them more energy than actually doing the work.

The consequences are obvious to those around them.

They don't like weekends with full schedules. Visiting the mother-in-law, organizing a picnic, taking their son to football training, cleaning out the garage, inviting the neighbors over for dinner—everything becomes a burden for them, and half the time nothing gets done at all. A Green glides under the radar and disappears completely. They really do need peace and quiet to be able to do what they do best. Peace and quiet make them feel good.

19.3.1 What You Should Do

On one level, the rest of us have to respect this attitude. We have to put ourselves into someone else's shoes and recognize how stressful it can be for these people to be constantly forced to activate themselves and be on the go when this runs against their natural behavior. In the midst of the 2020s, it's not possible to avoid all the bustle and activity of modern life—the wheels are spinning away so fast it's hard to cling on. The extroverts are the agenda setters now.

This means that a genuine Green often feels they are doing something wrong. They hear about everyone else's weekends, their activities, how they got moving and did one complicated project after the other; the only thing they feel is stress.

The solution is to allow the Green their periods of peace, quiet, and inactivity. They need this in order to function. This doesn't mean, of course, that they can sit on their backsides forever, but they do need to be allowed to do a reasonable amount of nothing.

Make sure you leave them some space.

19.4 WHERE EXACTLY ARE WE GOING? IS THERE EVEN A PLAN?

Stability and predictability are valuable to a Green. And when you think about it, it's very logical—it's a good thing knowing what's going to happen. We probably all have some measure of control dependency. We simply want to know. For Greens, this dependency is very strong. When Reds ask *What?* the Yellows wonder *Who?* When the Blues ask *Why?* the Greens want to know *How?*

A Green simply needs to know what the plan is. What needs to happen? When will things be taking place? What should they expect?

Just look at how it works at home. Who always has the same spot at the breakfast table? I know many of us are creatures of habit, but if you snatch a Green's chair, which they claimed as their own long ago, you unhinge their very existence and they'll lose all their appetite.

But their need for predictability goes further than that. It's about anything that even resembles change. In our society today, the only thing that's permanent is change. Nothing is totally predictable; everything rotates on its own axis and appears in new shapes and forms. And all this is extremely stressful for Greens.

19.4.1 What You Should Do

Since a Green probably won't come up with anything on their own, it will be you and I who will have to handle the planning. But maybe that's okay.

We can help ease Greens' minds by explaining every step of the plan. In short, we can tell them what's going to happen.

Here's what to do: Instead of just saying you've invited guests over for the weekend, you could explain that you will be having Helen and Steven over for dinner and you'll be offering a three-course dinner consisting of a starter, a main course, and a dessert. You'll fix the main course while your Green partner should follow this recipe to make the dessert.

You explain who is doing what. Who will buy the wine, who will buy the flowers, and so on. You might even explain on which day your Green partner has to do the shopping.

And who knows, maybe I'll write down the address of the flower shop with a list of exact instructions about what should be purchased.

Does this sound exaggerated? Not at all. Remember, they have other qualities, but Greens aren't world champions at taking the initiative.

Think of your family as a company—not everyone does the same thing, because we're good at different things. If you're better at taking the initiative, do it. But make sure your Green partner is on board. Otherwise, there's a risk they'll sneak out the back door.

19.5 WHAT YOU ALSO NEED TO DO WHEN YOU MEET GREENS

Okay, now you know how your Green friends would like to be handled. The result will be a calm and excellent relationship, and you will be good friends for many years. Nice, huh?

But you can't stop there, because unless you're a genuine Green yourself, you'll want to actually do something every now and then. And you'll need to have some appropriate strategies to kick-start your stability-loving friend.

So how do you push your Green ahead of you without them having to take any unnecessary risks?

19.6 WHY DOES EVERYTHING HAVE TO BE SUCH A TO-DO? MEH, I'M GOING TO BED!

I've said this before, but we need to spill more ink on this issue. Greens don't like friction of any kind. They back off when a discussion heats up or if you furrow your brow at the wrong moment. Everything could be a potential conflict, and that is a very bad situation for all Greens. They seize up and become silent and passive.

Let me illustrate what I mean with an example. Some years ago, I was speaking at a sales conference at which I was training salespeople in personal effectiveness. An attendee was playing with his mobile phone unremittingly, and when I—nicely and gently—asked him to write his text messages during the break, he completely stiffened up and stopped speaking.

He didn't respond to any questions or take part in any discussions. He didn't so much as lift his pen for the remainder of the day. He glared at me, and when I asked what the problem was, he just shrugged his shoulders.

He gave me what is probably the worst evaluation I have ever received. Although the conference was five days long, that one day was critical to him, and he truly cut me to shreds.

He had never encountered such a rude and incompetent consultant. He felt as if I had stuck a knife in his back. Obviously, this was a completely unreasonable reaction, especially considering we had agreed not to use our mobile phones during the working sessions.

But that didn't matter—this guy still thought I had wronged him wholly and entirely, and he punished me in the only way he could: through total passivity.

I phoned him afterward and confronted him about it. I really wanted to understand what was going on with this guy. He admitted that it was juvenile behavior and apologized. At least I think he did.

19.6.1 What You Should Do

If you have a comment to make about a Green's behavior, be very careful about how you present it. For example, if it involves criticism, you should deliver it in private.

Make sure the person you are talking to understands that you still like them but that you believe they and the group (work team, sports team, family, association) will function better if they switch things up. Don't ask them what they can do about their behavior; just ask them to do certain specific things.

It may be that they know what to do, but as usual, they won't lead the conversation—you'll need to do that.

Throughout the process, you'll need to use gentle and subdued body language, but under no circumstances should you compromise the message itself.

Say things like *I like you, but I don't like what you did*. Make it unambiguously clear that you are making a distinction between the matter at hand and personal feelings. This is especially true for those with people-oriented profiles: the Yellows and Greens.

You can also ask a Green afterward whether they're okay.

The Green may cut straight to victim mode, which means there is a risk you'll have a guilty conscience, and this may in turn lead you to start glossing over what you just said. This is a dangerous pitfall that is to be avoided. You must stand firm—no matter what. Greens will look for reasons to disregard the feedback. Do not give them any.

Tough on the issues; soft on the relationship.

That's the tune to stick to.

19.7 THINGS WERE BETTER BACK IN THE DAY. MUCH BETTER.

I realize I'm offering you a lot of work-related examples. When I'm talking about change, one of my favorite exercises is to ask everyone in the group who is afraid of change to stand up. Occasionally someone will stand up, but it's more common that no one moves. Even when I point out that I'm already on my feet, it's rarely enough to precipitate action.

Why? Because we all understand that change is inevitable and necessary if we're going to keep up with the world. Some people can admit that they dislike change, but this observation is only at an intellectual level.

And so we all sit quietly in our seats pretending there are no opponents to change to be found here. And besides, no one else is standing up.

My next question is *Who thinks that someone else in the group is afraid of change?* I ask anyone who thinks that to get to their feet. Suddenly the whole group stands up, and they look around in amusement.

So who doesn't like change?

Answer: *Everyone else. And because those other people are the problem, I don't need to do anything at all.*

The issue is widespread. The majority of the population has Green as its dominant quality. This is the main reason why we can't accept change with open arms. Everything new is evil, and it should be strongly discouraged.

Rapid change is the most difficult to accept. The faster it is, the worse it is. So the faster the wheels of society spin, the more frantic all those opponents of change become. We see this all the time in news reports. Yellows and Reds devise constant change, while Greens and Blues, who are in the majority, struggle to keep up. And the stress just increases while the Greens yearn for a return to the past.

19.7.1 What You Should Do

If you want Greens to accept change, you'll have to equip yourself with a good dollop of patience. Break down the process into small pieces and set aside a few weeks to persuade, win them over, and spell out the particulars. You must describe the process in detail, and since no one is going to take any notes, you'll have to go through it again, and again, and again until the message gets home.

The people you're addressing must be given the chance to sense the only possible solution. Once that feeling has developed, you're home free. But the road is long and complicated. You need to know exactly where you're heading, and you always need to remind yourself why you are going to all this trouble.

If you are Red, you'll be constantly seized by the urge to simply force your opinion on the group, but I hardly need to explain that you might as well shut down the company if you do that. It would spare everyone involved a great deal of time and suffering.

Make a plan and then follow it, step-by-step. And be patient.

I know I've just said this, but I'm going to repeat it:

Be patient.

19.8 SOMEONE NEEDS TO TAKE THE HELM IF WE DON'T WANT TO SINK TO THE BOTTOM

Let's be honest—taken in isolation, Green behavior does not lend itself to pronounced leadership. Especially since leadership is often all about the subject of the last section—change. Fortunately, this doesn't mean there are no good Green bosses—there are, in fact, many of them out there—but they don't grow on trees. They won't step forward in the same way Reds and Yellows do.

Often, you'll find it's the same in couples. A strictly Green partner is very unlikely to be the person driving big issues forward. It's simply too burdensome.

Besides, it's convenient not to have to take responsibility. I think all of us have a certain degree of laziness in us. It's liberating not to have to think, to avoid having to decide and to just be a passenger. Sometimes that's just the ticket.

Of course, it varies depending on the circumstances, but Greens have developed this laziness into an art form. They don't want any responsibility because (a) it can lead to conflict if someone doesn't agree with a decision; or (b) there may be lots of extra work and that's never good. And so they dodge it for as long as possible.

Responsibility is burdensome, requiring inner strength as well as an external drive to assume it. But at the same time, it's a measure of maturity, and it begins with taking responsibility for yourself and your own life.

Greens (and sometimes other colors too) have a tendency to blame everything and everyone but themselves.

A female acquaintance of mine some years back had an entire list of things she could blame if something didn't go her way. She blamed the government, the opposition, taxation, her employer, the economy, her education, her parents, her husband, and her children. Sometimes it was the weather's fault. She blamed everything and everyone except herself.

What did she gain from this? The jury's still out on that one. But she didn't have to take any responsibility herself.

You see, because there was always some other factor that was responsible for things, she never had to tackle her own problems and make real change. I remember I asked her to explain why she didn't appear on her own list, but I suspect she didn't understand the question.

Given the monumental passivity a Green person can demonstrate, we immediately end up with problems. If someone doesn't row the boat or take the helm, no amount of prayer will ever help. And Greens will remain seated, waiting for aid. (Usually, someone comes and helps out, so despite everything, they survive.)

19.8.1 What You Should Do

If you want to make headway with a group of Greens, you have to take command, firmly grasp the tiller, and, in some cases, simply get into the driver's seat yourself. Asking a group of Greens to solve a task is a nonstarter since they won't get to work unless you put them on track. They're too polite, too considerate. Too afraid to step on someone's toes and thus much too indulgent.

A darn-it-I-thought-they-were-grown-ups approach simply won't work. Sure, they're adults, but they're children when it comes to such basic things as making decisions. And much of this is because once upon a time they made a decision not to make any decisions. So now someone else has to put their foot down (because Greens won't) and make a decision.

Negotiate the issue. Always discuss things in smaller, constituent parts. Divide responsibility up a little at a time. Who's picking up the kids on Tuesdays? If that falls on the shoulders of a Green, make sure it happens.

Who's going to call the grumpy plumber this time? If that falls on the shoulders of a Green, make sure it happens.

The first time a responsibility you agreed on slips through the cracks (if you don't think it's going to happen, then I'm sorry to say you're rather naïve), you have to follow up on it. Maintain that soft, friendly voice.

Oh dear, I think you must have forgotten to (insert whatever blunder has been committed by your Green here).

Do it and do it now. But at the same time . . . do it carefully.

Best of luck!

20

Adapting to Blue Behavior

20.1 WHAT A BLUE EXPECTS OF YOU

20.1.1 Think Everything Through Properly from the Very Start. Earlier If Possible!

A Blue prepares meticulously, regardless of what for. If you've planned to meet at a certain place at a certain time, you can rest assured they'll be there. The Blue will have reviewed the rules of the new parlor game your aunt gave you so they know how to play it; they will have analyzed every possible opening down to granular detail; and they will be ready to discuss just about any tactics for winning it. They will have a backup plan and a contingency plan for the backup plan, too.

They've thought of everything—and you should, too.

Being Blue is a little like doing military service: No excuses are allowed. If you get a flat tire, you should be prepared for it. In the unlikely event there's a puncture in the spare tire—who on earth left that in the Blue's car?—you must have a plan for that, too. You simply have to set aside time for all eventualities.

A Blue will have some critical questions if you say, *That's just the way it is.* The next time you meet them, their confidence in you will be tarnished.

20.1.2 What You Should Do

Make sure you can show you've done your homework and are well prepared. When a Blue is pondering over this or that, feel free to pull out the relevant binder from your bag. Don't make a big deal out of knowing the answer. You just deliver it in an orderly manner. They expected nothing less.

And—most important—if you don't have the answer, just say so. Acknowledge that you don't know. Don't offer an excuse just to get out of the situation. When the Blue discovers the white lie—and they will—you will fall from favor. It's not ideal to have to come back with the answer the next day, but it's definitely preferable to telling a fib.

A car salesperson who lived next door to me many years ago said that when she met Blue customers, she knew from the outset that the customer was more informed about a particular model of car than she was, since her job required her to keep track of some fifty different models.

Blue customers don't ask questions to find things out; they ask to confirm what they already know. My neighbor stopped even pretending. If she didn't know the answer, she acknowledged this and then went to find out—assuming there even was an answer to the question in the first place. It was the only way to win a Blue customer's confidence.

20.2 WE'RE NOT HERE TO HANG OUT AND HAVE A NICE TIME

This is a given if we're referring to a working relationship. Stick to the job. Be sure to stay focused on the task at hand. A Blue is not at all interested in your personal preferences or what you think about their choice of car, house, sport, or anything else unrelated to work. They're there to work. Period.

I remember one occasion when I thought I had gotten to know a new neighbor whom I must have seen five or six times. I'm sure you know the sort of person I'm talking about: He washed his car every Sunday afternoon regardless of whether it was dirty, because that was the thing to do.

We had passed the stage of greeting each other neutrally every time we saw each other, and by now we both knew when the other watered their garden.

On the seventh occasion, it occurred to me to ask him—no, I don't know what got into me—what he'd done over the weekend.

At first there was confusion in his gaze, and then he began to wring his hands. I immediately realized I had gone too far, and tried to salvage the situation by talking about the weather and how we might well see some precipitation one of these days. Naturally, I didn't breathe a word of what I'd been doing that weekend.

Around four waterings of the garden later, he cautiously informed me that he'd taken his family camping in a national park. Finally I had my way in with him.

What can I say? All it takes is bumping into someone you think you recognize at an annual neighborhood gathering. It might be the guy from three houses down the street. He definitely knows who you are, but you don't really know each other.

That means when you start asking personal questions, it all goes awry. The same is true if you tell him things about yourself and your family that he hasn't asked to be told. It can all become terribly embarrassing. In this respect, Blues are like Reds—they just don't want to know.

20.2.1 What You Should Do

Stick to the task. Work with checklists of strictly factual items—things you can tick off together with the Blue. If you're Yellow, put some of your spontaneity aside. For that matter, put away as much spontaneity as you can. Force yourself to do one thing at a time. Remind yourself that a Blue will rarely or never ask how things are going or show interest in your personal problems. Don't ask how things are going for them on a personal level, either. That should be self-evident from the word itself: *Personal. This is private. Stay away.* In time, they will open up if they want to. It's not that they don't like you; it's just that work comes first. Accept this and it will go well.

To solve this, imagine you are talking to ChatGPT. There's simply no receiver for this kind of social dialogue. At least, not if you want to feel it's real.

20.3 NO VISION NECESSARY, THANK YOU VERY MUCH

Your Blue friends aren't flitting about up there in the blue, blue sky. They're on the ground using their critical minds to judge whether things are realistic or not. While you may think they're boring, suspicious, or downright pessimistic, they believe they're simply realists. They want to know what reality looks like, not what the world looks like if you're a dreamer or a visionary.

I remember once, when I was working in the banking world, we were having a kickoff event and I wanted to inspire my team to do great things, the likes of which had never before been seen. I really went for it. I wrote things on the whiteboard and I dare say I used a lot of excessive body language. I finished my rousing speech by exclaiming, *Soon we will stand on the peak of success and look down on the market we've conquered. We, all of us, will be on top of that mountain!* What a victory it would be! Wow!

Hmm, not quite. While both Yellow and Red and, to a certain extent, Green employees smiled and felt stirred up, the Blues only said one thing: *We can't imagine ourselves up there. How did we get up there?*

20.3.1 What You Should Do

If a plan seems crazy, a Blue will never have any confidence in it. There's no point in playing on their feelings or trying to promote ideas that are way too wild. What you say needs to have realistic perspectives; otherwise, you won't get anywhere.

This is another case where the same is more or less true whether you are in a professional or domestic setting.

No matter what you want to convince a Blue of, you need to be prepared. That's the case whether it's a creative assignment at work or a wholly unnecessary bathroom-renovation project.

Think through what you want to say and what you want to convince the Blue of. Put the lofty vision to one side. It's probably sensible to consider the language you use. Skip the inspirational speeches that Yellows and Reds devour. You can ditch "fantastic," "wonderful," "awesome," "cool," and the rest of it.

Stick to the facts, and be clear. Impart details.

According to my calculations, the tiles will cost $41.92 per square meter. (Why $41.92 exactly? Because a fiddly, unrounded figure looks more authentic. It shows that you've genuinely made a calculation. This is quite different from saying, *About $40.* Oh no—$41.92. For more on this, see the next section on details.)

If you have an idea that hasn't been tested before, try setting reasonable goals. Don't say that you'll be dominating the field within three months or that your kids are going to win the Little League even though they've lost every match this season. You'll just be taken for a fool.

If you already suspect you have Yellow traits in your profile, you should really pause for thought here. You're already facing an uphill struggle when it comes to Blues. And be careful about the use of overly exuberant gestures. If possible, put your hands in your pockets while you talk. And try to stand still.

20.4 DETAILS: FACTS ARE THE ONLY THINGS THAT MATTER

Details are essential to communicating with a Blue. If you really want to get through to them, you must be very exact. Carelessness—a failure to pay attention to the details—won't be looked upon kindly.

And remember it's not about whether the details are crucial to any given decision. Say you want to get someone interested in your house. I don't know why—maybe you want to find out if this individual would like to buy it. Everyone can see what it looks like and its location. Right now, it may not matter much either way when it was built, but your Blue will simply want to know.

And they'll want to know exactly what things cost. If you're asked how much something costs, don't say, *Around $70*. Much better to say $69.50. That's an exact answer. The Blue is more interested in an exact price than a low price. They may well negotiate, but they will want to know the exact cost right away.

Rounded numbers and other types of estimates arouse suspicion. I don't know that your Blue friend would openly admit this, but doubt will have been awakened within them. How is it possible the number is so even? Is that really credible?

Always provide accurate information—that's the way to keep a Blue happy and settled.

20.5 THERE'S NO SUBSTITUTE FOR QUALITY

Quality is what drives a Blue. Everything else is secondary. Things can't be allowed to go wrong. A lot of their wider focus originates from a deeply rooted desire for everything to be perfect. A Blue is discontented if they're not allowed to perform their work to an exacting standard. That has nothing to do with what quality of work is actually required. It's simply due to their belief that things must always be done the proper way.

Of course, this takes a huge amount of time. But the advantage is obvious—if you do it right from the beginning, you will avoid having to redo it. This is actually a great way of saving time. But since a Blue does not think in terms of hours, days, or even weeks—but rather in months and years—they don't see the potential downside of these exacting standards. They want quality, and quality takes time. It's as simple as that.

Imagine that you're at your Blue friend's house for dinner. She's planned a meal for you and has carefully selected recipes, shopped for ingredients of the highest quality, and planned everything down to the smallest detail.

When you enter the kitchen, you see her slicing vegetables into

identical pieces with an air of concentration, measuring every ingredient with millimeter precision. You ask her why she is devoting so
much time and energy to preparing the dinner. You might even crack
a joke. *We're not going to talk to the food—we're only going to eat it.*
This won't fall on fertile ground.

Throughout the evening, you note how she carefully monitors the
preparation of each dish, tasting it and adjusting the seasoning with
a precision that would impress a professional chef. She talks quietly
but enthusiastically about each ingredient and how she picked them
to ensure the very best taste and texture in her dishes. She refers to
how many test runs she undertook before getting it right.

When you ask her why she's devoting so much time and effort to
making this dinner perfect, she tells you that quality is what makes
the difference.

After dinner when you're basking in the afterglow of that delicious food, you probably realize that each and every bite was an
explosion of flavor, and you can't help but be impressed by her commitment to creating the perfect meal.

20.5.1 What You Should Do

Don't be sloppy since that is a sure sign of poor quality. You should
be on your guard about using negative terms about the Blue spending
too much time on quality. Use words like "careful control," "properly
inspected," "the importance of quality." Let the Blue understand that
you too wish to ensure that what you're working on is of a high
quality.

This means you should prepare very carefully before any meetings with a Blue. Whether that's the condo association, the annual
barbecue, or a session at the gym with your new fitness coach. They
judge you by the merit of the work you create. Not by how funny
you are, not by who you know, not by whether you invite them out
for fancy meals. None of this means anything if you are careless.
When you are finished with a task—double-check it. If possible—
triple-check. Have someone else look at it. Only then should you
show it to a Blue.

20.6 WHAT YOU ALSO NEED TO DO WHEN YOU MEET BLUES

Just agreeing to a Blue's initiative would be like driving a car with one foot on the brake. Your Blue acquaintance, friend, or spouse simply likes to have the handbrake on. It's safer that way. Your task is most likely to get things moving, but you can't just hit the gas.

Instead, you need to find the right lever to pull and take off that Blue handbrake. Here are a few ideas in that vein.

20.7 HOW TO MANAGE AND BUILD RELATIONSHIPS SMOOTHLY—AND ABOVE ALL, WHY YOU SHOULD

A Blue has feelings like everyone else, and they appreciate people. It just looks a little different. Because most of a Blue's emotions are self-contained, they may seem a little cold. No facial expressions to speak of, no gestures, no emotional expressions at all. Blues may not seem interested in other people; they simply focus on the issue at hand.

This is a good approach if we're at the annual general meeting of the condo association or trying to deal with a particularly thorny issue with our electricity supplier. But every time other people, especially Yellows or Greens, are involved, a Blue's tendency to dissociate from others can be problematic. They simply don't realize that other people don't function in the same way. People want to feel like they can relate to this person. They don't want to feel like robots.

20.7.1 What You Should Do

Remind them that other people have visible feelings. Point out occasions when they have unnecessarily called attention to the shortcomings in a neighbor's house. Explain that they don't have to express themselves critically all the time. Show them people can take great offense when others criticize their home, car, spouse, or children.

Make it clear that the apology *I was just telling it like it is* doesn't cut it. They didn't say things as they were. All they said was what they thought or believed about a certain thing, based on their own assessment.

Question the value of constantly making critical comments. You should also explain that there is the truth, and then there is the truth. Not everyone wants "the truth" rammed down their throat all the time.

This isn't an easy task, given that Blues will think you're wrong. They've every right to criticize others and identify failures and short-comings. They can hardly ignore an error if they see it. You may have to explain that others won't appreciate this behavior.

Only time will tell whether this argument has gotten through to them.

20.8 DIGGING ALL THE WAY DOWN TO ROCK BOTTOM—AND THEN A BIT FARTHER

Have you ever listened to a Blue tell an interesting story about something that happened to them?

Let's say they got a flat on the motorway.

They'll begin by saying that their alarm clock, a Sony, rang a minute earlier than usual because it was Thursday and on Thursdays they like to gargle with Listerine for a little longer—the green kind, since a recently published taste test clearly demonstrated it's preferred by most people. Breakfast consisted of two seven-minute eggs and coffee. Gevalia has a new roast, but they don't much like it. At least 9 percent of the beans were damaged, which made them reflect on how bean structure affects the mouthfeel of the coffee.

Then they went to retrieve the newspaper from the mailbox. *USA Today* was offering 18 percent off for a three-month period. While they were getting the newspaper, they talked to their neighbor over the hedge—apparently he's a *The Wall Street Journal* reader—about the best lawn care methods for September. There's an interesting website that sets out details about autumn fertilizers—absolutely fascinating stuff. . . .

Before they've even made it onto the motorway, your lunch break is over and you're left wondering what that was all about. The thing is, once the highly introverted Blue has gotten started, they can't stop. You must be told everything.

Rather troublingly, they seem to remember . . . everything.

20.8.1 What You Should Do

It goes without saying that you need to intervene. This is one of the very few things a Blue shares in common with Yellows—they need to be steered toward a certain goal, for example, in conversation.

What's the goal? What's the point? What do they really want to say? You can, however, be much more to the point here than you would with a Yellow. Your Blue friend is nowhere near as sensitive as a Yellow. They can handle being told that they are being long-winded. They might well be crestfallen at your inability to appreciate all these fascinating tidbits, but that's probably because you aren't in possession of your faculties, not because you're at loggerheads.

Explain there are limits to how much detail is needed in any given project. We don't need to know the rent increase next year down to four decimal places before we draw up the household budget. If the car you're buying is just a shade thirstier than you planned, it really makes little difference, high fuel prices be damned.

A round percentage is more than enough to allow for a forecast. It's a balancing act, given that the truth is often in the details. But if you know you are unnecessarily digging all the way down to rock bottom . . . pull the handbrake!

Simply set a deadline: *I need an answer by this date. Dig as much as you want, but after this date I'll be moving on.*

20.9 ROME WASN'T BUILT IN A DAY— THIS HAS TO TAKE TIME

Haste is only for sloppy people. We can tell Blues to hurry up, but it goes in one ear and out the other. Speed isn't an end in itself. Often,

Blues slow down even more when they're experiencing stress, since in a high-stakes situation, you really don't have time to make mistakes. Better to be careful to avoid time-consuming fixes.

This may be true, but sometimes things are urgent, particularly in our fast-paced society—hurry to work, hurry at work, hurry home from said work. Hurry in school, in traffic, in the supermarket—everywhere, everything is urgent.

I don't encourage any form of behavior that may lead to stress-related illnesses. But sometimes you have to speed up in order to stay in the race. There's a schedule and other people and their priorities to adhere to. Outwardly, the Blue is quite unmoved. But not even Blues can shirk their responsibilities toward the rest of the world, much as they would like to. They work at their own pace without worrying all those people around them suffering from burnout—after all, they only have themselves to blame.

20.9.1 What You Should Do

Calmly and methodically tell the Blue that next week they'll need to work at a faster pace. Explain exactly why this is so important. State that there are only thirty-eight hours left for this task and this time must be devoted to the right activities. Point to the big picture. Give them valid reasons why they should go against their instincts.

You can readily prove your point by highlighting the long-term plan: *We must stay on track or we'll miss our next deadline.* If, for example, you're talking about renovating your house, it might be helpful to negotiate in advance when everything will be ready. Blues will always find something that needs a little extra polish. But that isn't always acceptable.

If the in-laws are arriving in four weeks' time, they're arriving in four weeks' time. Calculate how many hours you'll need for the renovation project and decide which activities are to be prioritized. Make sure the Blue sticks to their schedule and keeps moving forward once they've completed each task. Otherwise, the risk is they will spend five hours polishing the finer details—time they don't have.

If you have all the time in the world, well, that's another matter. But hand on heart—who really has that these days?

20.10 IF IT'S IN THE BOOK, THEN IT MUST BE TRUE

Can't we go by our gut feelings? Try saying that to a strictly Blue individual and see what happens. It's like forcing a vegan to watch a seal being clubbed to death. Gut feeling is the opposite of rational thought, and nothing could be more foreign to the Blue.

Wait a minute: Does this mean you should never use your own intuition?

Even Blue individuals have what we call a sixth sense or "nose" for what is right. The difference is that they don't trust it because it can, of course, be wrong. The problem is that it's impossible to prove anything with the help of a gut feeling.

The only things that count are the facts. And even the facts might not be enough. After all, there may be other facts that are just as worthy of evaluation.

20.10.1 What You Should Do

Tell your Blue friend that if they have to make a decision without all the facts, they can follow their gut. This can apply to work or ordering at a new restaurant. Speak clearly and loudly to the Blue, and explain that if they don't make a decision, they'll end up going hungry. Prove that it's better to do something than nothing.

Feel free to speak in terms of how it is logical to go with their gut right now since not all the facts are known. Explain that the quality will end up almost as good anyway—well, maybe it'll only be 95.3 percent, but you can't have it all—and that they might learn some valuable lessons that will help them in future decisions. Help them to calculate the risk. But move forward.

Announce that you are going to order your steak—and eat it—regardless of what your Blue does.

20.11 DECISIONS MADE HERE

Because the Blue experiences the decision itself as less important than the path to the decision, stagnation can occur. After painstakingly collecting facts and meticulously studying all available conditions, you finally come to the moment of truth—the decision. There is a risk that everything can grind to a halt. *On the one hand . . . but on the other hand . . .* Let's take a closer look at this issue.

An acquaintance I've known for more than three decades wanted to buy a new car. Over eight months he test-drove sixteen different makes. Sixteen! Can you even think of sixteen different brands of car?

Over fifty different models in different combinations: different engines, chassis, transmissions, interiors, colors. He tried everything.

Fabric versus leather upholstery. Gas versus diesel. Automatic versus manual.

He put together comprehensive Excel spreadsheets examining fuel consumption and depreciation, and he handed out graphs to various car salespeople for their input.

After considerable internal torment, he bought a Volvo V90, then Sweden's most popular car, in the bestselling color, silver. This particular model was the most tested car in the Swedish motoring press that year. You would think he could have picked that car just by reading about it.

Why did you do that? I asked. *Why did you run this borderline crazy market research project before buying the same car as everyone else?* His wife wanted to know the same thing.

His three teenagers wanted to know, too. *Why?*

His answer?

Why not?

20.11.1 What You Should Do

You can definitely help out. Equip the Blue with the crucial piece of the puzzle. Gently and carefully steer them in the right direction, or failing that, in any direction at all.

Pay attention to the point when the decision process stalls. Suppose you need to hire a new teenager from the local neighborhood to mow your lawn while you're on holiday in Thailand for five weeks. You might whittle the short list down to two equally strong candidates. On the one hand you've got Filip, whom your neighbor has used, and on the other you've got Sara. On the one hand. On the other hand.

It's all gone fine so far. Your Blue spouse has been documenting everything meticulously and keeping you abreast of all measures and steps. The process has been followed to the letter.

In order to get something to happen, provide the decision-maker with the necessary data required for them to make a decision about one of the candidates. Push them to make a choice. Remind them that as the discussion is being prolonged, the grass is continuing to grow.

Point out there isn't a lawnmower on earth that will be able to get through that if your Blue doesn't get a move on.

Explain that everything has been properly considered and that, regardless of which candidate they choose, all the risks have been eliminated. And you could point out that it's just a lawn, not a nuclear power plant.

20.12 FINAL CONCLUSIONS ON ADAPTATION

Now you have some basic information about how you can interact with the different colors so you can get to where you want to go. The first step is to try to tune in to the frequency of others and then adapt to them. In this way, you gain their trust and they are able to recognize themselves in you.

So the basic rule is to meet a Red with Red behavior, Yellow with Yellow, Green with Green, and finally Blue with Blue. You've done your work with pacing. Then it's time to get them on board by making certain demands. Keep these straightforward at first, then make them a little tougher.

You may think it sounds simple.

The difficulty comes, for example, if you are Yellow and must adapt to a Blue. You might need more training here. It depends on what color you are, how strong your self-awareness is, and how willing you are to make headway with a specific contact in your everyday life. (You can always do what Adriano did—you can continue being yourself.) The next step will be to start leading the person away from common pitfalls.

Imagine you're booking a trip to New York. You call your travel agent (not that we do that anymore, but play along!) and ask for a ticket to New York. Their answer will be *No problem.* But then they'll ask where you'd like to fly from.

Imagine you answer that question with *Who cares? Just get me a ticket.*

How will they solve this challenge? Answer: They won't.

In all communication—physical or verbal—a starting point and a goal are needed. And the starting point in each verbal communication will always be you.

And this is where it gets interesting. How do you get to New York? Presumably not the same way as I do, since we're not in the same place.

When we talk about adapting to a Green, it might entail an adjustment of our tempo. But how? If you're a Yellow, you need to slow down. But if you're a Blue, you actually need to speed up. If you're a Red, you need to sit down for a minute first.

As you have seen, each color has its obvious weaknesses. But a Blue can help a Yellow become more concrete, and the Yellow can perhaps persuade the Blue to loosen up and be a little more spontaneous.

It's all about working together, about meeting one another in the middle, and about helping each other to maintain a smooth life.

21

Stress Factors and Energy Thieves

21.1 JUST WHAT IS STRESS?

We talked about anger and aggression in a previous chapter.

Anger is one thing. Stress is another. Sometimes one is a consequence of the other, but not always. Some people become angry because of stress; others become stressed because of anger. When we speak about stress, we often mean the feeling of having too much to do and too little time to do it. There's not enough time to do everything at work, and on top of that, factor in the time needed to go to the gym, meet with friends, spend time with family, and engage in recreational activities.

Then we have the outside world. Social media. We should eat better, drink less, and exercise more. We should spend more time with our children—quality time. But how are we supposed to do it all?

It's important to be clear that the feeling of stress that makes us feel chronically bad is often caused by things other than stress. If you feel pressure and the weight of high expectations on you and your actions, you may be stressed even if you have plenty of time.

Pressure, demands, and expectations create stress and can make you feel low and paralyzed by inaction, and they can also lead to difficulties sleeping and physical pain. Simply put, the feeling of stress arises when we experience greater demands and expectations than we can cope with.

21.2 DIFFERENT PEOPLE REACT DIFFERENTLY TO STRESS: WHAT A SURPRISE!

Seriously, though, all of us react differently to stress. Different people can experience the same event in different ways, and a person can experience similar events differently at different times. The things you have been through in the past and how you are feeling right now all have an effect on how you act and react.

If you're well rested and feeling fine, you could experience a tough week at work as an invigorating challenge, despite your heavy workload. But if you're tired and feeling down on yourself, you may experience the same week as horrible and demoralizing.

How does communication style affect your stress levels? Basically, it says nothing about your stress threshold—i.e., how much stress you can tolerate. But it can tell us something about what stresses you out, and how you are likely to react to stress. In this regard, our driving forces affect us a great deal—they're what motivate us to get out of bed in the morning, tear off to work, and really give it our all.

It's easy to see how we can get stressed by feeling that we are spending too much time on the wrong things—tasks or areas of life that we don't find rewarding.

If you understand what your key driving forces are, you can probably identify your stress factors and thereby ensure you don't end up falling into the stress trap unnecessarily. If you're familiar with other peoples' behavioral profiles, you can also avoid some big pitfalls. A lot of stress can be avoided if you know how to deal with specific individuals.

I'm going to set out a few brief facts that you may find useful. Think about where you are. Be aware that stress is often an energy thief. There's no getting away from the fact that we do our best work when we are experiencing a degree of harmony.

The rest of the chapter is written with an element of irony, and I urge you to read it in that way.

21.3 STRESS FACTORS FOR REDS

If you would like to stress a Red out, you can try one of the following to lower their self-confidence:

21.3.1 Take Away Every Form of Authority

Not being involved in decision-making is really difficult for a Red. They always think they have the best ideas and therefore they believe they should be the one in charge of the project.

21.3.2 Achieve No Results Whatsoever

If we're not making immediate headway, then all our work has been a waste. Such an insight can trigger severe stress reactions in a Red, and those around them should be on their guard. They'll look for scapegoats.

21.3.3 Eliminate Any Kind of Challenge

If everything is too easy, it becomes boring. Red behavior hinges on one thing: the ability to handle problems and difficult challenges. If there are no problems to solve, then Reds will lack stimulation. They'll become passive, believing they have absolutely nothing to do. They can slow down the pace, and this can be difficult to reverse.

21.3.4 Waste Time and Resources and Work as Inefficiently as Possible

Just sitting around doing nothing is a waste of time. Not that this is necessarily what we're actually doing, but, in the mind of a Red, if you don't get the maximum productivity out of your time, it's wasteful. This is particularly stressful for a Red manager, because they're likely to be evaluated on the organization's efficiency.

21.3.5 Make Sure Everything Becomes a Routine

Mundane and repetitive tasks are the kiss of death for a Red. It's deadly boring. Reds lose their concentration and will find something else to do. Routine work is not what they're good at. They're lousy at details, and they know it. Someone else needs to take care of the dull, routine work, because a Red believes they have a better understanding of the big picture.

21.3.6 Make a Bunch of Stupid Mistakes

Mistakes are one thing, but stupid mistakes, well, that's something completely different. It's so overwhelmingly unnecessary. If a Red believes their colleagues are brainless, they go crazy: *Why don't they understand what they're supposed to be doing? How hard can it be?*

21.3.7 Remove All Control over Others from Them

A Red's need for control can be considerable. And it's not about controlling facts and details. They want to control people. What they do, how they do it, and so on. Without this control, a Red gets very frustrated.

21.3.8 Tell Them Regularly to Cool Down or to Lower Their Voices

They get angry when people say they're angry when they're not (yet). They will always be a little more hot-tempered than the average person, but this doesn't actually mean they're angry. And it's precisely this accusation that can make them angry—really angry.

21.4 WHAT DOES A RED DO WHEN THEY'RE STRESSED AND UNDER PRESSURE?

That's easy! They blame everyone else. As a Red is often surrounded by idiots, it's easy for them to single out scapegoats. And they can easily overdo it when they take someone to task for having made a mess of things. Be aware. That's my advice to you, because you'll feel the sting of their wrath.

Reds are always more demanding than other colors. They expect a lot from themselves, and they expect a lot from you. When under stress, they're also excessively demanding and driven—much more than usual.

The Red will shut out their colleagues. They will become closed, burrowing into the task at hand and working even harder. Remember that their anger and frustration are lurking just beneath the surface, so please be careful about what you do in their presence.

21.4.1 What Do Reds Need in Order to Manage Their Stress?

If you have the authority to give a direct order, the answer is simple: Ask them to get a hold of themselves. It actually works. Another way to make it easier for Reds in stressful situations is to send them home and tell them to do some physical exercise. Send them to a place where they can compete in some kind of competition, expending their energy on winning something that will be of no importance to the group. When they come back, most of their aggression will have dissipated.

21.5 STRESS FACTORS FOR YELLOWS

If for any reason you would like to make a Yellow feel stress, try one of the following to get them off balance:

21.5.1 Pretend They're Invisible

You remember a Yellow's greatest weakness, right? *Look at me! Here I am!* If you want to get them off balance, simply make them feel invisible. If they're not visible, then they don't exist. They feel ignored and overlooked, and this is guaranteed to cause stress.

21.5.2 Declare Your Skepticism of Everything

Any person manifesting lots of skepticism comes across as very negative, which stresses Yellows out. They want to see the positive and the light, and they consider even everyday realists to be prophets of doom. Pessimism and negativity effectively kill Yellows' enthusiasm and cause them to feel tense.

21.5.3 Put Them Inside the Box as Much as Possible

Just like Reds, Yellows shun routine, repetitive tasks, and jam-packed schedules. They happily create schedules for others, but they can't follow them themselves. Force them into one of your plans and you'll see your Yellow f(r)iends begin to unravel.

21.5.4 Isolate Them from the Rest of the Group

For a Yellow, the absence of someone to talk to is perhaps the worst thing ever. Because they need to talk, there must be someone there to listen. Being trapped in an office space with only a desk for company is a punishment worse than death. It's like being deported to North Korea.

21.5.5 Make It Clear It's Inappropriate to Joke at Work

No joking around and no sense of humor? Is this a funeral home? I once got exactly that comment from a Yellow who discovered that busy management consultants didn't have time to monkey about. She was very stressed out by all the seriousness and left before her probation period was over.

21.5.6 Push Them to Think Carefully—in Advance

Suppressing a Yellow's spontaneity is like holding down the lid on a saucepan when the milk is boiling over. It simply doesn't work. It creates a terrible mess, and everyone gets dragged in as the Yellow—loudly and intensely—invites them into their stress spiral. Remember that a Yellow's stress will always be noticed. Don't believe otherwise.

21.5.7 Bicker and Fuss Incessantly over Trivialities

Having to face incessant confrontations is exhausting. This is something of a paradox, because Yellows aren't afraid of conflict like Greens. But if there's too much squabbling, it will disrupt their desire for fun and positivity, which causes stress. They can cope with bickering, but when it becomes too much, Yellows won't be at the top of their game, and they can lose their usual luster.

21.5.8 Try a Little Public Humiliation

A Yellow who has been given negative feedback in the presence of others won't be a pleasant sight to behold. They'll probably never speak to you again. Moreover, they'll also become incredibly defensive, and you'll achieve nothing at all.

21.6 WHAT DOES A YELLOW DO WHEN THEY'RE STRESSED AND UNDER PRESSURE?

Be prepared for the fact that they'll draw attention to themselves even more than usual. Their ego drives them to seek out more attention and affirmation since they have to compensate for the negative feelings of stress. This means they'll actively look for attention, which makes them feel better. The risk is they'll talk too much, take up too much space during meetings, and in relationships, they'll force themselves into the center of everything.

Maybe you thought this wasn't possible, but they also run the risk of becoming excessively and unrealistically optimistic. You've never experienced a real challenge until you've tried to cope with a truly stressed-out Yellow. They'll come up with plans so wild and outlandish not even they believe in them. But this is perfectly natural for them.

21.6.1 What Do Yellows Need in Order to Manage Their Stress?

Let Yellows throw a party. They need to meet people in social contexts. This need is often urgent. They can sink very deep into their own misery if they remain stressed for too long. When things are at their worst, suggest a pub crawl, a party, or a simple barbecue. It doesn't need to be fancy, but make sure they get to enjoy themselves for a while. Also, make sure it's FUN!

21.7 STRESS FACTORS FOR GREENS

If for any reason you would like to get a Green to feel stress, I propose the following unpleasant things:

21.7.1 Take Away Every Form of Security

Give them tasks they've never done before without explaining anything whatsoever to them. But, at the same time, expect perfect implementation. Leave them alone in meetings with people who make unreasonable demands of them. Don't support them when things heat up in a conversation. Deliberately send a disgruntled Red to rant at them. Stress will soon follow.

21.7.2 Leave Lots of Loose Ends

Unfinished tasks and loose ends are deeply disturbing. Greens like to know how things fit together, and when they don't understand how the process works, it won't go well. Unfinished projects—things that have been started but are drawn out without any end in sight—really mess things up for Greens. This is why Yellows are phenomenal at causing stress for Greens.

21.7.3 Hang Around Them Constantly

If a Green doesn't get their private space, if there's nowhere they can withdraw from the world, they get very stressed. They like other people, of course, but they need to be alone with themselves, too. Deprived of this possibility, they seize up completely.

21.7.4 Make Lightning-Fast Changes and Unexpected Dodges on the Field of Play

This is the specialty of Reds and Yellows: quick decisions they don't always explain. Greens are miserable when they're forced into making unexpected and rapid changes, and they often respond by sinking into a state of absolute apathy. The worst kind of change is when a Green gets an order in the morning, and just as they begin to reflect on how they will do it, a counterorder comes. Nothing will ever be the same again.

21.7.5 *Would You Be So Good as to Do It All Again? I Needed It Done Yesterday.*

Having to redo a task is synonymous with failure. If something must be redone, it can only be because your work wasn't good enough the first time. In other words, negative feedback. By extension, this means you're not good enough as a person, which is, of course, extremely stressful. Greens are left assuming everybody hates them.

21.7.6 *Look! We Can't Agree on Absolutely Everything!*

Disagreements in a work group or in the family inevitably lead to stress. Only troublemakers enjoy conflict. Friction in the most important group, the family, is particularly serious. A Green won't know what they should do.

21.7.7 Force Them into the Limelight

Under no circumstances do Greens want to take center stage when they're in larger groups. Groups of more than three people would be considered large groups unless the Green knew everyone very well. Making such demands of Greens can only end badly, because they will just stare down at their papers. Everyone will be able to see how uneasy they are, and the rest of the group will also be stressed. Not good.

21.8 WHAT DOES A GREEN DO WHEN THEY'RE STRESSED AND UNDER PRESSURE?

They become very reserved and almost cold. Their body language becomes rigid and closed, and if you're the one who triggered their stress, they won't have anything to do with you. Some Greens exhibit strong apathy. They become cold and unsympathetic even toward people about whom, in normal circumstances, they care very much.

They also become very hesitant and uncertain. Stress makes Greens insecure and afraid of making mistakes. This can occur at work but also at home. If a child gets sick, a Green becomes passive and simply looks on, because they're afraid of doing the wrong thing. They'll also internalize the blame for the situation and may become completely closed up. At work, it may be slightly different. It depends. Many Greens end up in a rut of obstinacy or stubbornness, provoking those around them by refusing to change anything. Even when they see that a particular method is not working well, they may refuse to act. It may seem strange, but the typical Green stubbornness gets the upper hand and prevents them from doing anything.

21.8.1 What Can I Do to Help Greens Manage Their Stress?

Allow them to do—nothing. You read that right. Give them free time for meditative occupations like gardening, fishing, or other forms of relaxation. Consider sending them off to the cinema—not with a large group of people, but possibly on their own—or giving them a good book that takes two days to read. They don't really want to do anything. Let them do nothing until the stress subsides. Then they'll be back to their normal selves.

21.9 STRESS FACTORS FOR BLUES

If for any reason, you would like to get a Blue to feel stress, just upset every one of their calculations. . . .

21.9.1 *You Don't Know What You're Talking About*

You may think Blues don't take criticism personally, but if they believe that the criticism is untrue and unfounded, it can be very hard on them. Not because they're afraid of conflict, or that your relationship will suffer, but because their sense of perfection is being besmirched.

21.9.2 Get Management to Make a Spontaneous Decision

For Blues, change can be just fine, since they're under no illusions that everything was perfect to start with. But they need to know the motivations behind the change. They need an answer to the question *Why?* If it's not in the plan, then it's unplanned, and a lack of planning indicates poor structure—not good. Inevitably, this leads to headaches.

21.9.3 *That Actually Looks Very Risky, but Let's Do It Anyway!*

There's a certain amount of risk in everything. A Blue sees risks everywhere. Where a Red would say that jumping from a plane without a parachute is a huge risk, a Blue would say that it's risky to buy a new lawn mower. You never really know what might happen. And the faster things go, the greater the risks.

21.9.4 Oh Look! Here's Comes Your Entire Family—Unannounced!

It's a matter of order and structure, of working at a relaxed pace, or renovating the kitchen according to a clearly established plan. If half the family were to drop in all of a sudden, it would upset everything. You should never try to surprise a Blue. Since they may not have communicated their own plans in detail, this can create quite a problem.

21.9.5 Whoops-a-daisy! What Happened There?

Mistakes are made by blockheads and careless people. Blues don't make mistakes, so when everyone else makes a mess of things and disrupts their plans, a Blue may simply close the door and refuse to listen. They don't want to hear that the project has crashed; they just want to keep on doing their bit—even if that task no longer makes any sense.

21.9.6 Damn It! You're Such a Stickler!

Don't you have any imagination? We have to be a bit more flexible here. This is a great way to put a Blue on the defense. People who break the rules and go against the regulations are regarded with suspicion, and you need to keep them on a short leash. If a Blue realizes they're in the hands of an organization that pays no attention whatsoever to proper procedures, they may show considerable resistance.

21.9.7 We Just Have to Take Some Chances

A variation on the preceding point. Right is right, and adhering to that is the be-all and end-all, the alpha and omega. It even says so in the Bible. So when a Blue can't prepare themselves in their (sometimes extremely cumbersome) way, it triggers stress. They're the opposite of spontaneous. You simply can't force a Blue to respond to a situation before they've had time to acquaint themselves with the subject. Their answers will contain so many caveats they'll be of no practical use at all.

21.9.8 Surround Them with Overly Emotional People

Nope. Sloppy sentimentality is downright unpleasant. It's messy and awkward, and a Blue doesn't like it. Logic is what counts, and if you overlook this, they'll find it very trying. They'll make themselves scarce, and they won't forget that you're an overly emotional person who doesn't use your brain in the same way they use theirs.

21.10 WHAT DOES A BLUE DO WHEN THEY'RE STRESSED AND UNDER PRESSURE?

They become excessively pessimistic. Oh yes. It actually gets worse than usual. Suddenly everything becomes pitch black, and they fall into a pit of despair. Lethargy is common, and nothing is of interest anymore. Gloom and doom will rain down on all of us. They also get unbearably pedantic. When they feel stress, many people increase their pace in order to compensate. Not a Blue. They stomp on the brakes. Now isn't the time for making any mistakes. Those around them can expect constant criticism. They'll suddenly point out every little mistake they observe—and there are quite a few. They might also become an unbearable know-it-all.

21.10.1 What Can I Do to Help Blues Manage Their Stress?

They need privacy. They must be given time and space to think. They want to analyze the situation and understand the connections, and they need to be given time to do that. If you give them space, they will come back—eventually. But if they fall too deeply into despair, you may need to offer them more proactive help.

21.11 CONCLUSION

What can we learn from studying different people under stress? When under stress, an individual's normal conduct and behavior are often reinforced and exaggerated. A Red becomes even tougher and more aggressive toward those around them; a Yellow becomes more sulky and unstructured; a Green becomes even more passive and noncommittal than usual; and a Blue can become completely closed off, splitting hairs so thin not even Google could spot them.

The most important thing is to avoid stressing people unnecessarily. Of course, you knew that already, but it can be helpful to understand what actually causes stress for each profile. To push a Red is not as stressful as pushing a Green or a Blue. On the contrary, you have to push a Red for them to bounce back. If everything went too smoothly, they would get bored.

Add to this each individual's driving forces and the picture begins to come into sharper focus. Suddenly, we realize there are reasons why people today are so stressed.

The situation, your profile, the time of day, the level of work, the group, the weather—lots of things cause stress in our lives. But if you are aware of these factors, you can deal with things much more easily.

The Most Common Combinations

22.1 THE REASON WHY FOUR COLORS ARE REALLY MUCH GREATER THAN FOUR

Are we really set in our behavioral ways forever? Do we never change?

You're right to ask. This is an interesting and simultaneously complex question to answer. Everyone you meet has the potential to act according to any color, depending on the situation. When I give a lecture to five thousand people, I'm Thomas-on-stage and I come across as a vibrant extrovert who is able to joke with the audience just the right amount to ensure they have a good time.

Sure, I'm trying to teach people things and obviously I believe the message I'm sharing is an important one, but I'm also seeking to give the audience an experience. A lot of what I do can be referred to as edutainment—there's a dose of entertainment inherent in it. I simply summon more Yellow from my inner self than would normally be natural for me.

While this is taking place, every member of the audience—all five thousand of them—is sitting and listening attentively without talking. Everyone (well, I suppose not everyone—some people are still focused on their social media feeds) is behaving like a Green, regardless of their natural core behavior.

Let's say I maintain my very Yellow demeanor when fuses start to blow in my house. I don't take the incident seriously. I make up stories about what happens when you're not on the ball. I make jokes and clown about. I'm sloppy when it comes to details. Will that approach work when I check what might be constantly tripping my fuses? No.

In order to make sure I don't burn the house down, I become thoroughly meticulous for the forty-seven minutes it takes me to locate the fault. I actually behave in a very Blue manner. Investigating, checking, double-checking. Locating the fault and then solving the problem.

Once I'm safely ensconced in front of the TV again, I will probably return to whatever color I am in my natural state.

I quite simply change my behavior depending on context. We all have reserves of all four colors on hand, but we don't show them all at the same time. If we have a lot of one particular color in stock, you can generally see it in our behavior; if we have very little of it, it only emerges in exceptional cases.

But at the foundation of this are our four colors.

The point is simply that while we can all swing in somewhat different directions in our behavior, we all have a specific pattern that feels more natural to us. Some behavioral patterns don't require any adaptation—they're just there. And my overall recommendation is that you try to find a context in which you don't need to stray too far from your natural core behavior.

22.1.1 How Four Becomes Sixteen

A comment I've encountered with relative frequency in relation to the four colors is that it seems odd there are only four of them in the first place: Red, Yellow, Green, and Blue. Some people say this isn't enough because it suggests that there are only four types of people. Obviously this doesn't reflect reality, and the question most often comes from people who haven't had time to familiarize themselves with a model of this kind.

An alternative to the DISC model is the Myers-Briggs Type Indicator (MBTI), which boasts no fewer than sixteen personalities. Sounds brilliant, right? MBTI is another great tool for people who want to learn more about behavior. I'm also MBTI-certified, but the problem with the model—at least from my point of view—is the pedagogy behind it. You're assigned a letter combination you then struggle to recall.

But it's clearly true that sixteen is greater than four.

At the same time, DISC easily combines the various colors in its model in a number of different ways. When we add Red/Yellow (which signifies Red as the strongest trait and Yellow as the second strongest), Yellow/Green, Green/Blue, and Blue/Red, we quickly reach a total of eight variants. To that we can add Yellow/Red (which indicates that Yellow is the strongest trait and Red is the second strongest), Green/Yellow, Blue/Green, and Red/Blue. Hey, presto—that's twelve. Add Yellow/Blue, Blue/Yellow, Red/Green, and Green/Red into the mix and we have sixteen variations, just like MBTI.

22.1.2 How Sixteen Becomes Sixty-Four

This is where, in my opinion, the DISC model becomes more effective, since we can easily add a third color to any of the above combinations. And this third color may be the strongest or the weakest of the two previously mentioned colors, or indeed be in between them.

What about the fourth color? I hear you asking. *Where is it?* Well, is it *quite* visible but still the *weakest* of the four? Is it just ever so slightly *less* than the *second* weakest? Or is it practically *nonexistent*? The opportunities to describe a person's behavior expand and expand the more depth we go into.

But it doesn't stop there.

Since this type of analysis can now be done entirely digitally, the different colors can be combined in a tremendous number of variations.

The stock of each color scores between one and one hundred points. Theoretically, you can have any score at all for each color, one to one hundred for Red, Yellow, Green, and Blue. In addition, we have, in fact, two different profiles: a natural one and an adapted one.

22.1.3 How Sixty-Four Becomes a Whole Crowd

I suppose that would give us tens of thousands of combinations. (I'm afraid I'm not a good enough mathematician to figure out the correct number of variants, but ChatGPT says it is one hundred million combinations.)

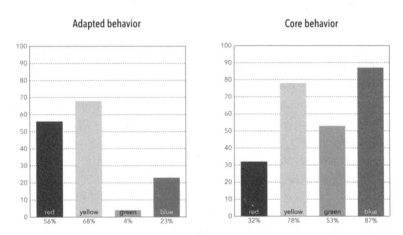

But that's not the case in reality. You see, no one has a full complement of all the colors. The statistics tell us that can only apply to a maximum of two colors. You can have one hundred points for both Red and Yellow (extremely extroverted and always putting the pedal to the metal) but that would have a high probability of very low scores for Green and Blue. Additionally, no one can have fewer than fifty points across all four colors. At least one color will always be above the fifty-point mark—probably a long ways above it, if the other three are some distance beneath it.

It's easy to get caught up in the technicalities, but that's how it works.

One of the tools I use contains somewhere between 19,500 and 19,800 combinations, purely algorithmic, and these combinations exist in reality and not just in theory. You'll have noticed by now that 19,500 is rather more than 16.

And that's how you have to look at this kind of model. As I wrote in the introduction to this book, you need to learn the basic ingredients first and then you can start mixing things like crazy.

The only way to get an accurate description of which profile applies to you is to conduct the analysis on an individual basis. Details of how to buy access to this tool are included at www
.surroundedbyidiots.com/en/disc-analysis/. It's not free—these are
very advanced models and should not be compared with anything
you can find online for free. There are reasons why things are offered
for free.

Nonetheless, let's take a look at the most common combinations
and see what we can learn when we add a little extra color to the mix.
Since there's a limit to how long a book can be, I'm going to offer
six examples of different combinations: Red/Yellow; Yellow/Green;
Green/Blue; Blue/Red; Yellow/Blue; and the most uncommon combination of all, Red/Green.

Let's dig in!

22.2 RED/YELLOW MOTIVATORS

22.2.1 Behavior

Red/Yellows are innovative, creative, enthusiastic, and flexible. They're
exceptionally receptive to other people's ideas, and quickly and intu-
itively recognize the possibilities in them. They like to visualize the
world as it will be tomorrow. They're inventive and initiate projects,

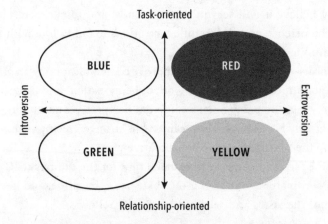

but they're often a little weaker when it comes to the actual implementation. Nevertheless, they're persistent when it comes to things that
interest them and they often come up with brilliant solutions.

Red/Yellows like variety. Inspiration and impulsive intuition
characterize most things they attempt. They are driven by a desire
for discovery that they perceive as their own unique gift. They often
successfully make use of what they've learned from previous projects
in their subsequent tasks.

A person with a combination of Red and Yellow is both challenging and socially engaged. They are confident and don't hesitate to
take the initiative, which means they're often regarded as driven and
result-oriented. They value their independence and aren't afraid to
take risks to achieve their goals.

At the same time, they have a friendly and optimistic attitude
toward people and relationships. They thrive in social contexts and
are good at building communities and commitment among members
of groups. They have no difficulty getting to know people and are
open to new opportunities and ideas.

22.2.2 Challenges

This combination of behaviors can also lead to challenges. Due to their
heavy focus on results and their own ideas, they can sometimes be
intolerant of those who think differently or take more time to understand the matter at hand. They also have a tendency to break the rules
if they believe it will serve their own ends, and to exaggerate their
own competence in order to influence others to fall in line with their
own thinking.

In order to create balance and improve communication with others,
it's important that these people work at being patient and listening to
others' views. By being open to different perspectives and taking into
account others' feelings, they can create stronger relationships and
achieve their goals in a more collaborative way.

These Motivators rarely have much time for their opposite, Green/
Blue Coordinators, who are far too systematic, sensitive, and keen on
order for the tastes and sensibilities of Red/Yellows.

22.2.3 In a Group

Red/Yellows are good at presenting themselves and their projects in a convincing and effective manner. They ooze charm and great confidence in their own abilities. Their self-esteem depends on acclaim for their performances. They're accustomed to doing many things at once, but these things have a tendency to be done very superficially.

Their strength lies in their engagement, enthusiasm, imagination, spontaneity, and ability to instill hope. Red/Yellows can be the engine running an entire group. They have mastered the art of convincing others and securing their wholehearted support.

Red/Yellows adapt easily to different assignments and adopt an attitude that suits the group they are a part of at any given time.

22.2.4 Areas for Development for Red/Yellows

- It's great to be hands-on but they need to beware of promising a quicker execution than they can deliver.
- Improve delegation—Red/Yellows tend either to do the job themselves or to provide inadequate instructions when delegating to someone else.
- Work on two-way communication—they tend to talk instead of listening.
- Red/Yellows should think about their work-life balance.
- They need to be aware that they may exceed their authority and can be dominant.
- They also need to be aware of a tendency to focus on crises and act impulsively.
- Red/Yellows may neglect the details unless they consider them important.
- They may also talk too much when offering criticism.
- It's good to show exuberant enthusiasm but sometimes that can be perceived as superficial.
- They should beware of absorbing information as fact without checking its validity.

That's what this combination can look like. It's important to remember there is a difference between a Red/Yellow (more Red than Yellow) and a Yellow/Red (more Yellow than Red). Sometimes the Red part is more prominent, sometimes it's a yolkier shade of Yellow.

This is usually connected to surrounding factors. As we've seen, the overall context can change how someone chooses to act, and this is particularly clear when seen in a combined profile.

22.3 YELLOW/GREEN HELPERS

22.3.1 Behavior

Yellow/Greens are open, participatory, and loving people who want to be liked and are protective. They want to feel they are a meaningful part of people's lives. They have understanding and empathy for their fellow human beings and derive satisfaction from helping others.

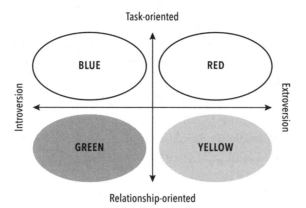

Yellow/Greens ask for others' views and help other people accept decisions. They modify their own emotions to suit others' needs, which makes them popular. If they don't get the attention they crave, they will continue to adapt themselves so much that they eventually suppress their own needs.

Yellow/Green Helpers like to think their family and friends are completely dependent on them. Their intrinsic value depends on how others see them. When Helpers give to others, they expect something in return—at least a little attention, if nothing else.

A person with a combination of Yellow and Green is open, patient, and socially engaged. They are a good listener and gather information by being receptive to differences. They pride themselves on their intuition and function best in a setting where they feel engaged.

In contrast to those who prefer to rely on facts and figures when they want to convince others, Yellow/Greens have a propensity to rely on their gift of gab. They approach people in a safe, diplomatic, and controlled manner. Yellow/Greens get along well with most people and can be fairly informal and relaxed when in company. This is also the case when meeting people they don't know—they try to make the newcomer feel comfortable. They judge other people on their ability to express themselves verbally and exhibit warmth. They have the ability to see the bigger picture. This manifests itself in the way they view relationships, the fact that they are aware of the feelings of others, and the way they focus on the real consequences of their own actions and decisions.

They are both good speakers and good listeners.

22.3.2 Challenges

One of the challenges for Yellow/Greens is they can be overly reliant on others' approval and thus risk being exploited. Despite being open and well-meaning, they can also be stubborn when their ideals and values are questioned. They have a tendency to avoid confrontation in order to maintain good relationships, which can sometimes lead to them failing to address a problem head-on.

It's important for people with Yellow/Green traits to balance their commitment to others with a need to set boundaries and stand up for themselves. By developing a stronger sense of self and working on dealing with conflict, they can better handle the challenges that arise in their relationships and professional lives.

The direct opposite of these Helpers are Blue/Red Organizers, whom Helpers regard as formal and stiff and too concentrated by half on the task at hand.

22.3.3 In a Group

Helpers like to assume a role that provides help or consultation and are very loyal to the group. Their preferred tasks include lots of relationships. The fact that they tend to disregard their own interests can help oil the wheels of collaboration. At the same time, Helpers can become too indispensable to their colleagues, who may come to rely on them too much, even in personal or private matters. This is particularly striking when Helpers work with others such as Organizers, or observers, who are very different from themselves.

Since Helpers have a tendency to feel inferior, they are drawn toward people in positions of power who make them feel safe.

22.3.4 Areas for Development for Yellow/Greens

- They should work on seeing criticism as constructive feedback, rather than taking it personally.
- Yellow/Greens should try to avoid becoming indecisive and passive when faced with a lack of information.
- They should also try not to rely on others to always make decisions.
- Yellow/Greens are uncomfortable about taking action against rule breakers—but sometimes this may be necessary.
- They may also keep their views to themselves, when actually they have something useful to share.
- Yellow/Greens need to be aware that they often underestimate their own abilities and focus on the shortcomings in themselves and others. They might try to be more positive.
- They also need to avoid the temptation to evade responsibility through exaggerating the difficulties in any given situation.
- They often have excessive optimism and a tendency to shower praise on others; these are positive things but they can appear superficial and frequently only motivate others at a shallow level.

- Yellow/Greens need to beware of neglecting the details and only focusing on results.
- They should also avoid making impulsive decisions without careful analysis.

22.4 GREEN/BLUE COORDINATORS

22.4.1 Behavior

Green/Blue Coordinators are systematic, thorough, organized, thoughtful, and questioning. They can absorb large volumes of facts and carefully evaluate, organize, and coordinate this information, provided that it is clearly described in the first place.

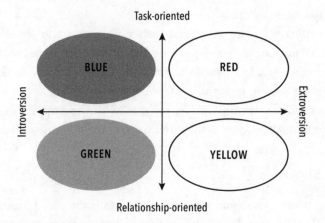

They are very practically gifted in their own areas of expertise, but they also have a tendency to undervalue their own skills—Coordinators' success tends to rely on others discovering and appreciating their talents.

They are very loyal and dutiful and often happy to work for the same employer for a long time. A person with a combination of Green and Blue is harmonious, responsible, and methodical. They are calm and controlled and strive to maintain a stable and reliable working

environment. They are meticulous and ensure that tasks are performed correctly and in full.

22.4.2 Challenges

A challenge for Green/Blues is their tendency to be self-critical and
to set high standards both for themselves and for others. They can
be reserved and feel uncomfortable showing emotion or opening up
to others. Their meticulousness and desire to adhere to established
methods can also make them reluctant to adapt to changes or new
working practices.

It's important that Green/Blues balance their pursuit of perfection
with flexibility and openness to new ideas and methods. By practicing being more expressive and open to change, they can better
meet the challenges that arise in their professional lives and in their
personal relationships.

Coordinators place great emphasis on analysis and logic. They
overlook nothing and are quick on the uptake, while never taking
anything for granted. They're patient and take an interest in the details, while having no trouble adapting to routines.

Coordinators struggle to get to grips with their opposites, Red/
Yellow Motivators, whom they find to be unreliable and gullible.

22.4.3 In a Group

Coordinators like to take on a role that entails the coordination and
control of a group. Given their desire to finish whatever they start,
their role in a group is to ensure that the job gets done from start to
finish. When a project is being planned, their ability to listen with
empathy while also structuring the material is particularly useful.
They do not impulsively embark on adventures and don't allow themselves to be distracted. If they feel threatened, they can defend themselves tooth and nail, which can come as a surprise to both themselves
and those around them.

Coordinators are happy to help with things they consider to be logical and sensible. However, they struggle to understand other people's needs and can be suspicious of their motives.

22.4.4 Areas for Development for Green/Blues

- Green/Blues often fail to take action against rule breakers and assume responsibility; these are areas to work on.
- They should try to avoid becoming indecisive and passive when faced with a lack of information.
- They should also be aware of their own tendency to exaggerate difficulties to avoid responsibility.
- Difficulty prioritizing tasks and meeting deadlines is common for Green/Blues and an area to improve on.
- They should try not to underestimate their own abilities!
- They should also beware of giving up in order to avoid conflict.
- A Green/Blue may oppose change without providing any clear explanation why—they should work on stating their reasons and avoiding knee-jerk reactions to change.
- They should consider whether they really require such a full explanation before accepting a change.
- Green/Blues may be poor at communicating their own views and need to work on expressing them.
- They should also be aware of a tendency to avoid making decisions due to a fear of making the wrong choices. If the worst happens, we learn from our mistakes.

22.5 BLUE/RED ORGANIZERS

22.5.1 Behavior

Blue/Reds strive for perfection and exactitude in their work. They are pedantic and picky about details and carefully adhere to established working methods and rules. They set high standards for themselves and others, and can be self-critical when their idea of what is right isn't met.

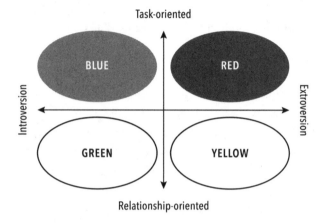

It's important for them to understand and follow instructions, and they get annoyed when other people don't do the same. Blue/Reds prioritize their work over relationships, and can be quite reserved toward others if they don't have the same work ethic and ambitions.

They are skilled at gathering and analyzing facts before making a decision, and prefer to work for a manager who clearly outlines their expectations and requirements.

Blue/Reds are results-oriented and strive to bring projects and tasks to a swift conclusion. They usually take the initiative and are eager to embark upon new projects. Blue/Reds are extremely focused on achieving their goals and can be pushy and analytical at the same time. The high expectations they set for themselves and others can lead to frustration if people are unable to match their tempo or commitment.

Blue/Reds are skilled at identifying problems and finding solutions, but can be poor in their communication and can be perceived as cold or reserved by those around them. They need to work on being more flexible and tactful in their interactions with others.

Blue/Red Organizers are dedicated, rational, and independent. They like to establish norms and follow clear rules and ethics. They are sensitive to errors and injustices, and react strongly when these occur. They have high expectations of their superiors, and feel safe and secure when areas of responsibility and rules are clearly set out. However, they can be perceived as arrogant and pedantic by others due to their pursuit of perfection and exactitude.

22.5.2 Challenges

Blue/Reds can be so focused on the details and rules that it inhibits their ability to be efficient and flexible in dynamic working environments.

Their tendency to prioritize tasks over relationships can cause tension and misunderstandings with others. Striking the right balance between maintaining high standards and building positive relationships can be a challenge for Blue/Reds.

They can be poor in their communication and perceived by others as reserved or distant.

Blue/Reds' determination to quickly bring projects and tasks to a conclusion can lead to stress and impatience.

Flexibility and adaptability: Their propensity to be pushy and controlling can make it difficult for them to adapt to changing working environments or the alternative working methods of those around them.

Communication and relationships: Blue/Reds' lack of tact and empathy in their communications can give rise to conflicts and misunderstandings. Working to be more flexible and responsive to the needs and views of others can improve professional relationships and collaborations.

Organizers' blind spot is their direct opposite, Yellow/Green Helpers, whom they regard as too soft and emotional to be effective.

Both personality types face a challenge in balancing their strong driving forces and working approaches against the need to collaborate effectively with others and to deal with complex working environments in a constructive manner. Being aware of these challenges and working actively on personal development and improvement can help them achieve their full potential and be a success in their careers.

22.5.3 In a Group

If Organizers are happy in a group and consider everyone to be on the same page in terms of goals, approach, and rules of work, then their best attributes will shine.

The Blue/Reds' strength is the ability to organize, and to identify and exploit opportunities for improvement. Other strengths include the ability to concentrate, as well as use observant, realistic thought. What may cause problems during collaboration with others is the Organizers' inner critic, which is always assessing everything they think and do. Criticism from others can therefore be doubly painful to a Blue/Red. They dislike being told what to do or how to do it. They can also annoy others by refusing to give in.

22.5.4 Areas for Development for Blue/Reds:

- Blue/Reds need to work on developing empathy for the feelings of others.
- They should balance their trust between people and technology.
- They should also work on improving their communication and their ability to convince others.
- They should aim for more flexibility without the need for full explanations.
- Blue/Reds should work on using their own initiative and making decisions without the fear of lack of experience.
- They should aim to reduce their suspicion of new ideas and their requirements for support.
- They should also realize it's okay to delegate responsibilities and thus avoid overloading themselves.
- Blue/Reds could try a motivational leadership style instead of being demanding!
- They should also focus on finishing projects before new ones begin.
- Finally, they should strive for stability and patience in prioritizing and negotiations.

22.6 CONTRADICTORY YELLOW/BLUES
AND BLUE/YELLOWS

22.6.1 Behavior

Yellow/Blues and Blue/Yellows have different ways of approaching their work and relationships, which means different challenges for each type.

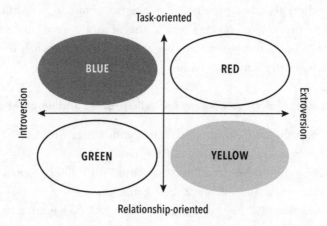

Do you get Green when you mix Yellow and Blue? It's quite possible. Yellow/Blues are known for their warm and social approach to influencing others by establishing personal relationships. However, they can sometimes avoid conflict and reprimands in order to maintain good relationships, which can affect their ability to be consistent and involved in the decision-making processes.

Meanwhile, Blue/Yellows are focused on order and quality in their work, which sometimes leads to high expectations of their colleagues and frustration when the facts are presented in a disorganized fashion. They strive to make decisions based on quality and have a strong sense of the consequences of their actions, which can make them cautious when faced with big decisions.

Despite their different approaches, both Yellow/Blues and Blue/Yellows have a desire to maintain good relationships and influence others in a positive way, even if they encounter challenges relating to their unique personalities and ways of working.

22.6.2 Challenges

Both Yellow/Blues and Blue/Yellows face challenges when it comes to striking a balance between being friendly and candid, while also dealing with the pressure of making decisions. Yellow/Blues strive to please and avoid conflict, which can make it difficult for them to rebuke others or to make decisions that may cause tension. Blue/Yellows have to balance the need for exactitude and logical thinking with the pressure of making quick and accurate decisions, which can lead to difficulties handling big and urgent issues when there is insufficient information on hand.

22.6.3 Areas for Development for Yellow/Blues and Blue/Yellows

- They should be aware of potential difficulties with time management and control of time use.
- They should beware of overestimating their ability to motivate others and influence their behavior.
- Additionally, they need to recognize a lack of attention to detail, unless those details are considered significant. Sometimes those details may be important.
- It's great to be positive, but they should avoid excessive optimism about their own abilities and those of their colleagues.
- They should be aware that using praise excessively as a means of motivation can appear superficial to others.
- They should ensure decisions are based on proper analysis.
- It's also important that assessment of other people, especially friends, be realistic.
- They should avoid the tendency to be long-winded and verbose when offering criticism.
- They should also be aware of the temptation to surround themselves with like-minded people and to give up their own standpoint in order to avoid conflict. This may feel comfortable but it isn't always the right way forward.

- In a group, they should be aware they may be perceived as Red since they know all the answers and argue in favor of them.
- They should try to avoid becoming defensive and using others' mistakes to bolster their own position.

22.7 ENIGMATIC RED/GREENS

The attentive reader will have noticed that at the beginning of this chapter I mentioned the combination of Red and Green as the most unusual of all combinations.

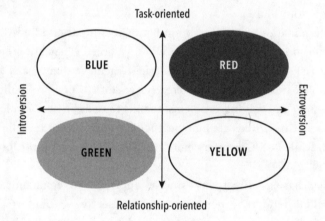

I believe this merits a brief explanation. When I say Red and Green, I'm referring to instances in which the proportion of each color is distinct and at about the same level in an individual. This also means the contributions of Blue and Yellow are considerably lower and may not even be visible.

What does that mean? Well, it produces an individual who is both prone to conflict and yet simultaneously averse to conflict. Someone who wants to express their strong views in most situations but who often holds back. Someone who thinks relationships take too much time and often get far too messy, while also wanting to be friends with everyone.

This is—in short—a complicated profile.

But why is this particular combination of colors so unusual? Not a clue. In my thirty or so years in this business, I've encountered this Red/Green profile just a handful of times, and all those people I met were very stressed. Likely as not because of these inner tensions.

Anyway, what follows is a description of what it can look like.

22.7.1 Behavior

Independence and goal-orientation: Both personality types are independent and have a strong vision. Green/Reds prefer to work according to a plan and have a stable, structured approach, while Red/Greens are more dynamic and innovative, always eagerly seeking new solutions.

Determination and risk-taking: Both Green/Reds and Red/Greens are determined and have a strong will to succeed. They are prepared to take risks and make changes in order to achieve their goals.

Problem management and creativity: Both types are skilled at identifying and solving problems, thanks to their critical and logical approach. Green/Reds are more methodical and focused on following a plan, while Red/Greens are more creative and always on the lookout for new solutions.

They have a direct and sincere approach to communication. Green/Reds tend to be more reserved and selective with information, while Red/Greens are more outgoing and can sometimes be obstinate in their views.

They are considered stable, reliable, and responsive to the feelings of others. They prefer to work individually or in small, familiar groups. They are motivated by logic and have a methodical working style.

They are often perceived as bold, unabashed, and competitive. They are driven by a strong sense of self-esteem and the desire to win. They are creative and visionary, but can sometimes fall short in terms of empathy and flexibility in their communication.

22.7.2 Challenges

They show resistance to change and a lack of flexibility, which creates communication challenges and difficulties in dealing with criticism. Red/Greens also tend to take big risks without carrying out sufficient analysis, which can be problematic.

22.7.3 Areas for Development for Red/Greens and Green/Reds

- They should endeavor not to take criticism of their work personally.
- These people may sometimes need help prioritizing new tasks, and they should be open to this.
- They should also strive not to take it to heart if their personal convictions are questioned.
- They should recognize when they have difficulty prioritizing tasks and meeting deadlines.
- They should be aware of suppressing their own views on various issues.
- They find it difficult to address violations of the rules or slapdash working and need to work on this.
- They should beware of becoming underconfident when urgent decisions need to be made without sufficient information.
- They should try not to underestimate their own abilities.
- It is also possible that these people may make ill-considered comments that can be perceived as personal insults. They should be aware of this and think before speaking!
- They should avoid setting unreasonably high standards for both themselves and others, as these may make goals unrealistic.

22.8 MIXED PROFILES: A SUMMARY

So there we have it: some of the most common combinations. But as I mentioned before, there are more out there. Add a little Yellow to a Blue/Red and they will be perceived as more open and easygoing. Swap the Yellow for Green in that same person and they will seem a little softer.

Or take a decidedly extroverted profile—how about our Red/Yellow?—and add a dash of Blue. You'll see the tempo come down a notch and the analytical traits will intervene to weigh up the Yellow's craziest of plans.

We could go on and on, but as I've emphasized, you need to understand the basic ingredients in the mixture before you can drill down into the details. A book with all the 19,500 combinations would not sell at all.

22.8.1 Some Statistics

About 5 percent of the population present almost solely one color.

About 80 percent present a combination of two colors. These combinations can be any two colors and in any order.

The remaining 15 percent present a combination of three colors. The author himself belongs to this group.

The most common color is Green, but as the data above suggests, this is most usually found in combination with another color.

Red is the most unusual color. Around 9.5 percent of the population present Red as their strongest factor.

In purely mathematical terms, this makes wholly Red profiles very unusual indeed. Only half a percent of the population are solely Red. So if you bump into a pure Red, you'll be sure to notice. That is, if we're to believe my wife, who happens to be one of them.

What the Colors Can't Reveal

23.1 AN EXPLANATION OF WHAT FEELS WRONG ABOUT THE FOUR COLORS

One question I've been asked frequently following the worldwide success of *Surrounded by Idiots* is whether it's really true that all Reds behave the same way. Or Yellows—or any other color.

And the answer to that is clear: No, they don't.

Why not? How can two individuals with pretty much the same combination of colors still be perceived as quite different?

This question is very relevant and the answer isn't that there's something wrong with the system. No, the answer is simply that there is a difference between *how* you behave and *why* you do it.

And the question of *why* leads us to the elements of an individual that the DISC model simply cannot explain. Fortunately, there are plenty of tools we can use to add further insight on human behavior.

So let's spend some time exploring this issue of *why* in further depth.

23.2 AN INDIVIDUAL'S DRIVING FORCES

The factors underlying our driving forces are our values and our interests. When these combine to create desire and commitment, we can refer to them as a driving force.

If, however, those values and interests don't give rise to any desire, then they are not a driving force. For example, you might think you should do the right and responsible things in life (this is a value) and understand that it's important to get education and training so you can earn money (this is an interest) without these things actually arousing any particular desire to do anything.

If, however, the same value and interest trigger a desire and therefore create energy, that's a driving force. The person in question *wants* to get an education. Getting an education becomes something that feels right and important to this person.

If their interest diminishes (they finally bag their dream job and no longer need to upskill), that desire and driving force may also diminish and be replaced by entirely different ambitions. Of course, the desire and therefore the driving force to follow the same path may also remain strong, even if the person has secured a job. It varies from person to person. There are those who constantly want to learn new things, regardless of other circumstances.

There's a big difference in how efficiently we approach a task, depending on whether it's done with passion and the desire to succeed, or whether it's done half-heartedly.

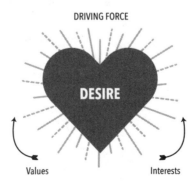

Our driving forces—the things that make our hearts beat faster—are what make the difference. If a task aligns with our driving forces, we mobilize extra reinforcements and energy to make a success of it. We become passionate, and throwing ourselves into the task wholeheartedly is easy.

23.2.1 Driving Forces Explain Why We Want to Do Certain Things

Behind effective actions we find a desire and a reason rooted in a person's driving forces. There may be various driving forces behind a single action.

Who would bother to read a book about the origins of rhetoric? Well, there are actually plenty of reasons why you might.

1. Someone might think it's an important and exciting topic. Reading the book will enable them to learn more, regardless of whether there's any actual value to them from knowing more about rhetoric.
2. Someone else might read the book cover to cover because the content appears to be useful. For instance, you can use it to earn money by organizing a course on rhetoric. A lot of people out there need to become better speakers, so there ought to be a market for it.
3. Yet another person might plow through the book because it's part of their personal development. They see it as a step toward becoming a better rhetorician.
4. A fourth sees the book as an obvious must-read—they believe the book's contents can help them help others become better at whatever it's about.
5. A fifth individual sees a book on rhetoric as an opportunity to get a head start and perhaps boost their personal qualities in certain contexts. Being able to express yourself well gives you a certain power over others.
6. And finally, perhaps you decide to read the book because it seems to align with your own values. Or you might really like the ancient Greeks.

23.3 THREE LEVELS OF DRIVING FORCES

23.3.1 Personal Driving Forces

Not all driving forces work the same way. We'll start by talking about personal driving forces, which are the most deeply rooted core motivations an individual possesses. These come straight from our innermost selves and are the result of personal experiences, values, and beliefs. They give us an immediate sense of inner satisfaction. For example, an individual's personal driving force may be to strive to be honest and fair in all situations, and they feel an immediate sense of satisfaction when this principle is adhered to.

23.3.2 External Driving Forces

External driving forces are those influenced by external factors, such as the values of an organization or society at large. These values are generally weaker than personal driving forces. However, if these align with an individual's personal driving forces, that can engender strong motivation and a sense of purpose in them.

For example, if an individual prioritizes environmental protection and works for an organization that also prioritizes this, it may give them a sense of harmony and fulfillment. If the driving forces are not in harmony, it can instead cause disappointment. This is because the personal inner satisfaction (derived from the personal driving force) is not achieved, despite the fact that the organization's driving force has been achieved, or vice versa.

23.3.3 Displaced or Inactive Driving Forces

These are driving forces that exist within us but are yet to rise to the surface. In many ways, these driving forces are the most deeply rooted ones we have.

A driving force of this kind can remain waiting in the wings for much of someone's life but emerge and become tangible when the time is right. This may be because previous driving forces have been fulfilled or because a repressed motive has been awakened through maturity and self-awareness.

A common example is when an individual leaves a successful career to pursue another passion or lifestyle. For example, someone who has previously focused on their career and financial success may discover a hidden passion for art or nature and choose to pursue this instead.

A previously repressed or inactive driving force may therefore have been activated, either because other driving forces have previously been satisfied and fulfilled, or because the person has matured and affirmed a driving force that was previously repressed.

23.3.4 Driving Forces in Flux

Driving forces can change over time, and sometimes this can happen quite quickly. This can occur for several different reasons:

- The interest underlying a driving force may have changed. A clear example of this is people who spend a long time striving to become financially independent. If that goal is achieved, the interest and driving force can change direction toward other goals and other driving forces. If you win the lottery, you may feel you're home free on the financial front.
- Our values can also be influenced as we mature and gain impressions of events and other people, and that too can affect our driving forces. For instance, this can apply to people who get involved in a range of organizations after suffering from illness or having an accident that strongly affected them.
- Our values and interests are also affected in the long term by the social currents that influence us externally. There's a whole bunch of things happening in the world around us and naturally those influence us, too.

23.3.5 Driving Forces That Influence Each Other

Most studies show that two or three driving forces dominate a person's approach to life. Sometimes there is an interplay where the person's strongest driving forces come to the fore in different situations. When the strongest driving forces work together, you achieve the strongest motivations.

It is also the case that a person's weakest driving forces can have a significant impact on their commitment and motivation. The weakest driving forces can create a real aversion toward the characteristic traits of the driving force in question.

For example, someone with a very low theoretical driving force will—out of pure principle—be opposed to the theoretical pursuit of knowledge.

23.3.6 How Driving Forces Affect Our Behavior

Our driving forces are like the engines of our lives and don't just control our behavior at work; they also influence us in countless situations and areas of life as a whole. Let's take a closer look at how these driving forces play a crucial role in our daily lives.

23.4 OUR TASKS

Driving forces govern what we choose to dedicate our energy to and where our passions lie. This means they have a significant impact on our professional lives. Finding a job that fits like a glove can be a real challenge. For example, someone with a strong social driving force may feel most satisfied when they are working in customer service, while they will experience less enthusiasm when engaged in sales. At the same time, an individual with a strong practical-economic driving force will feel more motivated and energized by tasks that involve financial planning or strategy.

23.4.1 In a Group

When people with different driving forces have to work together, they focus on different aspects of the task at hand. This means that they bring different perspectives and skills to the group, which can be advantageous for the whole. For example, someone with a strong traditional driving force can contribute stability and security in established methods and routines, while someone with a strong theoretical driving force can offer analytical thinking and problem-solving skills.

23.5 MOTIVATIONAL FACTORS

Different people are motivated by different rewards, depending on their driving forces. While someone with a strong social driving force may prefer the gratifying feeling of helping others as their primary reward, someone with a strong individualistic driving force can be far more motivated by personal success or recognition by the outside world. No one option is more right than any other; we have to accept that we're all wired differently.

23.6 PERSONAL DEVELOPMENT

Different driving forces also lead to different forms of personal development. The same is true in relation to growth, both at an individual level and in groups, but also in whole organizations. For example, an individual with a strong aesthetic driving force can develop their creative abilities through artistic expression, while someone with a strong practical-economic driving force can focus on developing their business and leadership skills, which will obviously serve the organization as a whole.

23.6.1 Individual Strengths

Each individual has unique strengths that stem from their driving forces. By understanding and using these driving forces efficiently, both individuals and those around them can benefit from their full potential. For example, a person with a strong theoretical driving force can be a top-class performer in the fields of research and problem-solving, while someone with a strong social driving force can stand out in their customer relations and teamwork.

23.6.2 Individual Weaknesses

Alongside their strengths, each driving force also has associated weaknesses that need to be developed and strengthened. For example, a person with a strong individualistic driving force can sometimes be overly focused on their own goals and needs at the expense of others' perspectives and needs.

23.7 UNDERLYING STRESS FACTORS

In many cases, the driving forces are the underlying source of stress, and different individuals are stressed by different factors depending on their driving forces. It's important to be aware of these stress factors in order to manage and mitigate them efficiently. For example, someone with a strong practical-economic driving force may feel stressed by economic uncertainty or by being unable to achieve their financial goals.

Right, there you have it: the basics on how these issues affect us. But what driving forces are out there? I'm sure you could rattle off all sorts of phenomena that motivate different people to do different things. There are those who say that everything humankind does stems from a very limited number of basic instincts.

A common assumption is that this boils down to just two things: sex and power. Others think it's *all* about sex. Well, except for sex, which is about power.

I suspect that's a little too simplistic as an explanation; I believe people are generally more advanced than that.

23.8 THE PURSUIT OF KNOWLEDGE AND TRUTH

People with a strong theoretical driving force have an inherent desire to explore and understand the truth behind phenomena and events. They prefer an intellectual and rational approach to achieving their goals, rather than allowing themselves to be pulled along by emotions. Their curiosity leads them to seek out similarities and differences, and to carefully observe and discuss a range of subjects.

Through systematic reasoning and logical thought, they are able to find the answers to the questions they pose. They're skilled at using existing knowledge and experience to analyze and comprehend the situations they are faced with. This makes them excellent problem solvers in their fields.

Despite their pursuit of truth, their focus on the past can limit their ability to deal with future challenges. Their driving force is often a deep thirst for knowledge and a passion for gathering this knowledge for the sake of it.

23.8.1 General Features

- They reason their way to solutions: They use systematic reasoning to solve problems and understand complex subjects.
- They are curious: Their strong curiosity drives them to explore and learn new things—constantly.
- They want to be well-read and have a lot of information: They strive to be well-informed and appreciate having an extensive knowledge base.
- They want to understand things and put them in context: They strive not only to learn facts, but also to understand how the various parts work together.

- They emphasize objectivity and rational thought: They
  prefer to base their views and decisions on objective facts
  and logic.

The theoretical driving force can manifest itself in various ways depending on the individual's other driving forces and behavioral patterns. This combination affects their approach to the pursuit of knowledge and problem-solving in a range of situations.

The driving force can manifest itself as a spectrum. But what does this mean? The implication is that, in practice, each driving force has two different perspectives. You can think of it as two sides of the same coin, if you prefer. But it's not a black-and-white case of one or the other; just like with extroversion and introversion, people are all to be found on the same spectrum. You're usually somewhere in the center of this spectrum, and the same is true for all driving forces.

THE DRIVING FORCE CAN MANIFEST ITSELF ON AN AXIS

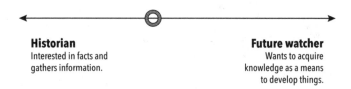

Historian
Interested in facts and
gathers information.

Future watcher
Wants to acquire
knowledge as a means
to develop things.

As you can see from the illustration above, a theoretician may seek out knowledge to understand what has happened on a very exact basis (historian), or they may be very focused on obtaining new knowledge in order to influence the future (future watcher). The circle indicates where the person in question may be on the scale.

23.8.2 Possible Limitations

- These people may have difficulties dealing with practical
  problems. For them, most things boil down to theoretical
  reasoning.
- They don't set aside time for people who see things differ-

ently from themselves, especially if they're emotional and have very few facts to support their views.
- They can end up digging down into the details, which can entail delays.

23.8.3 Stress Factors

People with a strong theoretical driving force can be stressed by this:

- Their quest for the truth and to understand contexts and connections can become a burden if they are confronted with a person who doesn't feel the same degree of joy at the pursuit of knowledge.

23.8.4 Good Communication Is Achieved By:

- Focusing the conversation on logic, objective facts, and experiences.
- Focusing on problem-solving.
- Referring to existing research. This is important.

23.8.5 Weak Theoretical Driving Force

A person who has a weak (or very weak) theoretical driving force is negative or indifferent to the intensive pursuit of knowledge. References to scholarship and knowledge that they can't see with their own eyes are of no value.

23.8.6 Example

Imagine you're at a party hosted at your friend Anna's. She's known for her passionate interest in science and philosophy. During the course of the evening, you end up in lively discussion with her about the mysteries of the universe and various existential issues.

While the other guests dance and chat, you and Anna sit in the corner and plunge ever deeper into an intellectual discussion about quantum mechanics and the philosophical meaning of time and space. You're mostly nodding along since you don't really understand a word of what she's saying, but Anna is deeply engaged and her reasoning flows freely as she examines various theories and hypotheses.

All of a sudden, you notice the party has continued without you and you've become so engrossed in the conversation you've both lost track of time. Even though the other partygoers are trying to include you in the laughter and dancing, you're completely absorbed in your thoughts and discussions.

In fact, you realize that you've missed much of the party, but for the two of you, the intellectual exchange has been the true highlight of the evening. For the two of you, the pursuit of knowledge and truth is what really drives you, and nothing can compete with the exciting world of ideas and theories.

23.8.7 Conclusion

A theoretical driving force can lead to a deep fascination with intellectual subjects and a strong desire to understand complex contexts.

People with a strong theoretical driving force can sometimes become so engrossed in their thoughts and conversations that they have no sense of time and lose touch with what is going on around them.

While they may miss out on certain social events, the intellectual stimulation and exchange of ideas is what brings them the most joy and satisfaction.

23.9 STRIVING FOR PRACTICAL BENEFITS AND USEFULNESS

People with a strong practical-economic driving force have an inherent desire to make efficient use of all available resources in order to achieve tangible results. For them, all resources are valuable—these can be time, money, or other assets.

Their driving force also means they want financial and economic security not only for themselves but also their families, both in the present and the future. Their approach to managing their financial assets varies. Some prefer to spend, while others prefer to save for the future.

Identifying and exploiting what is practical and useful is a key tenet of this driving force. They are often creative when it comes to solving practical problems and planning for future needs. This ability can be expressed in a number of ways ranging from saving money to organizing their lives in an efficient and safe way.

The goals of people with this driving force can vary widely. Some strive to accumulate material assets, while others focus on a practical and stable living situation. Regardless of their individual goals, they can be very goal-oriented and have the ability to adapt and stretch their goals if and when they reach them.

Some set the bar low, while others set it so high it takes them their whole lives to achieve their goals. Sometimes they set loftier and loftier goals as they achieve their original goals. This can, in turn, lead to people with this driving force becoming wholly focused on work and forgetting all about the concept we know as free time.

23.9.1 General Features

- Forward-thinking: They're focused on achieving results and making a return on their investments.
- Practically inclined: Their mindset is practical and action-oriented.
- Efficient at management: They're skilled at managing and reusing resources in a smart way.
- Business-focused: Many have an interest in business and finance.
- Strong in time management and results: They're good at planning their time and working toward achieving tangible outcomes.

The practical-economic driving force can manifest itself in various ways depending on the individual's other driving forces and behavioral patterns. This combination of driving forces and behaviors affects how they approach their goals and handle different situations in life.

It's the same thing as with the theoretical driving force. Either you want to preserve what you've already achieved (manager) or you're working hard to create something new (producer).

THE DRIVING FORCE CAN MANIFEST ITSELF ON AN AXIS

Manager
Wants to preserve what has already been achieved.

Producer
Wants to use resources to create new things and develop things.

23.9.2 Possible Limitations

- They may be workaholics. They can't stop chasing results.
- They can end up focusing too much on their own gain.
- They can have difficulty with tasks they don't perceive as efficient or that don't generate clear outcomes.

23.9.3 Stress Factors

People with a strong practical-economic driving force can be stressed by these things:

- A perceived waste of resources, time, and materials.
- Investments that yield insufficient or no returns.

23.9.4 Good Communication Is Achieved By:

- Focusing conversation on the returns on investments that have already been made.
- Establishing the accuracy of whether time and resources invested have generated the anticipated return.

- Ensuring that the promised return on investment is of value to these people.

23.9.5 Weak Practical-Economic Driving Force

A person with a weak practical-economic driving force is not interested in returns on their investments. Time and money are invested without much thought. The outcome is of little importance.

23.9.6 Example

Imagine you're at a flea market with your friend Johan. He's known for his sharp financial know-how and his ability to cut a great deal. You're strolling around and Johan is imbued with a sense of anticipation as he searches for items that might be either useful or valuable.

While other visitors to the event turn up their noses at old furniture and pointless trinkets no one really wants, Johan stops at every table to examine each item. He uses his keen eye to assess the potential and value of each old object, and he doesn't shy away from haggling with the stallholders.

Gradually, you notice that Johan is captivated by his pursuit of a bargain and opportunities. He demonstrates astonishing creativity as he devises different ways to use or sell the objects he finds. For him, it's not just a case of spending money—it's about making smart investments and making a return on what he puts in. He simply can't help thinking that he can secure a better price for these things elsewhere.

After a few hours at the flea market, Johan has filled several boxes with his treasures, and as you leave he's beaming with satisfaction. For him, this visit wasn't just a fun day out with a friend—it was also a strategic opportunity to manage his resources and make smart financial choices.

23.9.7 Conclusion

People with strong practical-economic driving forces strive to use their resources optimally and are good at making smart investments.

They often show great creativity when it comes to finding practical solutions and business opportunities.

While they may be focused on financial successes and returns, their driving force is not only to maximize their profits but also to maintain and reuse their resources in an efficient manner.

And take note of this: It doesn't have to be about money. It's all about resources.

23.10 STRIVING FOR INNER BALANCE AND SELF-REALIZATION

People with a strong aesthetic driving force seek inner harmony and a feeling of self-realization through experiences of beauty and aesthetics. For them, experiences are not just a sequence of events; they are an opportunity to appreciate beauty and harmony at any given moment.

Their inner vision leads them to pursue different ways of expressing their emotions and experiences. Enjoying the beautiful details of life is a central part of their being, and they appreciate loveliness, symmetry, and form in all they do. While they are not necessarily artistically talented, they have a deep interest in aesthetics in life.

For some, this driving force may be reflected in their work, where their desire to acquire beautiful things or to experience the beauty of nature can serve as a motivation for hard work. For others, satisfaction is derived from living a harmonious life and surrounding themselves with whatever they find beautiful and inspiring.

23.10.1 General Features

- A feeling for beauty and harmony: They have a natural ability to appreciate the beauty and harmony of life around them.
- Self-realization is important: They strive to achieve a feeling of inner balance and personal development.

- Enjoying the beauty of life: Enjoying the small details in life is an important part of their lifestyle.
- Interest in aesthetics: Regardless of artistic ability, they prioritize anything that is expressive, moving, and beautiful.
- Balance and enjoyment: Maintaining a balanced lifestyle and having time to enjoy the beauty around them are important to them.

The aesthetic driving force can manifest itself in various ways depending on the individual's other driving forces and behavioral patterns. This combination influences how they integrate beauty and harmony into their lives and how they relate to the world around them.

23.10.2 Possible Limitations

- These people may have difficulty focusing.
- They can be perceived as illogical dreamers.
- They may lack an aptitude for practical solutions.

THE DRIVING FORCE CAN MANIFEST ITSELF ON AN AXIS

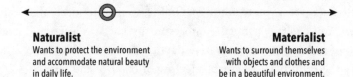

Naturalist
Wants to protect the environment and accommodate natural beauty in daily life.

Materialist
Wants to surround themselves with objects and clothes and be in a beautiful environment.

23.10.3 Stress Factors

People with a strong aesthetic driving force can be stressed by these things:

- Disorder in form, harmony, and beauty in themselves or others, or in their surroundings.
- Objective truths that are not influenceable.

23.10.4 Good Communication Is Achieved By:

- Focusing the conversation on subjective experiences—whether of the individual or others.
- Trying to establish form and harmony.
- Striving to remove pain and discomfort.

23.10.5 Weak Aesthetic Driving Force

A person with a weak (or very weak) aesthetic driving force is negative toward or uninterested in form and harmony, as well as subjective experiences and creative modes of expression.

23.10.6 Example

You visit your friend Stefan, who is known for his pronounced sense of what is beautiful and harmonious in life. As you step across the threshold into his home, you are met with an atmosphere of tranquility and beauty. Every object in his apartment appears to have been carefully selected to create a sense of harmony and well-being. Everything works together. Materials, shapes, colors. Nothing is there by chance.

Stefan invites you to take a seat in the beautifully decorated living room. You can't help but be impressed by the way each and every item of furniture and decorative detail seem to be positioned in exactly the right place to create a feeling of balance and beauty.

During the conversation, Stefan becomes impassioned as he tells you about his interest in art, design, and the aesthetics of beauty. He tells you about his latest discoveries and talks about how he spends his time exploring art exhibitions, hiking in the great outdoors, and making beautiful things with his own two hands.

You can tell that Stefan really does live in the here and now and appreciates every moment of beauty and harmony he experiences. For him, it's not just about appreciating beauty; it's also about creating it himself and sharing it with others.

23.10.7 Conclusion

People with a strong aesthetic driving force strive for an inner balance and self-realization by enjoying the beauty in life.

They have a sense of what is beautiful and harmonious and spend their time surrounding themselves with beauty in their daily lives.

While they may be perceived as illogical dreamers, they have an ability to create and experience beauty that enriches their lives and brings them a sense of well-being.

And—important—they don't have to be arty. It's all about the pursuit of harmony.

23.11 STRIVING TO HELP OTHERS AND ALLEVIATE DIVISION

People with a strong social driving force have a deep desire to help and support their fellow human beings. Their benevolence and selflessness reflect their inner love for people and their belief that love forms the basis of all human relationships.

These individuals are sensitive and understanding, and they often have great empathy toward others. Their ability to empathize with other people's thoughts and emotions allows them to provide support and assistance even in the most demanding of situations. Their joy is derived from being able to contribute to the well-being and development of others, and they are willing to help others even if it involves personal sacrifice.

23.11.1 General Features

- Feeling joy in helping and supporting: Their satisfaction comes from being able to help and support other people.
- Seeing the potential in other people: They believe in and encourage other people's abilities and potential for development.

- Standing up for others: Their compassion and empathy mean they are ready to support and help others, even when doing so is difficult or entails personal sacrifice.
- Eager to contribute to others' development: They are keen to be a positive force in other people's lives and strive to help them with personal growth and development.

The social driving force can manifest itself in various ways depending on how it is combined with other driving forces and behavioral patterns in the individual. This combination affects how they interact with others and what type of support and help they offer in various situations.

23.11.2 Possible Limitations

- These people may be very self-sacrificing.
- They may have difficulties setting boundaries.

THE DRIVING FORCE CAN MANIFEST ITSELF ON AN AXIS

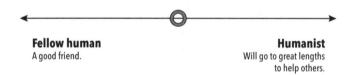

Fellow human
A good friend.

Humanist
Will go to great lengths
to help others.

23.11.3 Stress Factors

People with a strong social driving force can be stressed by these things:

- Too much concentration on economic and financial results.
- Decisions or actions that don't take into account other people's feelings.
- Not being able to be of service, or wanting to help but being unable to.

23.11.4 Good Communication Is Achieved By:

- Focusing on how things can be improved for others.
- Discussing how discomfort and conflict will decrease and how people's opportunities will increase.

23.11.5 Weak Social Driving Force

A person with a weak (or very weak) social driving force is uninterested in supporting and helping others.

23.11.6 Example

Meet Sofia: She's a woman with a strong social driving force who always seems to have a positive attitude and a smile on her face. She's known in the neighborhood for her helpful, considerate manner, and it's not unusual to see her involved in local and charitable initiatives helping those in need.

One day, you spot Sofia on the street; she has stopped to talk to an elderly neighbor who seems to need assistance carrying her groceries home. Without hesitation, Sofia offers her help and carries the heavy bags all the way to the neighbor's front door. You notice how grateful the neighbor is for Sofia's kindness and care.

In conversation, Sofia describes her range of volunteering activities and how she is passionate about making a difference in the lives of others. She talks about the people she has met and how her ability to put herself in their shoes has enabled her to offer help and support when it is most needed.

You notice how Sofia really does live in accordance with her belief that love is the basis of all human relationships; her desire to help others is a natural extension of this conviction. For her, it's not just about offering practical help—it's also about being there for others on a deeper, more meaningful level.

23.11.7 Conclusion

People with a strong social driving force strive to help people and show empathy for their situation.

They are inclined to put other people's needs ahead of their own, and take joy in being able to contribute to others' well-being.

While they may experience difficulties in setting boundaries and risk becoming too self-sacrificing, their willingness to help others is a central pillar of their identity and philosophical outlook on life.

23.12 STRIVING TO WIN, GAIN POWER AND CONTROL

Individualists are driven by a strong desire to achieve power, control, and success. They are often very competitive and are energized by challenges and opportunities to show off their abilities. For some of these people, their primary goal is to achieve personal power, influence, and recognition, while others prioritize control over their own lives.

It's important to understand that the individualistic driving force is about more than just wanting to dominate or control other people. For some, it's about having the freedom to act and the ability to shape their own destiny without external influences. These individuals are often inclined toward leadership roles and utilize their driving force to achieve success in their careers and personal lives.

23.12.1 General Features

- They strive for power, influence, and success: Their primary goal is to achieve power and control over their own situation, and to be successful in their endeavors.
- They desire freedom of action: They value their independence and strive to gain control over their own lives and decisions.
- They eagerly lead others: Their strong personality and driving force make them good leaders and they often thrive in roles where they can exercise influence and control.

- They are powerful careerists: They're ambitious and focused on achieving their career goals, and they are prepared to work hard to achieve success.
- They are competitive: They thrive in competitive environments and are motivated by the opportunity to outperform others and show off their abilities.

The individualistic driving force can manifest itself in different ways depending on how it is combined with other driving forces and personal characteristics. This combination affects how individuals act and interact with other people, as well as which strategies they use to achieve their goals and aspirations.

23.12.2 Possible Limitations

- They pick their tactics and strategy in life and follow them doggedly for good or ill.
- They can make others feel steamrolled.
- They always want to get their own way.

THE DRIVING FORCE CAN MANIFEST ITSELF ON AN AXIS

Self-steerer
Wants to be able to control
their own life.

Controller
Wants power to be able
to influence others.

23.12.3 Stress Factors

People with a strong individualistic driving force can be stressed by these things:

- Real or perceived threats of a reduction in or loss of position or power.
- The inability to advance or the lack of opportunity to do so.
- Being forced to report to someone they don't respect.

23.12.4 Good Communication Is Achieved By:

- Focusing on possible routes to promotion or success.
- Talking about how their professional role and influence can be used to help others.
- Inviting them to participate in decision-making processes.

23.12.5 Weak Individualistic Driving Force

A person with a weak (or very weak) individualistic driving force doesn't care much about their career and is negative about or uninterested in people with strong individualistic driving forces.

23.12.6 Example

Lisa is a woman with a strong individualistic driving force who always seems to be in control of her life. To her friends and colleagues, Lisa is known for being ambitious and for relentlessly pursuing success. She thrives when challenged and is driven by the desire for personal power and good performance.

One day, you see Lisa taking on responsibility for a project at work. She confidently delegates all the tasks and makes all the strategic decisions to ensure the project's success. Her confidence and decisiveness are apparent as she navigates obstacles and leads her team with implacable confidence.

In a conversation Lisa shares with you her ambitions to progress in her career and her goal of becoming a leader in her field. She talks about her indefatigable pursuit of success and her desire to do what it takes to achieve her goals. For Lisa, personal power and influence aren't just ambitions—they're critical components in her identity and peace of mind.

You can tell that Lisa's competitive nature drives her to constantly seek out opportunities for growth and progress—both professionally and in her personal life. She really thrives in environments where she is in control and can have a significant impact, and where she is able to use her leadership skills to inspire and motivate others to surpass themselves.

23.12.7 Conclusion

People with a strong individualistic driving force strive for control and power, and often show competitive and ambitious traits in their efforts.

They are driven by the desire for personal success and recognition, and seek out opportunities to lead and influence others.

While their independence and decisiveness can lead to success, they can also encounter challenges in balancing their pursuit of power with the needs and perspectives of others.

23.13 STRIVING TO FOLLOW THE "RIGHT WAY"

People with a strong traditional driving force are driven by a deep desire to live in accordance with an established set of values or a system that provides clear guidance on what is right and wrong. Their moral compass guides them toward the "right way"—as they see it. This system may be rooted in religious faith, a philosophy, or other outlooks on life.

These individuals are often very focused on maintaining and preserving traditions and historical norms. They value stability and see traditions as important building blocks of society. At the same time, they can also be driven by a desire to influence and change the system in order to adapt it to their inner beliefs and to create a deeper meaning of existence.

23.13.1 General Features

- These people seek meaning in life: They strive to understand the overarching meaning of life and to seek an understanding of the world around them.
- They are often looking for a deeper meaning in life: They

aren't satisfied with superficial explanations and seek to find a deeper purpose to their existence.

- They often have spiritual interests: Many people with a traditional driving force have a strong interest in spiritual issues and seek out answers to the great existential questions of life.
- They follow their values: Their actions and decisions are controlled by their inner values and beliefs, even when that means going against established norms and expectations.

The traditional driving force can manifest itself in different ways depending on how it is combined with other driving forces and the individual's characteristics. These factors affect how the person navigates a course through life and interacts with their surroundings.

23.13.2 Possible Limitations

- They may have their own evaluation of what is right and wrong.
- They act according to their own values instead of those of the organization.
- They lack understanding for other points of view.

THE DRIVING FORCE CAN MANIFEST ITSELF ON AN AXIS

Conservationist
Wants to preserve systems, traditions, and regulations.

Reverser
Wants to create and change systems, traditions, and regulations.

23.13.3 Good Communication Is Achieved By:

- Focusing the conversation on the meaning of life.
- Adding spiritual elements to the conversation.

- Showing how your plans lead to the ideal state.
- Talking about how their ideas improve the world.

23.13.4 Stress Factors

People with a strong traditional driving force can be stressed by these things:

- Their beliefs not being understood by others.
- People who have completely different values from their own.

23.13.5 Weak Traditional Driving Force

A person with a weak (or very weak) traditional driving force is negative and unsympathetic toward people with a strong traditional driving force who live by strict rules.

23.13.6 Example

Henrik is a man with a strong traditional driving force who is characterized by his deep connection to traditions and values. He lives his life according to a well-defined set of principles, and strives to follow a clear moral and ethical pathway in life.

To his friends and family, Henrik is known for his loyalty to his values and his commitment to upholding traditions. He sees value and meaning in sticking to the tried-and-true way of doing things, and he's passionate about handing these values down to the next generation.

A typical day for Henrik sees him follow a structured routine that is rooted in his traditional values. He takes time to reflect on the meaning of life and seeks to live in accordance with his inner beliefs. For Henrik, it's important to be a role model to others through his way of life and his behavior.

During a discussion about the family's values and traditions,

Henrik expresses pride in his heritage and emphasizes the importance of following the way paved for him by previous generations. He is convinced that a strong, coherent set of values is the key to a meaningful existence and he strives to embed these values into all his actions.

You can tell that Henrik's traditional driving force provides him with a sense of security and stability in a world that is in constant flux. He tackles life's challenges with a calm and certainty based on the knowledge that he is acting in accordance with his innermost beliefs.

23.13.7 Conclusion

People with a strong traditional driving force strive to live in accordance with a clear set of values and principles.

They value traditions and see them as a source of stability and meaning in life.

By following their inner beliefs and values, they seek to be role models to others and to pass on their legacy to the generations following in their footsteps.

24

Combining Colors and Driving Forces

24.1 THE ANSWER TO WHAT YOU'VE BEEN WONDERING ALL ALONG

Okay, so we've taken a brief look at what's often found under the surface and might not be visible upon first glance. Overt behaviors are those actions and reactions that a person shows outwardly, and which are often visible to others. This is where the DISC model can come in handy, by describing an individual's actions based on the four colors.

However, as I mentioned before, there are also shortcomings in this, given that behaviors do not necessarily reveal the underlying motivators or driving forces. Why does person X behave in a particular way in a specific situation? These behaviors can be the result of all sorts of factors, including social expectations, external influences, and passing emotions. Of course, there are also situations where all colors will surprise even themselves by behaving in a certain way and where everything will be far from logical.

At the same time, the motivational factors that lurk beneath the surface represent the deeper, more complex driving forces and beliefs that steer a person's actions and behaviors in a certain direction. These motivators are more personal in nature and often rooted in the individual's values, beliefs, past experiences, and emotional needs.

Attitudes can also have an impact, as do preconceived notions and even prejudices grounded in ignorance.

But unlike overt behaviors—colors—these motivators are not always visible or apparent to other people, and they may therefore be more subtle and difficult to detect. And that's what sometimes makes it tricky to interpret certain behaviors. A Red giving a good friend a piece of their mind doesn't exactly make the most winning impression on you, does it? But if they're doing it to help their friend escape a bad relationship, that behavior might be excused—now we know what's behind it.

The purpose of getting involved in the friend's personal life in the first place is to help—a social driving force. But the method is a raised voice and something of a rant—Red behavior.

Does that sound strange? It's not really that strange. An organization I once worked for had, in fact, a very Red middle manager who had a big heart. She would push her colleagues without hesitation, but she was also very caring.

On one occasion, I had noticed a number of warning signs in a key employee who was clearly on the brink of burnout. When she found out, the Red middle manager was on her feet quick as a flash, making for the employee in question. She scolded the person for not telling her about the overload and ordered them to take some time off. The colleague was sent home because the manager was worried about their mental health.

Sure, it both looked and sounded peculiar. I think all of us watching the incident thought that. But it was perfectly logical when you take a closer look.

Here's another: Years later, I crossed paths with a translator of French technical manuals. She was almost painfully Blue, dry as tinder, a really stony-faced lady. I don't think I saw her smile once in the four months we worked together.

Deadlines in her projects would often be missed because she wanted the manuals to *look good*. She worked with extraordinary intensity on the layout and design of every single page. Font size and typeface, colors, the position of images. The whole caboodle. How come?

That's easy. She had a powerful aesthetic driving force. It had to feel and look right. The way to a beautiful product was Blue behavior. Accuracy, a wealth of details, tenacity.

The difference between overt behaviors and underlying motivators is overt behaviors represent what is seen on the outside, which is the first thing people see. These are what create the very first impression, one an individual is often judged by.

And as we already know, it can be hard to shake off a first impression down the line.

The underlying motivators represent the deeper, more complex driving forces that underpin these behaviors. Understanding both overt behaviors and underlying motivators is important if we're to acquire a more complete grasp of someone's behavior and motivations.

But it means we need to be observant, and we need to use our imagination. It requires us not to make any sweeping judgments of people until we've actually understood them.

And that requires us to actively try to avoid judging people too quickly. That could be a mistake.

My basic tips for avoiding a catastrophic misstep here are these:

1. Try to find out what an individual's driving forces are.
2. Adapt your communication to suit the individual's color.

Why start with the driving forces when these aren't even visible? Well, that's the whole point. If you work on analyzing behaviors, you'll quickly get good at it. But figuring out what's hiding under the surface is much harder—so turn your focus to that.

24.2 DRIVING FORCES AND BEHAVIORS

Driving forces and behavioral styles—both individually and in combination—affect the way we act and behave. People who have the same driving forces can act and behave quite differently depending on their behavioral profile. A Green individualist and a Yellow individualist set side by side will look completely different. As ever, the colors affect the individual's behavior. Likewise, people who are the same color can act in differing ways depending on their driving forces. A Red with a theoretical driving force will feel different from a Red with a practical-economic driving force.

It's important to understand and be able to identify what distinguishes a driving force from a behavioral type. The pursuit of knowledge and wanting to learn new things are both examples of a theoretical driving force. Being meticulous and exacting (not to mention the gathering of wide swathes of information) is a behavior.

People with theoretical driving forces can behave in different ways as they go about their pursuit of knowledge: Reds will be goal-oriented, Yellows will be outward-oriented, Greens will be stable, and Blues will be detail-focused.

Blues may have driving forces that are entirely separate from the theoretical one that compels them to acquire accurate knowledge. It might be to help others (social driving force) or for their own personal development (aesthetic driving force).

Social Greens aren't necessarily driven by a social driving force. Behind their actions, there may be other driving forces, but they behave in a social and stable manner in order to achieve those driving forces' goals.

With six interacting driving forces and four behavioral dimensions all intersecting and affecting one another, we're dealing with a relatively complex system. As such, it's very important that we avoid gross generalizations and that we instead take each individual for the human being they are.

By the way, this is another answer to the question *Are there really only four categories of people?*

24.3 CORRELATION BETWEEN DRIVING FORCES AND BEHAVIORS

The following table lays out the statistical relationship (correlation) between driving forces and behaviors. This data is based on a specific

DISC tool that has then been combined with a specific driving force tool. I'm afraid I can't indicate which version this is drawn from, as that would provide an unnecessary competitive advantage for certain tools over others, which isn't my intention.

Okay, what does all this actually mean? According to these statistics, Yellows (high I) tend to have a strong individualistic driving force and vice versa.

	RED	YELLOW	GREEN	BLUE
Theoretical	-0.01	-0.04	-0.13	+0.15
Practical-economic	-0.04	-0.10	-0.02	-0.09
Aesthetic	+0.10	-0.02	+0.16	-0.04
Social	-0.97	-0.17	+0.46	+0.08
Individualistic	+0.20	+0.39	-0.44	-0.09
Traditional	-0.50	+0.001	-0.16	+0.21

Greens (high S) tend to have a strong social driving force and a weak individualistic driving force.

Beyond that, there are no statistically significant correlations to be found between driving forces and behaviors.

However, this does not mean there is a lack of Greens with strong individualistic driving forces or that there's no such thing as a Yellow who completely lacks such a driving force. Or indeed that there are no Reds with a strong social driving force, or no Yellows with a strong theoretical driving force.

24.4 WHAT CAN WE USE ALL THIS FOR?

Take a look at the following illustration. It shows an example of a person who is mostly pragmatic, receptive, efficient, and investigative. Those are this person's drivers. The way they behave is based on the colors, but the reason for that behavior is found in the driving forces.

Intuitive	THEORETICAL–KNOWLEDGE	Investigative
Unforced	PRACTICAL–ECONOMIC–BENEFIT	Effective
Pragmatic	AESTHETIC–SURROUNDINGS	Harmonious
Selective	SOCIAL–OTHER PEOPLE	Generous
Collaborative	INDIVIDUALISTIC–INFLUENTIAL	Controlling
Receptive	TRADITIONAL–VALUES	Principled

We can take a look at the first driving force: the theoretical one. This person is drawn less toward intuition and more toward the investigative side. In what ways is it possible to pursue knowledge?

Little of this is really connected to the colors.

24.5 THEORETICAL DRIVING FORCE VERSUS BLUE BEHAVIOR

We need to understand the difference between a driving force and a behavior.

24.5.1 Behavior

Being thorough, exacting, and analytical.

24.5.2 Driving Force

The pursuit of knowledge and wanting to learn new things.

As you can see in the previous illustration, we need to be able to distinguish between behavior and driving forces. The pursuit of knowledge is a driving force, while being thorough with facts and details is a behavior. But there's no connection between the two.

A Blue theoretician will want to know all about something and they will dedicate a lot of time to finding it out. The risk is that everything else grinds to a halt. They want to know everything and will be extraordinarily busy getting to the bottom of every element of any given process.

But a theoretician doesn't necessarily need to act Blue. Here's an example:

To make it interesting, let's go with a Yellow theoretician, mostly because you didn't expect that. They also want to know how things work, but they go about this in a different way. They are probably more likely to watch YouTube than they are to read a book. And instead of writing down everything they learn, they'll talk to all sorts of people and force them to listen to their fascination with the boxing skills of kangaroos, how to build apps, or whether there really are alligators in the New York sewers. The same desire for knowledge is found in both individuals, but they have completely different methods of pursuing it.

24.5.3 The Yellow Theoretician

I'm thinking of a guy I knew quite well some years ago. Petter was practically a caricature of Yellow behavior. Some of the things he said and did were so astounding that when I use him as an example in my lectures, I can sometimes see the skepticism writ large on the faces of the audience. *Do people like this really exist?*

I digress. Petter was a constant motormouth who talked about anything and everything, and he was messy beyond belief and stressfully unstructured in his ways. But at the same time, he was incredibly fun to have around. He could tell a story like almost no one else.

The interesting thing about Petter was that he also had a very distinct theoretical driving force. This fact meant that among those who actually knew him, he wasn't perceived as being as poorly read as you might expect a Yellow to be. Yellows often open their mouths without having connected to their hard drive first, and if you're not ready for that, then you can be surprised by a torrent of words that aren't actually saying much at all.

Petter, however, tended to find things out. He was incredibly curious in his nature, but he went about it in a Yellow way. One time, we were in his kitchen and I noticed several thick bundles of papers lying around. They were on the shelves, on a chair, on the table. Paper of every kind, stacked up. Messy, as often is the Yellow's way.

I ventured to ask what they were and he confided that he could never throw out stuff that came in the mail. Advertising, municipal flyers, free newspapers. The lot. Direct marketing. Forms he'd requested. Printouts of everything imaginable. He had to check through them to see whether there was anything of interest.

His wife told me there were more stacks of papers like this around the house. Petter simply couldn't bring himself to throw the stuff out because *he wanted to read it all*. Unfortunately, his Yellow profile meant that he wasn't able to bring any structure to this. Instead, all that happened was he cluttered the house with piles of paper, which to my eyes looked like they should be sent off for recycling.

There was another very illuminating incident. He called me one Sunday morning. Since I'm often up early, it didn't really matter, but you do tend to wonder what has happened when someone calls you at eight on a Sunday morning.

Petter was bursting to tell me something: "Thomas! Did you know that the moon . . . is older than the earth?!"

The reason for his wild enthusiasm was he'd been watching a bunch of YouTube videos all night—wearing headphones (and I would guess copious cups of coffee might also have been involved)—and he had found out that the earth was apparently younger than its own moon. Fascinating stuff. I admitted I was not aware of this fact—and to this day I am unable to confirm whether or not it's true.

But since Petter had learned this new fact and since he was so strikingly Yellow, he immediately felt compelled to tell someone. Whom did he know who might be up and about at that time on a Sunday?

Hi, Thomas!

Theoretical driving force, Yellow behavior.

It's not enough to just interpret your own colors or those of someone else. There's more to keep track of. The more you learn about this, the more tools you'll have in your arsenal to achieve really good dialogue with those around you in the workplace. Your partner, too.

Think about your own driving forces. By being aware of them, you can gain a greater understanding of your own actions in many different situations.

And the fact is once you're aware of what you're really passionate about, you'll find it much easier to summon your energy. Personally, I now feel much happier in my skin and far more settled in life than I was before I understood my own driving forces. Perhaps the same might be true for you?

If we approach this with leadership, then it's clear—to me at least— that there are managers who have taken on their jobs for the wrong reasons. And we also find a lot of bad and useless managers here.

24.6 THE AUTHOR'S OWN PROFILE AND WHAT WE CAN LEARN FROM IT

Now it's time for me to share a closely guarded secret—the answer to the question I'm asked hundreds of times a year. I usually try to dodge giving an answer, but here's the truth.

The following two graphs describe my communication profile. The left-hand graph shows my adapted profile—that's how I behave when working. The right-hand graph is my core profile, which means that my character is somewhat different when I'm not at work. My colors are mainly Red, Blue, and Yellow. There's quite a lot of all three, with Red coming highest, followed by Blue, and then slightly less Yellow—but there's a lot less Green. Hardly any at all, in fact. As you can see, the difference between the two graphs isn't all that dramatic, but nonetheless there is one. Since the right-hand graph is my true self without any adaptation, I think we can safely say it's mostly me.

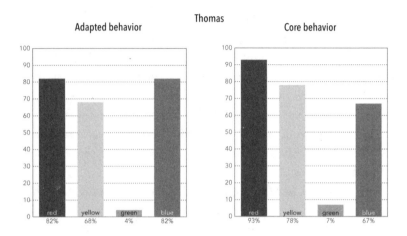

Thomas

Adapted behavior · Core behavior

24.6.1 The Difference Between Me When I'm Working and When I'm Not Working

According to these visuals, yours truly is somewhat less dominant when working than when not working, but I'm also less inspiring. On the other hand, I'm more analytical when working.

What does this tell us? Not very much, actually, since adaptation isn't the deciding factor in whether I need therapy or not.

All joking aside, making too many adaptations—ergo, too great a difference between core behaviors and adapted behaviors—can lead to problems. Long story short, it's for the best if I can be as much myself as possible when at work. But it does give rise to specific behaviors that I now understand rather well.

I can be incredibly impatient when my Red traits are taking the lead, but I can also be fairly analytical (ahem, I mean I'm slow) when my Blue self takes over. Just ask my wife. She's got even more Red in her than I do, but barely any Blue. Actually, scratch that: There's no Blue in her whatsoever. Details are her kryptonite.

Sometimes I plan far too much and search for holes and gaps in just about everything. And I still occasionally get completely stuck on tasks. What's more, because there is very little Green in me, I can be careless at taking in what other people are saying. It takes effort. I'm not proud to admit this, but I accept it's one of my weaknesses.

24.6.2 How Does This Mix Actually Work?

I realize the combination of lots of Red and lots of Blue sometimes makes me rather insensitive. But it also helps me do my job properly.

This is particularly true when I'm mentoring successful people across Europe (I'm an advisor to lots of executives). Let's look at an example: The CEO of a listed company (I appreciate this is bordering on bragging, but don't forget there's plenty of Yellow in me) asks me for advice on how to oversee their motley management team.

These people are on painfully tight schedules and already surrounded by yes-men. The last thing they want is to pay top dollar for a coach who just rambles on endlessly. They want the truth.

If I'm not appreciated for delivering the truth, that's just something I have to live with. My role in this is to be uncomfortable. I don't lose sleep over the fact that not everyone loves me or what I do.

It's all perfectly logical and I'm sure it'll be the same for you. You know your strengths and you're largely aware of your pitfalls.

24.7 TIRED OLD MEN

I was once at a conference where I was trying to listen to a series of presentations from a string of British psychologists. I say "trying" because the whole setup was mortally dull. They all seemed alike and were the polar opposite of entertaining.

Violent mental restraint was required on my part to stop myself from pulling out my phone and doing something else. I hate it when people do that and I consider it disrespectful. The knowledge these psychologists possessed—and no doubt it was extensive and valuable—was not the kind that I could listen to simply because it would be fun in and of itself.

And after being exposed to four (or was it five?) of these guys, I was so desperate I was ready to beat a retreat.

I stayed because I finally managed to find a reason to do so. Going back to why I had even shown up in the first place, I reminded myself I would be able to use the messages these speakers were imparting to me. There had to be something of worth here for me, and that aligned with my practical-economic driving force.

It's true. My theoretical driving force is quite weak. Together with a practical-economic driving force, this means that I prefer to confine my learning to things I need for my job.

Hmm. There's something in that. I read widely about psychology, behavior, and everything else that makes people tick. I'll often spot an interesting title—or a provocative one, such as *Surrounded by Idiots*—and think I ought to read it. Sounds exciting! This is a fairly frequent occurrence and I now own an extensive library specializing in subjects related to my profession.

But I don't read all the books I own. Some of them I'll only flip through; others I'll read a few chapters. Yet there are others I'll read cover to cover.

That's what happens when it's my assessment that the content is actually of use to me. Reading three or four hundred pages because something is fascinating isn't for me. It takes too long and life is too short.

But there are people who do the exact opposite. They'll read any book if it's on an interesting subject. It doesn't matter to me if you're reading this book for that reason, but it's not why I would do something. I'm too short on time.

How do I know? Well, my practical-economic driving force tells me. It strives for an efficient use of time, which means there is most definitely not time to read nonfiction tomes like others read novels. I'm not saying it's the right method—I'm just explaining what I do. If I want to be entertained, I read a thriller.

But it doesn't end here.

24.8 THE RIDDLE OF THE UNKNOWN DRIVING FORCE

Sometimes you need to dig a little deeper, right? As I mentioned at the beginning of the book, many years ago I worked in a bank. It was an acceptable job in many respects. I saw a lot of things, did a fair bit of traveling, and got to participate in various important projects. I trained people all over Sweden in sales, I made progress in my career, and I made a decent enough living.

All those activities stimulated my practical-economic driving force. The most important thing for me was generating results. I needed to see with my own eyes that my efforts were gaining a return. I'm not really talking about money here, even if that was part of it.

But there was something bothering me. No matter how hard I worked, I was less and less happy, even though I was doing most things right. I was being praised, I was getting promoted regularly, I was given a raise and a natty job title. Bank vice president at thirty years of age. That kind of thing. I even dimly recall a bonus of some sort, late on.

But something was wrong. My motivation was plummeting and no matter how hard I worked, it only got worse. In the end, it was so bad that I was having difficulty getting out of bed in the morning, and that had never been a problem for me before.

By fluke, I started trying out something that had been a long-term dream of mine—writing books. We don't need to delve into why it was my dream, but I've always been attracted to the idea of creating something from scratch on a blank sheet of paper. I have a very visual way of thinking and I like it when I get to use my imagination. That's one of the reasons why I prefer reading a book to watching a movie. In a film, everything is already done and set, but with a book I can create my own pictures using my imagination.

Not to mention writing the book all by myself. Wow!

As soon as I started writing, I found I was happier in life. I rediscovered my motivation, and I regained energy for all sorts of things. The fact is that I felt more harmonious. My entire self felt better.

At the time, I didn't really understand how these things were connected. But then I did a driving force analysis and suddenly all the pieces of the puzzle fell into place. When I realized that my second strongest driving force—almost as strong as my practical-economic one—was aesthetic, I realized why I had lost my vim at work.

I wasn't really creating anything anymore. Everything was regulated and there was basically no room for creativity. Everything had to conform to something.

The strange thing was when I was writing in the evenings and on weekends—with young children at home and a lot of business travel to boot—I became happier in my work, even though nothing about the job had changed.

Writing somehow made me a more complete person. The reason for this is the aesthetic driving force makes people strive for harmony and balance—and that's exactly what I got. My whole life came into balance.

The aesthetic driving force also explains a number of other decisions in my life. You see, I can't have the same car as my neighbor. Note: My car does not have to be in any way fancier or more expensive than everyone else's, but it does need to be different. This is because aesthetes want to feel unique. You could interpret this as Yellow behavior, but you'd be wrong. Yellows want to be first, but they also want whatever is popular.

If I were to spring for a really fancy car, I'd prefer a Jaguar or a Maserati to a Mercedes or a Cadillac, simply because they're a little less common.

I still have difficulty choosing the same option as everyone else—regardless of what that choice relates to. Insofar as it is possible, I want to feel unique. Logical? Not one bit.

If there's a moral to this story, it's that you should follow your heart if you want to feel at your best. Not to mention that your perspective can change as you move through life. Many of us have found other values as we have aged—no surprise there.

Before you start to feel nauseous at this saccharine observation, let me clarify what I'm saying: Driving forces are more important than many people think. Doing what you really like and what actually stimulates you is more valuable than you might realize.

The Relationship Bible—in Miniature

25.1 HOW TO MAKE YOUR MARRIAGE LAST (LONGER)

I don't usually give relationship advice, but I've learned the hard way that driving forces and core values are more important to a functioning relationship than mere behavior.

Blues and Yellows can live together quite happily if their lives include things that stimulate both their driving forces. If one of them is chasing money and the other is more aesthetically inclined, there will be a collision of priorities. And that's when problems will arise. They'll have a hard time listening to each other's arguments since they also don't communicate the same way.

There are very well-documented statistics that tell us around 50 percent of all marriages in the industrialized world fail. Not the greatest odds of success, to be honest. But I think this issue of driving forces and communication styles is one of the most likely reasons why this is happening—it's not infidelity or growing apart or parenting young kids being tough on everyone involved.

I think when partner one and partner two (it doesn't matter whether the relationship is gay or straight) each start to realize that the other person is prioritizing the wrong things, friction occurs.

And if they're not skilled communicators, it can be a real challenge to talk those issues through. Hence the relationship risks breaking up.

It's one thing not to be able to agree on how to plan your holiday, but it's quite another if one partner doesn't even want to go on the trip. There's nothing left to discuss.

There are an awful lot of couples where one partner is Red and the other is Green, or one is Blue and the other is Yellow. Two tough combinations, as we've already established. But they can figure it out if they both want the same things in life.

Once again—the driving forces are more important than behavior and, in turn, personality.

25.2 OPPOSITES ATTRACT? OR SHOULD THAT BE PEOPLE WHO ARE THE SAME?

Looking for the perfect partner? Keep on searching—I doubt they exist. And if you're waiting for a clone of yourself, then perhaps it's time to adjust your antennae a little. Sure, having interests in common is great—you can both laugh at the same jokes and shed tears over the same old movie. But what if you both hate fighting? Who will step up and handle the dreaded conversation with the call center operative whose computer says your bill hasn't been settled?

I'm quite clear on my own views here—the ideal partner isn't a mirror image of you. Imagine a world in which all your strange habits, your small and annoying quirks, were reflected back at you—day in, day out. Twice as much indecision about what to have for dinner, twice the reluctance to throw out old newspapers. No thanks.

Conclusion: You should not be identical.

At the same time, you don't really want a partner who is your absolute opposite. If you're an adventurous extrovert who loves nights out and wild travel adventures, while your introverted and taciturn partner prefers to set up a blanket fort in the living room to shelter from the apocalypse, perhaps you need to rethink your relationship. It's difficult to build a bridge when you're standing on either side of the Grand Canyon.

The ideal solution, I guess, is to find someone who is just the right distance away from you on the personality spectrum. Not too similar, not too different. Just right. Someone who shares your interest in bingeing Netflix series but might prefer thrillers as opposed to your penchant for comedies. That makes action-comedies the perfect choice. Or someone who appreciates your passion for good food and is happy to step in when it's time to make something more advanced than pasta with ketchup.

What I'm saying is you should look for someone who complements you, rather than complicates you. Someone who can take the lead in the household adventures you'd prefer to avoid, and who can teach you a thing or two about life outside your comfort zone. And most important, someone who can laugh at the situations in which you're different, because it's often in those moments that the secret to long-lasting love lies.

How do I know this? Because my wife and I laugh all the time. At ourselves, at each other, at nothing in particular.

Remember, a good relationship isn't about having a copy of yourself as your partner. It's about having someone who shares your outlook enough to make life harmonious, but who also challenges you here and there and enriches your worldview. It's the perfect blend of similarities and differences that keeps the spark alive.

Well, if you ask me, anyway.

25.3 AN EXAMPLE TAKEN FROM REALITY

Now that we've gotten to know one another, let's get real and use my own (and my wife's) behavior profiles to see whether this theory aligns with reality.

Just how similar or different are we? Well, take a look at the charts on the next page.

As you can see, these profiles are far from identical. However, based on the theory that similar colors work well together, things don't look too bad. We both have plentiful supplies of Red. Of course, my wife's score is the highest—she regularly scores at least 98 percent on the Red

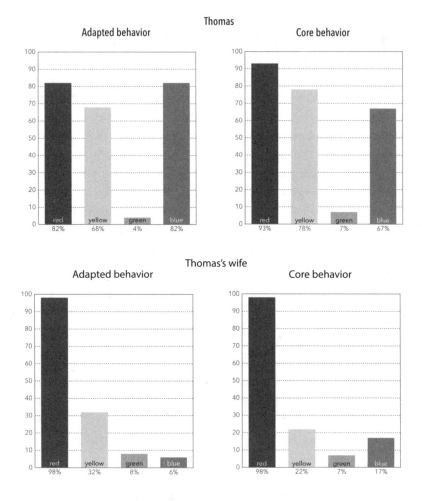

scale. (And she's a little annoyed not to make it to the full one hundred. *Ninety-eight? What's going on here? How do you get one hundred? I want to take the test again!*)

That being said, we're very complementary when we're under time pressure. I can elevate my own Red and match her without any great difficulties. And we get an insane amount of stuff done.

But as you can see, it's far from the whole picture. After all, my poor wife is forced to suffer my relatively high Yellow score. When I'm in a good mood, I'm pretty talkative—far too talkative, or so

I've heard on more than one occasion. And she can impart that view pretty bluntly:

My God, you do talk. So, so many words.

In the early days of our relationship, I was honestly a little miffed to hear that, but I got over it long ago. Now I know why she says it, and unfortunately she's right. Sometimes I really do talk too much. It's great on stage when I'm giving a lecture, but it's less ideal if we're watching TV.

But as we noted earlier, Yellows and Reds are a good combination since both profiles are extroverts. Both are relatively active and like to stay busy. The Red/Yellow part of me knows how to deal with her Red traits.

The challenge she faces in the shape of my high Blue score is more of a problem. Not to mention my own challenge, given that she has hardly any Blue. If there's one thing my wife struggles with, it's detail. I'm sure you remember hearing about my wife. Of course, she understands on an intellectual level—she's as sharp as a tack and has two advanced degrees—that sometimes you have to keep track of the details. And she doesn't like doing it.

I, on the other hand, sometimes prioritize details at the expense of pace. So this is where we have our disputes, where it can't be hidden. But we usually resolve it—98 percent of the time.

And I expect you're now wondering how we do that. You might well ask.

To some extent, we're a little maladjusted on all this communication malarkey. We talk a lot about how we talk. We communicate about our communication. If there's something one of us doesn't understand, we don't challenge the other person with a throwaway *What are you talking about?!*

Instead, we start by saying, *I've got a comprehension question.*

It's the signal to the other person not to take the least bit of offense. Obviously, something is unclear and it needs to be better explained.

Feel free to steal the idea—it's surprisingly effective.

But the really interesting thing is when we also look at our driving forces. Here we find the reason why we get along so well.

We like the same things. We're driven by the same things. Our core values are extremely well aligned. We want the same things. And this allows us to bridge our differences in communication styles without any great difficulties.

- We both have a very high practical-economic driving force.
- We both have a high aesthetic driving force.
- We both have a medium-high traditional driving force.
- We both have a very low theoretical driving force.

Right off the bat, that's four strong matches. That means we behave and navigate in our marriage and our shared life with the same core issues at the backs of our minds, more or less always.

However, perhaps the most important driving force, the one that really solves problems, is the individualistic one.

When I work with management teams on these issues, my message is always the same: You need a mixture of behavioral profiles to achieve full dynamics in that group.

But you need coherent driving forces. You need to be where you are for the same reason. Your driving forces need to match. Except in one very specific case: the individualistic one.

If too many people have an individualistic driving force, you end up with a very high number of conflicts. You see, individualists always want to be in charge and make the decisions. Once upon a time, this driving force was known as the political driving force, which I dare say hints at its obvious limitations.

It's about power. Power over oneself. Power over others. Power over the meeting, the agenda, the decisions. Power over life itself. It's simply not possible to tell them what to do, or how to do it. They hate obeying orders.

If more than one person in the room scores highly on this metric, friction is bound to follow. There's no way around it. And it doesn't matter what your spread of colors is. For example, even Blue/Green managers will challenge their CEO. It may be done in a subdued tone, but they won't just accept everything they're asked to do.

That's why you shouldn't have more than one or two people like that in a group.

How many individualists should there be in a marriage? Well, if you're in it for the long haul, one is more than enough. And that's the case in our marriage.

So who—out of my wife and me—is the individualist?

That's for me to know and you to find out. 😉

26

A Simple Unscientific Test

Let's test you, dear reader, to find out which colors are dominant in you and your behavioral patterns. Here is a series of questions to turn your mind to. It goes without saying you won't try to pretty up your answers to cast yourself in a better light . . . you'll be completely candid, right?

Some of these multiple-choice responses may seem very simple, but the fact is you'll struggle to choose in some cases. There's no need to play it safe—whatever you end up choosing will tell you everything you need to know.

On your mark, get set, go!

1. When faced with a problem, how do you usually solve it?
    A. I consider the situation carefully and think through all possible solutions.
    B. I go by my gut feeling and improvise a solution.
    C. I plan a strategic and systematic approach to dealing with the problem.
    D. I get right down to business and solve the problem through action.

2. How do you prefer to spend a day off?
    A. Planning an excursion or an activity with family or friends.

B. Exploring new hobbies or attending cultural events.

C. Relaxing at home with a book or watching a movie.

D. Doing chores around the house or making plans for the weeks ahead.

3. Which of the following statements best describes your approach to teamwork?

A. I enjoy motivating others and creating an enthusiastic atmosphere.

B. I want everything to be well organized and for everyone to stick to the plan.

C. I like to take the lead and make decisions on behalf of the group.

D. I listen to everyone and try to make sure no one feels left out.

4. What is most important to you in a friendship?

A. That my friend is spontaneous and funny.

B. That my friend is reliable and consistent.

C. That my friend is determined and energetic.

D. That my friend is understanding and empathetic.

5. How do you handle conflicts with loved ones?

A. By immediately discussing the problem and finding a solution.

B. By listening and trying to understand the other person's point of view.

C. By looking for compromises and avoiding imposing on anyone.

D. By trying to lighten the mood.

6. How do you usually react to change?

A. I adapt quickly and see it as an opportunity to try new things.

B. I feel uncomfortable and prefer it when things are predictable and stable.

C. I see change as a challenge and a chance to show what I can do.

D. I take my time and try to understand how the change affects me and others.

7. What type of work do you enjoy most?
A. Tasks that require exactitude and order.

B. Tasks where I can be creative and express myself freely.

C. Tasks that require quick decisions and leadership.

D. Tasks where I can work in a relaxed environment without stress.

8. What kind of holiday do you prefer?
A. An adventure filled with new experiences and activities.

B. A quiet and relaxing time on a beach or surrounded by nature.

C. A well-organized trip with a clear itinerary and things worth seeing.

D. An energetic and action-packed holiday where I can challenge myself.

9. What role do you most often take on in social contexts?
A. I'm the one who keeps conversations going and entertains others.

B. I'm the one who plans the meetups and makes sure it all works.

C. I'm the one who makes sure everyone is happy and feels included.

D. I'm the one who often initiates activities and leads the group.

10. Which leadership style suits you best?
A. One that is dynamic and inspiring, and creates a vision for others to follow.

B. One that is meticulous and methodical, with a clear focus on rules and routines.

C. One that is direct and decisive, ready to make tough decisions when necessary.

D. One that is supportive and caring, and looks out for the team's well-being.

11. How do you react when things don't go as planned?

A. I get frustrated but quickly find new solutions.

B. I adapt and try to see the positive in the situation.

C. I get worried and want to analyze what went wrong.

D. I don't let it worry me and I focus on supporting others.

12. How do you prioritize your personal goals?

A. I set ambitious goals and strive to achieve them quickly.

B. I set goals that are fun and stimulating to work toward.

C. I set realistic goals and carefully plan how to achieve them.

D. I set goals that are important to my personal well-being and relationships.

13. How do you usually deal with your emotions when you are upset?

A. I express them openly and directly.

B. I keep them to myself until I've had time to think them through.

C. I seek support from family or friends.

D. I try to distract myself with something fun or different.

14. Which of the following expressions best matches your approach to life?

A. *You only live once.*

B. *Think first, act later.*

C. *A tree with strong roots laughs at storms.*

D. *Lead, follow, or get out of the way.*

15. How would you describe your ideal home?

A. Colorful and filled with beauty and inspiration.

B. Organized and efficient with everything in the right place.

C. Warm and welcoming, a place where everyone feels at home.

D. Practical and minimalist, designed to maximize productivity.

16. When you get an unexpected day off, what are you most likely to do?

A. Plan a spontaneous excursion or activity with friends.

B. Use the day to catch my breath and relax on my own.

C. Reorganize my home or catch up on projects I've been putting off.

D. See it as a chance to tackle personal goals or to exercise.

17. How do you usually react to an unexpected visitor at your door?

A. I'm filled with enthusiasm at this pleasant surprise.

B. I'm reserved and would have preferred to know about the visit in advance.

C. I'm generous and hospitable—I'm happy to invite them in for a coffee.

D. I'm a little annoyed but I adapt to the situation.

18. Which activity would you most prefer to avoid at a party?

A. Overly formal contexts.

B. Loud and playful activities.

C. Activities where I am the center of attention.

D. Sitting still and talking—I prefer to be active.

19. How do you handle a day when everything seems to be going wrong?

A. I try to laugh at the situation and not take it too seriously.

B. I take a break to reflect and plan how I can improve matters.

C. I seek comfort and advice from my family or close friends.

D. I redouble my efforts to gain control of the situation.

20. What kind of gifts do you prefer to give to others?

    A. Personal and thoughtful gifts that reflect the recipient's interests.

    B. Practical gifts that the recipient really needs.

    C. Unique and unexpected gifts that come as a surprise.

    D. Gifts that encourage activity or personal development.

Well, there we have it. This wasn't the real analysis but was instead a simpler, more playful way to learn more about you and your potential profile. Sometimes you will have wanted to pick more than one of the possible answers; sometimes you won't have wanted to pick any of them.

And that is kind of how this works. Sometimes you simply have to choose a path, and doing so can provide valuable clues about the real you.

Turn to page 371 at the back of the book to find out how you got on in this straightforward quiz.

What can you use your results for?

You can reflect on yourself and your patterns of behavior. Why not run your results by people who know you really well? Just ask them whether they see the same thing as you.

If they do, that may be down to one of two things:

1. You're really self-aware. You all perceive you in more or less the same way, which is great.
2. They don't dare contradict you, because they know how you'll react.

I mean it: Don't take this deadly seriously. I simply want you to start reflecting on who you are and how you'd like to be regarded by those around you.

Are there elements to your profile that you're pleased with and that work well? Brilliant. Develop and expand them.

Maybe you'll go back to the color that matches the biggest share of your answers and read through how others might perceive you. You might realize there are some issues you need to get to grips with. If that's the case, don't be sad. Instead, congratulate yourself on reaching this exceptional level of insight. There are plenty of good things here for you to get started on.

Good luck!

A Short Reflection on History

27.1 TO BE HONEST, NOTHING'S CHANGED

27.1.1 The Background to Everything You've Read So Far

If you're not interested in history, or references, or research, or things that take time from your very full life, you can skip this chapter. For everybody else, once upon a time . . .

In all cultures, there has always been a need to categorize people. When the Stone Age came to an end and we became more reflective as people, we discovered that all over the world people were different. What a surprise.

But how different *are* people, really? And how have those differences been described historically? There are probably as many methods as there are cultures on earth. But I'll share some examples.

Which of the ancient Greeks should we use this time? Hippocrates? Hippocrates, who lived four centuries before Christ, is considered the father of medicine. Unlike many other physicians of that time, he wasn't superstitious. He believed that disease originated in nature and didn't come from the gods. For example, Hippocrates believed that epilepsy was caused by a blockage in the brain. Nowadays this is common knowledge, but back then it was revolutionary.

Humoral pathology, or the theory of the four humors or four

bodily fluids, has to do with the four temperaments. According to Hippocrates, our temperament is the fundamental way we react. It's our behavior or our natural frame of mind. Our temperament controls our behavior.

Hippocrates believed that your health is good when the four humors—blood, yellow bile, black bile, and phlegm—are in balance. When we vomit, cough, or sweat, for example, the body is trying to rid itself of one or more of these substances.

The word "chole" comes from the Greek *xanthe chole* and means "yellow bile." Therefore, a choleric person is controlled by yellow bile or the liver. Fiery and temperamental, choleric people sometimes frighten those around them with their powerful ways. "Choleric" can be translated as "hot-blooded."

The Latin word *sanguis* means "blood." A sanguine person is controlled by the blood, by the heart. Creative and happy-go-lucky, they spread positive vibes around them. Full of heart, and therefore optimistic and jolly, they have a cheerful manner. A synonym for a sanguine person is an optimist.

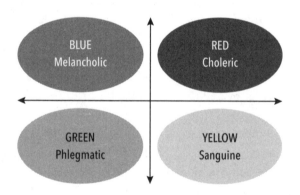

A phlegmatic person gets their influences from the brain. "Phlegm" simply means mucus. Mucus is viscous, which symbolizes a phlegmatic person's temperament. A phlegmatic person is sluggish and slow in movement.

Finally, a melancholic person has an excess of black bile—the Greek *melaina chole* means "black bile," found in the spleen—and is therefore often perceived as melancholic and gloomy. A common synonym for a melancholic person is a pessimist.

And there we have Hippocrates and his theories in a nutshell.

27.1.2 Body Fluids and Weather Types

Some five or six hundred years after the death of Hippocrates, a man by the name of Galen came onto the scene. He theorized there was a connection between different types of weather and our bodily fluids. These two parameters supposedly influenced our behavioral patterns in one way or another.

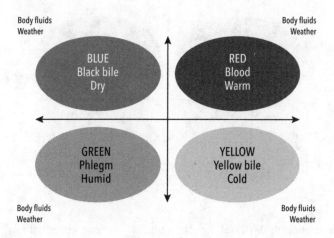

27.1.3 The Aztecs: An Indigenous People with a Calendar That Gave the Whole World the Meemies in 2012

The Aztecs were an indigenous people who lived in Central Mexico from the fourteenth century for a period of around two hundred years. They were a very advanced people who lived in close proximity to nature. Among other things, they were famous for predicting the end of the world in the year 2012—that's when they stopped counting future time. (When the end didn't arrive, a theory arose that they had simply run out of big enough boulders on which to carve their calendar.)

Anyway, when they tried to divide people into different categories, they used something they knew well—the four elements: fire, air, earth, and water. To this day, the four elements are used to describe different frames of mind, although nobody really knows if the Aztecs were the first to come up with this idea. But we do know for a fact that they used this idea, because they left carvings illustrating this approach.

Fire people were exactly as it sounds: fiery, explosive, a bit hotheaded. They were warrior types who wielded the sword to get their own way. Leaders.

Air people were different. They were also determined but considerably more easygoing. They swept in like a captivating wind, kicking up a little dust in the process.

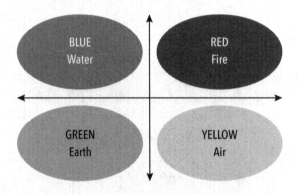

Earth people worked for the village, for the community. They exemplified stability and security. They were there to create longlasting things, to build for the future.

What about water people? Water was an element the Aztecs respected. Water can crush everything in its path, but you can also bottle it—if you know how to do that. Quiet and secure, water people observed everything that was happening.

As you can see, these divisions bear quite a resemblance to the theories propounded by Hippocrates—they're only different names for the same thing. Another of the ancient Greeks, Empedocles, made the same observations about natural elements. And he knew—just as we know using DISC theory—that the various elements could be mixed in countless different ways.

27.2 THE REASON WHY THE LANGUAGE OF COLOR ONLY WORKS ON THOSE WITH GOOD MENTAL HEALTH

William Moulton Marston created a systolic blood pressure test that was used in an attempt to detect fraud. The discovery resulted in the modern lie detector.

But Marston was also the author of essays on popular psychology. In 1928 he published his work *Emotions of Normal People*, in which he investigated the differences in the behavior patterns of healthy people.

Earlier, both Jung and Freud had published studies involving mentally unstable people, but Marston was a kind of pioneer who provided the foundations for what later became known as the DISC model.

However, the term "DISC" was introduced some years later through Walter Clarke's vector analysis. As you've seen, this is a model used to categorize the different types of human behavior. Marston's work has been an endless source of valuable insights about behavior and human interactions. He found a way to demonstrate how people were different. He noted distinct differences between personalities, which formed the basis of the model used in this book.

- Dominance produces activity in an antagonistic environment.
- Inspiration produces activity in a favorable environment.
- Stability produces passivity in a favorable environment.
- Analytic ability produces passivity in an antagonistic environment.

The term now used all over the world is "DISC profiles." This is based on the four initials of the above model. Marston used the word "compliance," but the word I've used in this book is "conscientiousness" since that's a better description of this type of individual.

The dominance trait in any given individual relates to how they approach problems and deal with challenges. But it's also the only thing that can be measured. Inspiration refers to a person who likes

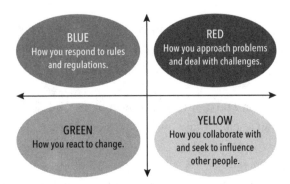

to influence others. A person with this trait will always be able to convince others. In simple terms, you could say that dominance is about acting, and inspiration is about interacting.

The degree of stability is measured primarily by how receptive an individual is to change. A strong need for stability means a person is resistant to change, while someone who enjoys change will have a lower need for stability. This leads, of course, to a number of specific behavior patterns—like a nostalgic belief in the long-lost "good old days," for instance.

Finally, analytic ability shows how willing someone is to follow rules and regulations. Of course, this also produces certain characteristics that are interrelated. Here we find those who can't accept that things go wrong. Quality is important.

As you've no doubt observed, everyone has the same colors regardless of whether we're talking about modern psychology or the indigenous peoples of Central America. The colors aren't critical; they're only a way to make it easier for those who aren't familiar with the system to make sense of the profiles. As a consultant, I've trained people in this area for the best part of thirty years, and I've found that the colors streamline the learning process.

Marston finished researching this topic sometime in the 1930s, after which he seemed to become preoccupied with other things. Many others have used his research and developed a tool that, according to the most recent data, has been used by nearly fifty million people over the past thirty-five years.

For example, the American Bill Bonnstetter made invaluable progress in creating definitive tools that help analyze the whole system.

But it's always helpful to remember that although in theory there's no difference between the concept on the page and the practice, in the real world there's a very big difference indeed.

I've described the four main traits Marston pointed out, but do remember that most of us are a combination of multiple colors.

The Colors in a Slightly Wider Context

28.1 WHAT HAPPENS OUTSIDE OUR OWN LITTLE PADDLING POOL?

You can basically skip this chapter because it doesn't offer any clear conclusions. Despite that, I have a couple of reflections on the issue of the different generations and their attitudes . . . if you're interested. Not to mention the differences we might observe in different corners of the world.

28.2 DOES MY AGE HAVE ANY BEARING ON MY PERSONALITY?

Let's start with the challenge we face with different generations. Young people are—in some ways—very different from older people. Or perhaps it's the older people who are a bit weird these days.

A frequent question I get when I'm out on tour lecturing on behavior and other patterns is whether this is something that changes over time, or something that stays relatively stable through the generations.

It's an interesting question, but the answer is complicated and far from straightforward.

Generational patterns are fascinating phenomena that provide a snapshot of how the environment in which we're raised, our values, and the historical events that touch our lives can all influence us. The idea that young people today might prioritize differently from the way I did as a young man is one thing to consider. Of course, each generation has its own unique experiences and influences from the time they grew up in, and these shape their outlook on the world and their approach to interacting with it.

The historical and cultural contexts into which each generation is born—for example, events such as wars, economic crises, technological progress, and so on—all have an impact on how a generation is shaped and which values they carry with them into adult life.

Personally, I'm not a big fan of labeling people by slapping their generation across their forehead. Of course, even I can see some deviating patterns, but it's far too blunt a tool, if you ask me.

We need to broaden our horizons.

Lumping a couple of billion people together is pretty idiotic, in my opinion. It may be well-intentioned, but it's still wrong to do so.

28.3 WHAT HAPPENS IF WE COMPARE DIFFERENT GENERATIONS?

28.3.1 Baby Boomers

The baby boomer generation, born in a time of extreme economic growth and optimism after the Second World War to parents who had seen two major conflicts, has often been associated with values such as individualism and forward thinking.

28.3.2 Gen X

I'm a member of the notorious Generation X, and when I read reports about myself and my generation, there's almost nothing in them I recognize (besides one single thing: we're not very sensitive, but there is a reason for that—keep reading).

What often emerges from various studies (or perhaps they're just observations, really) is that we're supposedly very tech positive, we think highly of social media (especially Facebook!), and we love news and innovation. You could say we're very trend-sensitive.

The truth is, of course, quite different. In practice, I've got some definite issues with technology, especially in the IT department. My grasp of it is fine, but I'd hardly say I'm interested in it. I've never understood social media. And the idea that I would even be mentioned in the same breath as early adopters is downright ridiculous. I'm always last to everything.

But it gets worse. There's also something up with my work ethic. I'm generally assumed to be a lazy slacker whose willingness to do my bit is doubtful. I'm primarily interested in personal experiences, thanks to my absent parents.

Once again, the truth looks a little different. I'm a workaholic, damn it! I don't have friends or free time. Fine, I'm exaggerating, but I really do like working. I dare say I do far more of it than is good for me.

Generation X was raised in a period of political and cultural upheaval in the 1960s and '70s, and is known for its tendency to question established norms and its focus on personal liberty and self-actualization. While I'm sure there are many people in my generation who are just like that, I have a hard time believing there would be more people of my own age with that outlook than there are among people who are older or younger.

Today's youth bear the burden of the climate change debate. Just what will the world look like in a century's time? There's certainly cause for concern on that front.

However, my generation grew up during the Cold War. We didn't know for sure whether we'd still be here in two hours' time. I grew up some three hundred miles from the world's biggest submarine base—chock-full of nuclear weapons. In the port of Murmansk, they had everything they needed to wipe us all out. Perhaps that's why we're perceived as insensitive, hard as nails, and generally unfazed? We were always somehow on the brink of disaster.

Of course, these various factors have affected us all differently.

But have they given us different personalities? Even though our values have changed—as surely they have—I wonder whether we have really changed.

28.3.3 Millennials

The millennial generation has often been described as more open to change and socially aware than the generations that went before it. They have grown up with rapid technological development and globalization, which have shaped their view of the world and their way of interacting with it. Millennials have also experienced events such as the global financial crisis in the 2000s and the issue of climate change, which have influenced their values and priorities.

28.3.4 Gen Z

Generation Z comprises the youngest group of adults at the time of writing; they have grown up in a world that is increasingly digitalized and globalized beyond what even millennials experienced. They don't know a world without the internet. They have grown up with smartphones, social media, and instant access to information, and these things have shaped their communication style and social behavior. They have no idea what it's like to wait to see the latest movie or listen to the newest music.

Generation Z are also powerfully engaged in issues such as environmental protection and social justice, which may reflect their increased awareness of global problems and their desire to be agents of change.

Sometimes they're described as both more inclusive and more individualistic. They're supposedly more rational but behave more emotionally. They have more negative emotions and are more averse to conflict, but they are simultaneously very aggressive and outgoing on social media. Preconceptions like these are downright contradictory and only add to the confusion. I don't really know who benefits from these types of studies, which are, frankly, far from reliable. To support my point, consider this: How big is Generation Z?

At nearly two and a half billion people, we're supposed to believe they're all the same? No way.

28.3.5 Can Any Conclusions Be Drawn from This?

You may well ask. With the passing of time, and as society has developed and changed, people's behavioral patterns have also changed—at least in part. We consume our news differently, we hang out online more, we're generally swifter to act—and much of this is thanks to digital tools. These changes can be ascribed to a range of factors, including cultural changes, social dynamics, and technological progress, which in combination have shaped the way individuals exist in and interact with the world around them.

Things move much more quickly nowadays—especially bad news. The digital revolution and the emergence of social media have had a significant impact on the way young people communicate, interact, and create their identities. To deny that would be stupid.

Additionally, family structures and social trends influence generational patterns. Changes in family dynamics, such as the increase in divorce rates and subsequent increase in single-parent families, can affect the way different generations view marriage, parenthood, and family life as a whole. Likewise, changes in the education system, labor market, and the use of technology all shape young people's attitudes toward and expectations of the future.

In short, generational patterns are complex and multifaceted phenomena that reflect the diversity of influences and experiences each generation encounters. By studying these patterns, we can increase our understanding of how society changes over time, and how different generations are shaped by the era in which they live. In turn, this can help us navigate and adapt to the challenges and opportunities that arise in an ever-changing world.

But does that make us different types of people? Does it give us other personalities? Let's take a look at a couple of tangible examples.

28.4 EXTROVERSION VERSUS INTROVERSION

When I was at school in the seventies and eighties, there were innumerable requests that the children should sit still and work quietly in their exercise books. Group work wasn't unheard of, but it was a relatively limited part of the day. You were assigned a task and you tried to complete it. The teacher would often prowl about between the desks making sure everyone was doing their best.

An important element was that there needed to be relative calm in the classroom. People needed peace and quiet in order to work. If everyone just sat there yacking away, it would be impossible to think and the work would suffer as a result.

So what did the teachers do?

They told everyone to be quiet and get on with their work. If you wanted something, you had to raise your hand. Asking another pupil to explain something to you was—if not off the cards entirely—very much frowned upon.

My poor parents were tearing their hair out. Why? Well, what they tended to hear at parents' evening was along these lines: *Sure, he's good in class, but can you get him to stop talking constantly?*

This was quite simply a model that suited introverted pupils much better. They preferred to work in silence and be spared having to discuss anything too much. Whether this is the best educational model out there is up for discussion, but that's not the point.

The system prioritized introverted pupils.

The extroverts had a harder time of it.

Nowadays, it's the reverse.

The system prioritizes extroverted pupils.

Modern teaching in schools—at least in my home country of Sweden—is heavily based on social interaction. This takes the form of group work and extended projects where pupils are expected to work together. You are supposed to be able to stand up in front of the class and give presentations; you're supposed to write assignments and then read them aloud; and above all, you're supposed to have goals, ideas, and visions for the future. Add social media to the mix and there's no doubt about it: It's extroverted youngsters who are seen and heard the most.

And the introverts have a harder time of it.

My purely personal view is that both systems are as bad as the other. Just as open-plan offices—invented by extroverts but largely populated by introverts—don't suit everyone, so a school system in which one in two kids doesn't fit in is not a system worth having, right?

Everyone tries their best to keep up, but an introvert hardly becomes an extrovert just because they're dumped into an environment like this. Adaptation is a difficult task.

28.4.1 So Is There Really No Difference Between the Generations?

Social change certainly plays a key role in shaping people's behavior. Urbanization, globalization, and technological progress have all served to transform our social interactions and have given rise to new opportunities for, and challenges to, our individual development. For example, increased access to the internet and social media has led to a greater sense of belonging and community for some people, while it has also increased the risk of social isolation and virtual alienation for others.

So who seeks out this particularly pulsating life?

My pet theory is that the big cities are inhabited by a surfeit of extroverts and have far fewer introverts. In big cities, the tempo is higher and the volume is a little different for entirely natural reasons. People are more anonymous and the stress and activity levels are often high—too high in many cases.

28.5 MEASURABLE CHANGES IN THE FOUR COLORS

There's one thing that can be measured based on what this book is about. That thing is the distribution of the four colors in the general population.

Statistically, the population of the world is actually slightly different nowadays than before.

We have slightly more Reds than we used to.

We have slightly more Yellows than we used to.

We have slightly fewer Greens than before.

The number of Blues remains unchanged.

So what does this mean?

If we look at the analyses done using the DISC model each year, there is a faint but measurable pattern observable.

In my part of the world—Europe—we're gaining slightly more extroverts with each passing generation.

The change is small, it's progressing very slowly, but it is indeed measurable.

The reasonable conclusion is that (at least statistically) my children will be different from my parents. Once again, though, these changes are small and I'm in no way claiming that this is a watertight conclusion.

And it's definitely going slowly enough that we cannot proclaim there are any great differences between the personalities of generations like the millennials and Gen Z. When we talk about the differences there are, I still argue that attitudes and values are more important.

Perhaps expectations, too.

An interesting question here is how much we can rely upon self-assessment tools like DISC, MBTI, Big Five, or anything else that is based on an individual's own assumptions and interpretations.

An individual's own preferences can most definitely influence the results; there's no point pretending otherwise.

I have experienced Greens making themselves Red in analyses since they would prefer to be Red. Astonishingly, I've also witnessed the exact opposite: Reds who have heard they're too insensitive their whole lives trying to get assessed as Greens.

This is one of the reasons why all consultants worth their salt carry out personal feedback sessions with the reports in front of them.

But that brings us to an important question: If it's the case that younger people are somewhat more extroverted than previous generations . . . is it because they're actually more extroverted? Or is it because they know they're *expected* to be more extroverted?

I'm afraid I have no good answer to this question. I can only speculate, but rationally I can't rule out that this might be the case. Subconsciously, you steer your answers in a direction that you know will fall on fertile ground, rather than being 100 percent honest at all times.

However, it's worth noting that this relationship doesn't apply everywhere. There's a big difference between different parts of the world.

28.6 CAN GEOGRAPHICAL DIFFERENCES AFFECT MY COLORS?

Where you live right now probably doesn't matter all that much, but cultural variations can definitely lead to some differences.

If you compare Europe with the USA, we see an interesting difference when looking at Red/Yellows as compared to Green/Blues.

Right now, you find more extroverted profiles if you look at the American respondents than you do on average in Europe. That may not be particularly surprising to a European like me. But let me spell out why I think this is.

It's the same story: The difference isn't huge—we're talking about a percentage point here and another percentage point there—but it's definitely there to be seen.

What's really intriguing is that the difference is constantly shrinking. The gap is closing and in a couple of generations' time, it's likely that Europe and the USA will be identical. That means we'll see roughly the same distribution of the four colors, excluding all the other potential influencing factors.

How come? Is it just a cultural issue, or are there any other rational explanations for the whole thing?

28.6.1 A Theory About Cultural Differences

For a long time, Swedes have been considered to be standoffish and dubious about change—sometimes even downright suspicious. They prefer to keep themselves to themselves. They all think the same things. Consensus is an important parameter in Swedish society. Conflicts are rarely appreciated and Swedes generally speak up far too late. Instead, we clench our fists in our pockets and grit our teeth. We work harder and say nothing, at least not until we've closed the front door behind us when we get home. Then we can complain and whine as much as anyone else.

Of course, this is a very gross generalization—just as gross as saying that everyone in the same generation is the same. Just like any other nation, Sweden is not a single place. We have lots of subcultures and there's a difference in the temperament of natal Swedes versus that of the many new Swedes who have immigrated here. But we still have a certain reputation on the international stage. We've definitely shown ourselves to be more introverted than extroverted.

There are lots of major Swedish companies, and I'm not just referring to IKEA, Volvo, and Spotify. While we may have been a very rich country for a long time now, that wasn't always the case. If you go back to the nineteenth century, Sweden was very poor and many of its population suffered from hunger and malnutrition.

For that reason, around one million Swedes emigrated to the USA to make a better life for themselves far, far away.

Let's take a closer look at this for a moment. One in five Swedes—that's 20 percent of the whole population—left the country without really knowing what they were embarking upon.

There was no internet, no social media. There was no TV, no radio. There were newspapers, but there were virtually no telephones. Communication meant writing letters, but a letter sent from one continent to another sometimes took up to eight months to reach the recipient.

In summary, the flow of information and the opportunities to communicate were powerfully restricted.

But people went anyway.

And if you survived the voyage to the far side of the planet, who knew whether there was even anything there to live on? Or to live for?

All those stories about fellow Swedes who had found success and wealth may have been a hoax from start to finish. Because what were people supposed to say? That they'd moved across the ocean and failed miserably?

And if you found a job and somewhere to live, who knew whether they were any good? What if you ended up in even more wretched circumstances than you'd been suffering back in Sweden? You know what you already have, but you've no way of knowing what you'll get. Out of the frying pan and into the fire wasn't a great way to go.

So what does a situation like that require?

It requires risk-taking. It requires an acceptance that you simply do not know what awaits you. I dare say it requires a certain thirst for adventure and entrepreneurship. Faith in the future is required.

In short: Who ended up crossing the Atlantic?

My theory? Red and Yellow families, or at any rate those families led by a Red or Yellow. Tell it any way you like, but these qualities would definitely have been helpful.

Who stayed behind? The overanalyzing Blues, and the Greens with their aversion to change.

My guess is that the entire American continent ended up filled with people from all over the world who were more adventurous and extroverted than the average population. Modern-day USA is a fantastic example of this. Entrepreneurship is a part of the American soul.

There's a genetic factor to this, as we saw at the beginning of the book. And now we have a cultural factor, too.

Finding yourself on the other side of the planet creates certain specific behavioral patterns. Everyone had to work hard, and by and large they were left to fend for themselves. And this has simply been passed down through the generations.

I won't comment on whether the USA is, in fact—as its people often like to assert—the best nation on earth. But it's hard to deny there's still a tremendous entrepreneurial spirit and desire to create things there.

The same goes for those who didn't emigrate. They bolstered their approach to things on the home front in Europe and little Sweden. They stayed, they kept fighting with what they had, and they showed far more patience, with all that entails. Sometimes it's good; sometimes it's a limiting factor.

No, I don't have any proof for this theory—it's largely based on gut feeling and my personal interest in history rather than any evidence-based arguments. Once I'm retired, I'm going to research this very issue.

And, of course, after X number of generations, these initially distinct differences will inevitably be smoothed out. The statistics tell us as much. These two continents are growing closer together in terms of the distribution of behavioral profiles.

28.7 WHAT ABOUT THE REST OF THE PLANET?

I haven't been everywhere, and I'm sure not everyone's opinions align. But let me share a couple of brief examples with you.

I thought I might stick my neck out—from my Swedish, everything-just-so point of view—and tell you what my countrymen and I think of our neighbors in Finland. They're the most introverted people ever. They essentially say nothing unnecessarily.

Some of them barely respond when addressed directly. Being a little buttoned-up is simply part of Finnish culture. But they're also very good at making things happen. I've worked in Finland and I know that if a Finnish contact promises to get back to me before two o'clock on Monday, they will. There are few people I trust more than the Finns. They have an ability to say something and then deliver exactly as intended. All without talking too much.

Many years ago when I worked in banking, my employer merged with Finland's biggest bank. I became attached to various projects whose aim was to bring together the two different corporate cultures. There were always equal numbers of Finns and Swedes present in meetings. This was a Swedish version of showing goodwill.

We Swedes talked and joked and were pretty thrilled to have all these new friends. The Finns mostly sat there staring at us. After a silence you could have cut with a knife, one of them finally said: *My God, you talk a lot. When are we going to get to work?*

This tickles me a little, since long ago Finland and Sweden were actually one and the same country. But each has developed along completely different lines, culturally speaking.

An analysis would show that Finnish culture is Blue/Red. Very task-oriented. But, if we look at the statistics of DISC analyses done in Finland, we see no difference to those done in Sweden. The distribution between Red, Yellow, Green, and Blue is effectively exactly the same in each country, yet the cultures differ.

If you scratch the surface, you find both Green and Yellow Finns beneath that rather morose exterior. And once you've gotten to know them, there are few people who are as much fun as a Yellow Finn. Their sense of humor is priceless. But you need to get to know them to find that out. That your road to that point is via a shot of vodka (or three) is a myth. A cup of coffee works just as well.

The same is true of our other Nordic neighbors. We Swedes sometimes think we're just like the Norwegians, but that's not how they see it. I'm sure they also think we talk too much and that we're too focused on achieving consensus. Norway is probably the country in the world that most closely resembles Sweden, but despite that, they are typically blunter and more to the point than us Swedes.

The Danes? Same thing. They're also more driven and more likely to speak their minds.

Germans? *Alles in Ordnung.* They keep meticulous records of everything. Calculations, quality, long-term outlook. But there's also a lot of drive there. They're often perceived as rather Blue but with dashes of Red.

France? More laissez-faire. No less Red, but probably less Blue and more Yellow.

We can go on and on and if we look at the individual deviations between these nations, we find the same pattern: The distribution of the four colors is essentially identical.

If I were to look at every single nation on earth, I'm secretly convinced that the result would be the same, no matter where I looked. And that basically confirms what any tool you care to use will tell you: People everywhere are overwhelmingly more alike than they are different. The similarities undoubtedly trump the differences, but you need to penetrate the cultural filter to see that.

What can vary are driving forces, but I have too little data to offer further insight there. In some cultures, people are more driven by money (practical-economic driving force) while in others there are systems in place to care for one another (social driving force). In some parts of the world, you're only convinced of something if you see clear evidence and you understand how things work (theoretical driving force). In other parts of the world, people are more inclined to rely upon old values when making decisions (traditional driving force). And in some cultures, art is incredibly important and people appreciate beautiful environments more than anything else (aesthetic driving force), while others couldn't care less.

28.7.1 What Are We to Do with This Knowledge?

My general reflection here is to never buy the argument that group A is this and that, while group B is different. No matter who we meet, we need to get to know the individual—I believe that's the only way forward to ensure we humans understand each other.

But the most important thing of all is worth repeating:

Our similarities are infinitely greater and clearer than our differences.

And that's why I don't have much trust in people who build their power base by talking about how everyone else is different and claiming they're the only ones who are right. That leads to an ugly world, and in my view we can do better. Shame on them.

But that's just my own, decidedly personal and perhaps naïve outlook.

28.8 A POP QUIZ TO SEE HOW MUCH YOU'VE PICKED UP

If you'd like to test your knowledge, here are a few questions for you. Think of it as an entertaining exercise you can use to test your friends. Just how carefully did they read the book? How much do they really know about how people do or don't work? I hope these questions might be a springboard to compelling conversations, whether it's at your next company kickoff or around your dinner table at home.

1. What combination of colors would naturally get along socially?
 Two Yellows
 Two Reds
 A Yellow and a Red
 A Blue and a Green
 All of the above

2. What combination of colors naturally works well together?
 Greens and anyone else
 Two Yellows
 Two Reds
 Blues and Reds
 All of the above

3. Which profile will always want to be in charge of a project?
 Red
 Yellow
 Green
 Blue

4. Which person will prefer to do more testing or obtain more information before they make a decision?
 Red
 Yellow
 Green
 Blue

5. Which profile typically makes for the best surgeon?
 Red
 Yellow
 Green
 Blue

6. Which person can you always count on to arrive on time?

> Red
>
> Yellow
>
> Green
>
> Blue

7. Which person would most enjoy giving a speech?

> Red
>
> Yellow
>
> Green
>
> Blue

8. Which person breaks the rules over and over while trying to get the job done?

> Red
>
> Yellow
>
> Green
>
> Blue

9. Which person would most commonly know where they had saved an email from their boss?

> Red
>
> Yellow
>
> Green
>
> Blue

10. Which person is most willing to try new things if it gets the job done?

> Red
>
> Yellow
>
> Green
>
> Blue

11. Which person remembers personal criticism the longest?

> Red
>
> Yellow

Green

Blue

12. Which profile wants the latest fashions?

Red

Yellow

Green

Blue

13. Which person takes personal criticism most to heart?

Red

Yellow

Green

Blue

14. Which profile would like new challenges the best?

Red

Yellow

Green

Blue

15. Which person is the least organized but knows where to go to get what they need?

Red

Yellow

Green

Blue

16. Which profile is the fastest to judge others?

Red

Yellow

Green

Blue

17. What combination of profiles would form the best team?

Two Greens

Two Reds

A Yellow and a Red
A Blue and a Green
A mixture of all colors

18. Which profile tends to always want to be in charge of making decisions?

Red
Yellow
Green
Blue

19. Which profile will probably talk the most?

Red
Yellow
Green
Blue

20. Which profile is the best listener?

Red
Yellow
Green
Blue

21. Which profile would absorb new ideas the fastest?

Red
Yellow
Green
Blue

22. Which profile will not miss the final point in a list of instructions?

Red
Yellow
Green
Blue

23. Which profile would delegate a task and then still do it themselves?
> Red
> Yellow
> Green
> Blue

24. Which profile is most common in your social circle?
> Red
> Yellow
> Green
> Blue

25. Which profile most often initiates social activities?
> Red
> Yellow
> Green
> Blue

26. Which profile is most likely to carefully plan their finances?
> Red
> Yellow
> Green
> Blue

27. Which profile is most likely to engage in charity work or volunteering activities?
> Red
> Yellow
> Green
> Blue

28. Which profile is most likely to volunteer at their kids' school?
> Red
> Yellow

Green

Blue

29. Which profile is most likely to hold a traditional family dinner?

Red

Yellow

Green

Blue

30. Which profile is most likely to suggest an unusual holiday destination?

Red

Yellow

Green

Blue

31. Which profile has the easiest time adapting to changed circumstances?

Red

Yellow

Green

Blue

32. Which profile tends to have the most order in their home?

Red

Yellow

Green

Blue

33. Which profile is most inclined to get actively involved in social issues?

Red

Yellow

Green

Blue

34. Which profile is most likely to impulsively start a new hobby?
Red
Yellow
Green
Blue

35. Which profile is most likely to resolve conflicts by speaking out about them?
Red
Yellow
Green
Blue

36. Which profile prefers to spend an evening alone at home rather than have a night out?
Red
Yellow
Green
Blue

37. Which profile is most likely to question authority?
Red
Yellow
Green
Blue

38. Which profile is most likely to be the last to leave the office?
Red
Yellow
Green
Blue

39. Which profile is most likely to suggest a compromise in a conflict situation?
Red
Yellow

Green
Blue

40. Which profile tends to be the most detail-oriented in their projects and planning?
Red
Yellow
Green
Blue

You can find the answers on page 371.

A Final Example from Reality

29.1 PERHAPS THE MOST ENLIGHTENING GROUP PROJECT IN THE HISTORY OF THE WORLD

Since this copy of *Surrounded by Idiots* is a heavily updated and revised edition, I thought long and hard about whether to change the final example that featured in the previous English-language edition. But upon rereading it, it still made me smile. It stayed. First, it's something that really happened to me; second, it's both screamingly funny and an entertaining example of how things can really go wrong when you don't think. Enjoy!

This is what happened.

Some years ago I was leading a conference, and I decided to do an experiment with a group of managers from a telecom company. The participants were professional and intelligent, and all of them were without a doubt highly successful. They had excellent qualifications and were destined for brilliant careers.

I'd already made communication profiles for all of them—they had completed a self-assessment that showed which colors they were. We'd already done their analyses and I had prepared myself in exactly the way I suggest in the previous chapters that you might do, too.

I divided these important managers into groups with similar behavior profiles and I planned to give them all a task. I imagined it would be easy for them to get along. They'd certainly understand one another. There were twenty people in total.

I called the groups Red, Yellow, Green, and Blue. I mean, I had to call them something.

I handed out the task. They had to solve a specially constructed problem that was connected to their field and required cooperation. They were given an hour to complete it. I explained the challenge and all the groups eagerly accepted the instructions and got to work. In the meantime, I was left to my own devices.

After the groups had been working for a while, I went around to see what was going on in the various teams.

In the Red group, the noise level was high. Three people were on their feet loudly explaining why they were right about this particular issue. So three of them were in the middle of an argument, and the fourth—the only woman in the group—had decided to work alone. Completely unconcerned about the shouting match three feet away, she was writing so fast her pen was practically sparking.

When I asked if everything was okay in there, they all stopped and looked at me in surprise.

Is everything okay? I repeated anxiously.

Peachy! one of the belligerent guys said grimly. *Almost done here.*

I left them and continued on. The Yellow group was also working frantically. The energy in the room was almost palpable. Things were happening!

The discussions were lively, with everyone trying to convince the others of their own position. While the Reds were mad as hell with one another, there were nothing but smiles here.

Two of the Yellows were jockeying for space at the whiteboard, and another told me an amusing anecdote that had nothing to do with the subject at hand (although I admit it was truly hilarious).

The fifth manager in the Yellow group was doodling on a piece of paper and sending emails on his mobile phone.

I left them to pay a visit to the Green group. Inside the room, there was a strange calmness. Their voices were quiet, and they were nearly all listening rather than speaking. The chief goal here was stability and security. Five of the managers were sitting quietly, listening to one of their colleagues telling a sad story about his dog who had died of old age that same winter. He still missed his faithful companion. It was a tragic story.

The last manager had sketched out some suggestions about how they could solve the task I'd given them, but every suggestion ended with a question mark. She needed more input, and it looked as if she would have to ask for it. She was worried.

I moved on.

In the last group, the Blue group, I was faced with an almost unreal scene. The silence was absurd. It was almost impossible to tell whether anyone was actually breathing in there. After sitting with them for three minutes without anyone uttering so much as a single word, I was seriously concerned. To be sure, there was plenty of thinking going on beneath the surface—after all, this was the cream of the crop as far as the company's thinkers were concerned—but there was no prospect of communication.

A woman was reading silently through the task with her lips moving. I asked if they needed help getting started. I got a few hesitant nods in reply. They soon began a very thorough deliberation. They would absolutely get to the bottom of things.

It was obvious they were on the right track, but at an extremely detailed level. They discussed for a long time what their plan of action should be.

I remember glancing furtively at the clock. Half the allotted time had passed, but they hadn't produced anything concrete. Proposals had been put forward, but they'd been rejected by the others on a variety of technicalities. The problems were mounting. The risks were considerable on all sides.

Every word was chosen carefully and the advantages and disadvantages were weighed up carefully. They were far more interested in doing things properly than in actually getting things done.

I left them to their fate and went back to the large conference room.

Before the allotted time was up, the Red group arrived with triumphant grins. They congratulated one another for being the first back. They'd clearly won whatever this was. They laughed loudly and condescendingly at all the losers who hadn't even made it back in time.

I had to go and fetch all the other groups. The Yellow group was the slowest. I had to go back twice before they deigned to make an appearance. By then, two of them were talking on their phones, and a third guy had actually gone to fetch some coffee and cake. Carrot cake, if I'm not much mistaken.

Anyhow, when all the groups had returned, I let them present their work.

The Red group triumphantly approached the podium. They'd turned the task into a veritable race. They'd finished in thirty minutes even though they had been allotted an hour, and they made it clear to everyone in the room that this was how things should be done.

The rest of the time they'd spent phoning around their coworkers, checking what they were doing with their time. It was a sound presentation, a well-organized structure, and properly thought out. But about thirty seconds into the report, it was clear that the Red group had solved a completely different problem from the one I'd given them. It wasn't at all what I had asked for.

When I asked if they had actually read the instructions, they all began arguing. One of the men stated confidently that they'd adapted the task to reality. I was, in fact, the one who was wrong. They'd done a brilliant job.

He expected applause, but when the standing ovation didn't materialize, the members of the group shrugged and returned to their seats. A second after sitting down, the woman in the group began playing with her phone. A vital text message must be sent immediately.

Next up, it was the Yellow group's turn. This group consisted of three women and two men. All of them smiled and stood at the front. Who should begin? A brief deliberation took place before one of the women charmed her way to the podium.

She quickly plunged into her topic, presenting the exciting discussions they'd had for the past hour. She spoke for a while about the whole thing being an inspirational exercise; she described how she was going to use the insights she'd gained when she returned to her work.

Her presentation was very entertaining, and everyone laughed. I was also amused by the woman's story, especially considering that it only had one purpose: to camouflage the fact that the group hadn't solved the task.

However, the Yellow group did manage to get some applause, mostly due to the high entertainment value of their presentation.

Now it was time for the Green group. It took a while to get everyone up to the podium. While the Yellow group had squabbled about who was going first, the Green group was anxious.

Do all of us go up? Who should present the report? Should I? Shouldn't you do it?

At least half of the six participants looked as if they had a stomachache. Sure, this was the largest group, but every single one of them was nervous.

No one took command. After a moment of low-key deliberations, one of the men began to speak. He faced the whiteboard most of the time. He talked softly, turning toward the members of his team for support. He was so subtle in his observations that the message was hopelessly lost. With growing desperation, he looked at his team for help.

The purpose of the whole exercise was to highlight that no groups could function with the same types of individuals and that diversity was the only possible way forward. When the report was complete—of course, the Green group had not solved the task itself either, even though they had actually come further than the Yellow group—I asked if everyone in the group agreed with what had been said.

The unfortunate spokesperson said he thought it was probably true that most of them were more or less in agreement. I asked the group, and they all nodded in unison. At least four of the participants in the group had grim faces and their arms crossed tightly across their bodies—body language that proclaimed they were far from agreeing with what had been said. One of the women looked resentfully at the spokesperson. But, by Jove, she was in agreement.

Finally, the Blue group marched up in line and stood in alphabetical order, just as they had planned beforehand.

Arne went through the instructions, revealing that there were several points that had made the task challenging. Among other things, he commented on the sentence structure in the document I'd distributed. He spent a lot of time explaining that it was better to use "advisor" than "adviser," although both forms are technically correct, and he pointed out two grammatical errors on the very first page.

Then it was Berit's turn to go through the structure they had based their work on, although she was interrupted twice by Arne, who believed that a few further minor details needed to be clarified.

When Kjell took over, they still weren't even close to providing a solution to the problem.

Stefan didn't straighten out any issues, and when Örjan finally announced they needed more time to finish the task properly, chaos erupted in the conference room.

The Red group quickly branded the members of the Blue group complete idiots; the Yellow group felt it was the most boring thing they'd ever experienced; and the Green group looked like they'd eaten something that was off.

29.2 CONCLUSIONS TO BE DRAWN

This story is completely genuine although I've abridged it somewhat in order to get to the end.

The best way to form an efficient group is by mixing different types of people. This is the only way to achieve decent dynamics in any group. This seems intuitive, but despite this, most of the organizations I have encountered fail on this fundamental requirement when they recruit people. Managers bring in new people who are just like themselves. At least they understand them. Some refer to these situations as "aha experiences." I call them "oh no experiences."

Why the group project I've just told you about wound up the way it did, and what you can do to avoid similar incidents, is what this whole book has been about. I hope you found pleasure in reading it and joining in this exciting exploration of how people function, what makes them similar, and what makes them different. Because we are all different. Well, maybe not all of us. But many of us are quite different. If you keep your eyes open, you'll find out exactly how different.

It's not primarily about how to behave at work—although obviously that's important, since you're surrounded by lots of people you haven't chosen to be with.

For me, the most important thing has always been how to act around other people. Period.

Simple as that. It would be deeply unfortunate if I gave it my all during the day and then came home to my family and behaved however I pleased. What an idiot! Being a son of a bitch on home turf won't get you far.

There's an old saying that I don't know the provenance of—I've tried to find out who said it first, but there are so many alternative originators listed. So my apologies if I'm stealing someone's quote. Here's how it goes:

Nobody will remember your salary. How busy *you were. How many hours you worked. How many Gucci bags you owned.*

People will remember: The time you spent with them. If you kept your word. If they could count on you. And the one that is most personal to me:

People will remember how you made them feel.

In the end, that's what really counts. And this book is my contribution to helping you reach out to the people around you.

Make sure you look at your reflection in the mirror every now and then, and remember that we're all the idiot in someone's story.

Thomas Erikson,
April 2024–October 2024

Appendix

HELP ANALYZING YOUR OWN TEST RESULTS

1. When faced with a problem, how do you usually solve it?
A. I consider the situation carefully and think through all possible solutions. (Green)
B. I go by my gut feeling and improvise a solution. (Yellow)
C. I plan a strategic and systematic approach to dealing with the problem. (Blue)
D. I get right down to business and solve the problem through action. (Red)

2. How do you prefer to spend a day off?
A. Planning an excursion or an activity with family or friends. (Red)
B. Exploring new hobbies or attending cultural events. (Yellow)
C. Relaxing at home with a book or watching a movie. (Green)
D. Doing chores around the house or making plans for the weeks ahead. (Blue)

3. Which of the following statements best describes your approach to teamwork?

    A. I enjoy motivating others and creating an enthusiastic atmosphere. (Yellow)

    B. I want everything to be well organized and for everyone to stick to the plan. (Blue)

    C. I like to take the lead and make decisions on behalf of the group. (Red)

    D. I listen to everyone and try to make sure no one feels left out. (Green)

4. What is most important to you in a friendship?

    A. That my friend is spontaneous and funny. (Yellow)

    B. That my friend is reliable and consistent. (Blue)

    C. That my friend is determined and energetic. (Red)

    D. That my friend is understanding and empathetic. (Green)

5. How do you handle conflicts with loved ones?

    A. By immediately discussing the problem and finding a solution. (Red)

    B. By listening and trying to understand the other person's point of view. (Green)

    C. By looking for compromises and avoiding imposing on anyone. (Blue)

    D. By trying to lighten the mood. (Yellow)

6. How do you usually react to change?

    A. I adapt quickly and see it as an opportunity to try new things. (Yellow)

    B. I feel uncomfortable and prefer it when things are predictable and stable. (Green)

    C. I see change as a challenge and a chance to show what I can do. (Red)

    D. I take my time and try to understand how the change affects me and others. (Blue)

7. What type of work do you enjoy most?

    A. Tasks that require exactitude and order. (Blue)

    B. Tasks where I can be creative and express myself freely. (Yellow)

    C. Tasks that require quick decisions and leadership. (Red)

    D. Tasks where I can work in a relaxed environment without stress. (Green)

8. What kind of holiday do you prefer?

    A. An adventure filled with new experiences and activities. (Yellow)

    B. A quiet and relaxing time on a beach or surrounded by nature. (Green)

    C. A well-organized trip with a clear itinerary and things worth seeing. (Blue)

    D. An energetic and action-packed holiday where I can challenge myself. (Red)

9. What role do you most often take on in social contexts?

    A. I'm the one who keeps conversations going and entertains others. (Yellow)

    B. I'm the one who plans the meetups and makes sure it all works. (Blue)

    C. I'm the one who makes sure everyone is happy and feels included. (Green)

    D. I'm the one who often initiates activities and leads the group. (Red)

10. Which leadership style suits you best?

    A. One that is dynamic and inspiring, and creates a vision for others to follow. (Yellow)

    B. One that is meticulous and methodical, with a clear focus on rules and routines. (Blue)

    C. One that is direct and decisive, ready to make tough decisions when necessary. (Red)

D. One that is supportive and caring, and looks out for the team's well-being. (Green)

11. **How do you react when things don't go as planned?**
    A. I get frustrated but quickly find new solutions. (Red)
    B. I adapt and try to see the positive in the situation. (Yellow)
    C. I get worried and want to analyze what went wrong. (Blue)
    D. I don't let it worry me and I focus on supporting others. (Green)

12. **How do you prioritize your personal goals?**
    A. I set ambitious goals and strive to achieve them quickly. (Red)
    B. I set goals that are fun and stimulating to work toward. (Yellow)
    C. I set realistic goals and carefully plan how to achieve them. (Blue)
    D. I set goals that are important to my personal well-being and relationships. (Green)

13. **How do you usually deal with your emotions when you are upset?**
    A. I express them openly and directly. (Red)
    B. I keep them to myself until I've had time to think them through. (Blue)
    C. I seek support from family or friends. (Green)
    D. I try to distract myself with something fun or different. (Yellow)

14. **Which of the following expressions best matches your approach to life?**
    A. *You only live once.* (Yellow)
    B. *Think first, act later.* (Blue)
    C. *A tree with strong roots laughs at storms.* (Green)
    D. *Lead, follow, or get out of the way.* (Red)

15. How would you describe your ideal home?
- A. Colorful and filled with beauty and inspiration. (Yellow)
- B. Organized and efficient with everything in the right place. (Blue)
- C. Warm and welcoming, a place where everyone feels at home. (Green)
- D. Practical and minimalist, designed to maximize productivity. (Red)

16. When you get an unexpected day off, what are you most likely to do?
- A. Plan a spontaneous excursion or activity with friends. (Yellow)
- B. Use the day to catch my breath and relax on my own. (Green)
- C. Reorganize my home or catch up on projects I've been putting off. (Blue)
- D. See it as a chance to tackle personal goals or to exercise. (Red)

17. How do you usually react to an unexpected visitor at your door?
- A. I'm filled with enthusiasm at this pleasant surprise. (Yellow)
- B. I'm reserved and would have preferred to know about the visit in advance. (Blue)
- C. I'm generous and hospitable—I'm happy to invite them in for a coffee. (Green)
- D. I'm a little annoyed but I adapt to the situation. (Red)

18. Which activity would you most prefer to avoid at a party?
- A. Overly formal contexts. (Yellow)
- B. Loud and playful activities. (Blue)
- C. Activities where I am the center of attention. (Green)
- D. Sitting still and talking—I prefer to be active. (Red)

19. How do you handle a day when everything seems to be going wrong?

    A. I try to laugh at the situation and not take it too seriously. (Yellow)

    B. I take a break to reflect and plan how I can improve matters. (Blue)

    C. I seek comfort and advice from my family or close friends. (Green)

    D. I redouble my efforts to gain control of the situation. (Red)

20. What kind of gifts do you prefer to give to others?

    A. Personal and thoughtful gifts that reflect the recipient's interests. (Green)

    B. Practical gifts that the recipient really needs. (Blue)

    C. Unique and unexpected gifts that come as a surprise. (Yellow)

    D. Gifts that encourage activity or personal development. (Red)

POP QUIZ ANSWER KEY (TO SEE HOW MUCH YOU'VE PICKED UP)

1. What combination of colors would naturally get along socially?
   Two Yellows
   Two Reds
   A Yellow and a Red
   A Blue and a Green
   All of the above

2. What combination of colors naturally works well together?
   Greens and anyone else
   Two Yellows
   Two Reds
   A Blue and a Red
   All of the above

3. Which profile will always want to be in charge of a project?
   Red
   Yellow
   Green
   Blue

4. Which person will prefer to do more testing or obtain more information before they make a decision?
   Red
   Yellow
   Green
   Blue

5. Which profile typically makes for the best surgeon?
   Red
   Yellow
   Green
   Blue

6. Which person can you always count on to arrive on time?
  Red

  Yellow

  Green

  Blue

7. Which person would most enjoy giving a speech?
  Red

  Yellow

  Green

  Blue

8. Which person breaks the rules over and over while trying to get the job done?
  Red

  Yellow

  Green

  Blue

9. Which person would most commonly know where they had saved an email from their boss?
  Red

  Yellow

  Green

  Blue

10. Which person is most willing to try new things if it gets the job done?
  Red

  Yellow

  Green

  Blue

11. Which person remembers personal criticism the longest?
  Red

  Yellow

Green

Blue

12. Which profile wants the latest fashions?

Red

Yellow

Green

Blue

13. Which person takes personal criticism most to heart?

Red

Yellow

Green

Blue

14. Which profile would like new challenges the best?

Red

Yellow

Green

Blue

15. Which person is the least organized but knows where to go to get what they need?

Red

Yellow

Green

Blue

16. Which profile is the fastest to judge others?

Red

Yellow

Green

Blue

17. What combination of profiles would form the best team?

Two Greens

Two Reds

A Yellow and a Red
A Blue and a Green
A mixture of all colors

18. Which profile tends to always want to be in charge of making decisions?
Red
Yellow
Green
Blue

19. Which profile will probably talk the most?
Red
Yellow
Green
Blue

20. Which profile is the best listener?
Red
Yellow
Green
Blue

21. Which profile would absorb new ideas the fastest?
Red
Yellow
Green
Blue

22. Which profile will not miss the final point in a list of instructions?
Red
Yellow
Green
Blue

23. Which profile would delegate a task and then still do it themselves?

> **Red**
> Yellow
> Green
> Blue

24. Which profile is most common in your social circle?

> Red
> Yellow
> Green
> Blue

25. Which profile most often initiates social activities?

> Red
> **Yellow**
> Green
> Blue

26. Which profile is most likely to carefully plan their finances?

> Red
> Yellow
> Green
> **Blue**

27. Which profile is most likely to engage in charity work or volunteering activities?

> Red
> Yellow
> **Green**
> Blue

28. Which profile is most likely to volunteer at their kids' school?

> Red
> Yellow

Green
Blue

29. Which profile is most likely to hold a traditional family dinner?
    Red
    Yellow
    Green
    Blue

30. Which profile is most likely to suggest an unusual holiday destination?
    Red
    Yellow
    Green
    Blue

31. Which profile has the easiest time adapting to changed circumstances?
    Red
    Yellow
    Green
    Blue

32. Which profile tends to have the most order in their home?
    Red
    Yellow
    Green
    Blue

33. Which profile is most inclined to get actively involved in social issues?
    Red
    Yellow
    Green
    Blue

34. Which profile is most likely to impulsively start a new hobby?
    Red
    Yellow
    Green
    Blue

35. Which profile is most likely to resolve conflicts by speaking out about them?
    Red
    Yellow
    Green
    Blue

36. Which profile prefers to spend an evening alone at home rather than have a night out?
    Red
    Yellow
    Green
    Blue

37. Which profile is most likely to question authority?
    Red
    Yellow
    Green
    Blue

38. Which profile is most likely to be the last to leave the office?
    Red
    Yellow
    Green
    Blue

39. Which profile is most likely to suggest a compromise in a conflict situation?
    Red
    Yellow

Green
Blue

40. Which profile tends to be the most detail-oriented in their projects and planning?
Red
Yellow
Green
Blue

Index

About the Author

Maria Östlin

Thomas Erikson is a Swedish behavioral expert, active lecturer, and bestselling author. For more than twenty-five years he has been traveling all over Europe to deliver lectures and seminars to executives and managers at a wide range of companies, including IKEA, Coca-Cola, Microsoft, Oxford University, Stanford University, and Volvo.

Surrounded by Idiots has been a Swedish runaway bestseller since it was first published in 2014. The Surrounded By series has sold more than 10 million copies worldwide in close to 70 languages.

Read the entire
Surrounded By series
by Thomas Erikson

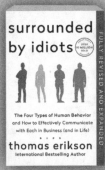

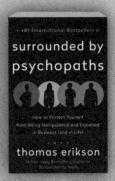

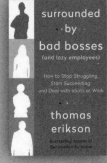

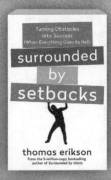

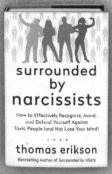